W9-BSM-530

CREDITS:

SUSAN MACKAY: Cover artist and graphic designer for

GUIDE TO WOMEN'S PUBLISHING

Back cover photograph of Polly Joan and Andrea Chesman: Paul Gibbons

Photograph of Joan Larkin: Barbara Adams

Other Photographs: Polly Joan

With warm thanks to Susan Shaw Weatherup, publisher BEFORE WE ARE SIX, for permission to reprint her letter to the authors as "ONE STORY."

Special thanks to QUEST: A FEMINIST QUARTERLY and SINISTER WISDOM for permission to reprint excerpts from their magazines.

Typesetting by Linda Andrews

TABLE OF CONTENTS

GUIDE TO WOMEN'S PUBLISHING

guide to
Women's Publishing

by Polly Joan
& Andrea Chesman

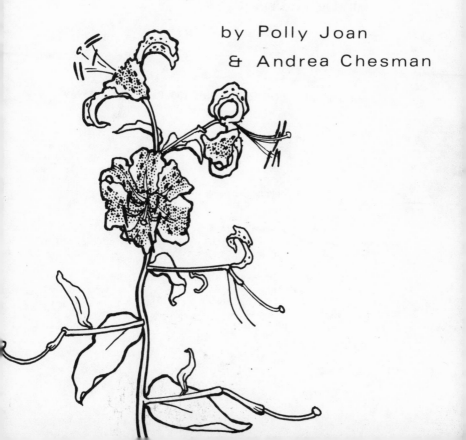

$4.95/Paper, ISBN 0-913218-79-0
$9.95/Cloth, ISBN 0-913218-80-4

Published by DUSTBOOKS, P.O. Box 100, Paradise, CA 95969

Library of Congress Cataloging in Publication Data

Joan, Polly.
    Guide to women's publishing.

    Bibliography: p.
Includes index.
1. Women publishers.   I. Chesman, Andrea, joint
author.   II. Title.
Z278.J54   070.4'8347   77-29143
ISBN 0-913218-80-4
ISBN 0-913218-79-0 pbk.

"We have woven together a kindof textured echo chamber, a flexible moving acoustical system, the new sounds we utter changing the space even before we hear each syllable. Our writing, our talking, our living, our images have created another world than the man-made one we were born to, and continuously in this weaving we move at one and the same time, toward each other, and outward, expanding the limits of the possible."

Susan Griffin

Reprinted with permission from SINISTER WISDOM, Vol. 1, No. 2, page 7. SINISTER WISDOM is available from 3116 Country Club Drive, Charlotte, NC. 28205, $4.50 per year.

FORWARD

Through a cold rainy summer and then a brief flash of fall, through the longest, hardest winter we had seen in years, and now amid the tulips and the iris, we have lived, breathed, talked women's publishing to each other for one full year. Over coffee each morning we told each other how we'd rather write poetry, how tired we were, how we wished we had never even heard of Feminism, until finally the coffee pot would be empty and we had no further excuses—we had to go to work.

Polly would go upstairs to her room in the big white farmhouse with the plants in the windows and the cats in the chairs and write about women's presses. And Andrea would trudge through snowdrifts to her yurt, build a blazing fire and immerse herself in women's periodicals. And somehow, no matter how negatively we began the day, no matter how much we complained about biting off more than we could chew, we would emerge at noon to wait for the mail, to wait to hear from one more press or magazine. Somehow our enthusiasm for our topic never waned.

Women's publishing is a much larger field than we had imagined. When we started, we had no idea of what we were getting ourselves into. Neither did we understand all of the contradictions we would face.

The title "Women's Publishing" was not chosen lightly. Often we were tempted by our politics to narrow the book into a more concise "Feminist Publishing." It is a debate that still rages within us. As a Virgo and a Taurus, temptation to be carefully defined or firmly grounded is particularly strong. Yet there is another side. There is a side that hates to cull weeds from the garden. Don't these plants have the right to exist too? If we have sympathy for weeds, why not for apolitical women's publishing? As poets, we make an analogy: weeds and spinach alike, were we not all nurtured by the same sun and rain—the Women's Movement? Is there really only one correct way to grow? When do fragile flowers die and weeds persist? When do weeds transform into edible fruit?

This book is full of weeds and flowers—but remember—many call wildflowers what others call weeds. Many will pick from this book a random bouquet. Bits and pieces will be read by writers looking for new markets, potential subscribers looking for new publications. To us the contents of this book represent far more than a helpful guide to women's publishing. This book is a document, an affirmation that women's publishing is a *reality*.

****

A book about women's publishing is a book about feminist politics. At times women's publishing resembles all small press publishing. Yet women's publishing is no more an off-shoot of the male small press than feminist politics is an off-shoot of the male Left from which many Feminists emerged. The analogy is important: feminist publishing is also feminist politics. It is not an alternative to male publishing. It is a political act as creative and diverse as the Women's Movement itself.

In the late 60's and early 70's women were more concerned with getting the *words into print* than with distribution. The effort to make the statement, the grit necessary for women writers to overcome the years of patriarchal rejection, to get angry enough to say *I AM I AM* by publishing a book, starting a women's press, all converged into that magical moment sitting in someone's kitchen or living room surrounded by brown cardboard boxes. Sometimes it wasn't until the smell of a new pot of coffee had blended sensually with the sweet sweet smell of printer's ink that the victory of publishing dissolved into the realities of "How are we going to distribute them?"

Despite this lack of forethought or experience with distribution, the spirit behind a movement can carry it a long way. In

2

the name of sisterhood, friends carted these books across the country to other friends who in turn sold or gave them to other friends. At the same time that feminist presses (books and magazines) were bursting into being, women's print shops were getting off the ground, and women's bookstores began springing up all over the country. The intensity of Feminism as a Movement, even with inadequate distribution methods spread through the "printed word." More than any other movement in history, Feminism had been identified with publishing.

Taking hold of the American doctrine that freedom of the press is the single most important access route to equality, Feminism has confronted the male heirs of the American Revolution with their own beliefs and strategies turned inside out for the sake of a *women's free press*.

Equally profound is the fact that, initially, poetry was the medium of the Movement. In the beginning it was feminist poetry books and magazines that spread the sounds of the American women's revolution. Art and politics converged. It was totally natural that they should. For a woman to publically confront her own rejection of female inequality was to call for revolutionary change in both human consciousness and institutions. This invocation to change came out of a woman's soul, the poems of the spirit.

While every revolutionary movement has had its poets and its poetry, no other movement has been so grounded in poetry as Feminism. So intense has been this identification that there was a time when the most articulate feminists in the movement were its poets. Women's consciousness-raising groups vocalized their pain and anger in poetry. Women's poetry readings were the focal points for spurring political action. Art and politics blended, personal experience and art converged. There was no separation between a woman's self and her art.

Today women's publishing is in a transitional stage. No longer in such a hurry to get the word into print, women's publishing is becoming more professional in approach. This book testifies that we are well on our way to conquering many of the technical and tactical obstacles to survival. Meanwhile, the necessary support services, writer's guilds, distribution companies, and directories spread the word and facilitate the needs of a growing field.

For it is a growing field, ever expanding, ever changing. Yet time and again we have discussed this book with women who have told us that, while the "idea" of a feminist press is a good one, nothing of "quality" has been produced yet. This statement, widely repeated, is pure myth! Over a million copies of feminist press books have been bought. We are supporting nearly 100 feminist bookstores and could support many more.

However, it is true that feminist publishing standards do vary. This is one of its greatest strengths. Even as the feminist press becomes more professional, we hope that women's publishing will never get so rigid that it can stringently define good and bad, because out of the most casual, most spontaneous expressions, are the seeds for new creation.

Up to this point the Women's Movement has resisted heroines, forming instead an intricate publishing network with many differing women's voices expressing our oneness in liberation, whether in poetry, fiction, diaries, herstory, or research. Hopefully, the Women's Movement and women's publishing will continue to be the voice of many.

The fact that there are many voices will probably effect changes in literature for years to come. From the literally hundreds of women-writer support groups all over the country will emerge the flames of new literature. It cannot help but happen, is already happening. There are too many women working too hard at writing for it not to catapult into a "new day" for literature.

Whatever else this book accomplishes, there is one assumption which underlies all of it: *The time has come to give women's publishing the full credibility it deserves!*

Polly Joan and Andrea Chesman

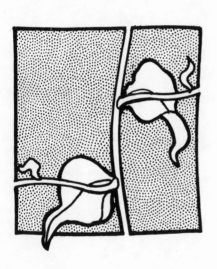

feminist
journals

LITERARY, ART CULTURAL AND POLITICAL JOURNALS

INTERWOVEN FORMS

Women's literary, art, cultural and political journals run the gamut of ideologies expressed in the Women's Movement. Goals and interpretations of what Feminism means vary from publication to publication. Some of these periodicals proselytize their brand of Feminism; some are women-oriented but have no political basis, some present a variety of viewpoints, espousing none. They have large readerships, or the potential for such, or they cater to a limited few. Where these journals all come together is as a space where women are free to express their thoughts, ideas, dreams, aspirations—creativity.

Poetry is the one art form that appears over and over again; it is the unifying feature of this chapter. It is fitting that this is so—poetry has been a unifying feature of the new Feminist literary movement of the 60's and 70's.

In the early sixties, poets were among the first artists to integrate their writing with a conscious feminist politic. Women began writing about their lives as women and previously taboo subjects such as menstruation, woman-love, motherhood, appeared in women's poetry. As the personal aspects of life came to be recognized as political choices, writing poetry became a political act. As Muriel Rukeyser wrote: "What would happen if one woman told the truth about her life?/ The world would split open." Obviously there was no place for this politically charged writing in male-controlled literary establishments. Women began publishing their own magazines.

This chapter is a sampling of the magazines women made in the United States and Canada. Throughout most of them, women's thoughts are expressed in poetry. This poetry is perhaps our greatest legacy from the sixties—where our voices begin—in chants—where the cornerstones of feminist culture are laid.

****

One can gather all the journals in this chapter into two broad catagories: the literary/art journals and the cultural/political journals. Into the first fall the publications which mainly publish art, poetry, fiction and criticism. While the cultural/political journals may also publish these forms, they focus on other expressions. Factual and theoretical articles, personal, photographic and journalistic essays, journal excerpts, and bibliographies all go into the making of the cultural/political journals. Often these publications are organized from a specific point of view: women's spirituality, feminist science fiction, country living, socialist/ feminism.

More important than the forms which distinguish the cultural/political from the literary/art journals are the differing goals of the two types of publications. Embracing the disciplines of herstory, psychology, sociology, politics, economics, as well as literature and art, cultural/political journals are committed to creating a new women's culture. Whereas many of the literary/art journals were conceived to provide a market for women's work (a "reaction" against male-oriented publication), women's cultural/ political journals are an assertive act of "creation" of cultural Feminism (not a "reaction" against male culture journals). In plain terms, this means that cultural/political journals are almost always politically radical. Literary/art journals may be radical, or then again, they may not. They may be "creative," or then again, simply "reflective" of the world around us (a male-oriented world where women are frequent victims).

Does it clarify the issues to understand the differences between types of magazines? Should I point out patterns among them, or espouse each one as a unique entity? Does it matter that I believe that there is a vast difference between *GILT EDGE* —"for women who happen to be artists" and *THE SECOND WAVE*—"The Magazine of the New Feminism"? Does it matter that I find *GILT EDGE* "reflective", and *THE SECOND WAVE* "creative"? Do the two magazines belong in the same chapter? These are questions I have asked myself. And, can I justify the presence of the few non-sexist (i.e. have male input) sources in this book about "women's publishing"? More importantly, can I justify imposing my personal comments about each periodical to the readers?

****

As a writer who sends unsolicited work out, I have been frequently frustrated by not understanding editorial policies of different magazines. To help writers understand more about magazine policies was my first priority. (All of the publications in this chapter consider unsolicited manuscripts when accompanied by an SASE.) Originally, my entire list of publications was comprised of Women Writing exchange contacts. Then I began to consult some media directories. (See *ADDITIONAL RE-SOURCES* for names and addresses.) Finally, I pursued every ad I saw in the newspapers and publications that were beginning to flow into my mailbox. I visited book stores and libraries. In the end I had contacted approximately 150 publications. (Some are listed in other chapters, some are no longer publishing. I did not hear from 30.) The rest is herstory—this book.

And herstory is just what this book is. My original intention, sharing information with writers, was soon expanded as I became more and more excited about what these journals represent. I have come to see all the publications in this book, and particularly the journals in this chapter, as part of the herstory of the Feminist Movement, a literary herstory. Consider, for example, *SPEAKOUT*. Publishing since 1971, *SPEAKOUT*'s casual, mimeographed format is a reminder of the early mode of feminist publishing when the very existence of a feminist publication was so exciting that little attention was paid to appearance. Each publication, however modest, was a joyful statement: "Feminism lives!" In 1977 *CONDITIONS*, a dignified, professional looking literary journal, published its first issue. What has happened between 1971 and 1977 is reflected in these two publications. Since 1971 the existence of the Feminist Movement has become more secure. And, women have learned all manner of publishing skills, from printing technology to administration, that enables them to raise money to publish more professionally.

If the contents of this book is part herstory, it is also an exploration of the intertwined and opposing facets and factions of the Feminist Movement today. Each publication in this chapter represents both a piece of the pattern *and* a unique entity.

Yet to do so, to name each one, was (and is) a great risk. As women, we have been so careful with our words, so aware of the power of naming. By naming we embrace, define, defend, understand, hold, create. As Susan Griffin says: "Our writing, our talking, our living, our images have created another world than the man-made world we were born to, and continuously in this weaving we move, at one and the same time, toward each other, and outward, expanding the limits of the possible." (*SINISTER WISDOM*, Vol. 1, No. 2). I have aked myself: Does the process of naming recreate a magazine, or does it create something new? Can I name and not compare? Can I achieve an adequate distance from the magazines and retain emotional honesty? What does honesty have to do with personal taste? One problem we have not solved in our Feminist Movement is how to criticize. How can I be critical, yet not criticize?

I read some feminist criticism. It was not helpful—too concerned with justifying the very existence of feminist criticism (that content is important, that historical context is important) to the male scholarly world. Hit or miss, I evolved my own method.

I have tried to be as descriptive of each publication as possible. To be positive and supportive, emphasizing each publication's unique strengths was my highest priority. I tried to

Reprinted with permission from SINISTER WISDOM, Vol. 1, No. 2, page 7. SINISTER WISDOM is available from 3116 Country Club Drive, Charlotte, NC. 28205, $4.50 per year.

eliminate the factor of personal taste—at the same time I recognize that such objectivity is impossible to attain. The result: hit or miss? A little of both perhaps. What I continually aimed for was to promote all of these publications in all their diversity—because I believe in them—all of them—as fertile grounds for the seed of Feminism.

I have come to gather this heterogeneous mixture of publications into one large chapter for two reasons. One, because the forms do interweave, with poetry a very common element. Two, because these publications are all naming—naming our present reality, our past and our future seen through women's eyes.

How do non-sexist journals fit into this vision? Most of them are feminist though not separatist. Take *SUNBURY* for example. Edited by a women, printing mostly women, publishing poems that confront patriarchal values, it is surely a Feminist publication. *SUNBURY* also publishes men. It is obvious to me that *SUNBURY* belongs with other Feminist publications. The few journals that have a male editor or co-editor are included because of their genuine commitment to publishing women and minority poets. There are possibly other non-sexist male publications. But I did not seek them out. One way to look at non-sexist publications is to see in them the degree of influence that Feminism has had on the literary world. In this way, even non-sexist journals are part of the herstory of Feminism.

****

A word of caution: the periodicals assembled here are highly volatile. Webster's defines volatile as having the power to fly, tending to erupt in violent action, easily vaporized, changeable, evanescent, transitory. By the time this book goes to press, some publications will have vaporized, succumbed to financial problems. Some will have changed formats. And some of them may be ready to fly—about to erupt into violent action—about to create something entirely new.

ALBATROSS Published bi-monthly
Box 112, $7 per year
111 S. Harrison St. 8½ x 11, 32 pages, saddle stitched
East Orange, NJ. 07017

With a breezy format and an unabashedly escapist attitude, *ALBATROSS* is one of the very few feminist humor magazines in this book. The editors describe *ALBATROSS* as a "radical-lesbian-feminist satire magazine (or a diversion for the deranged— depending on your point of view)." Feminist women who used to read *NATIONAL LAMPOON* but can no longer tolerate its sexism may find *ALBATROSS* just what they were waiting for. Certainly, *ALBATROSS* is a defiant answer to the charge that feminists have no sense of humor.

Not simply a humor magazine, *ALBATROSS* is also a general cultural journal where there is a little something for everyone. In addition to the humor and comix, *ALBATROSS* features serious poetry, news briefs, reviews of books and music and interviews.

AMAZON Published bi-monthly
2211 E. Kenwood Blvd. $3 per year, free to prisoners
Milwaukee, WI. 53211 Newspaper format, 24 pages

AMAZON, A MIDWEST JOURNAL FOR WOMEN is not easily classified: it is both a newspaper and a cultural journal. At first, one is tempted to see *AMAZON* as simply a newspaper. There are many articles dealing with news events such as the opening of a feminist bookstore, and political analysis dealing with issues like "battered wives"; the format is that of a newspaper. But the *AMAZON* collective would probably disagree. They would point out that each issue is themed, and writers and storytellers are solicited to contribute on the themes they have announced, such as "Dedication to Motherhood", "Country Women", and "Money."

Whether *AMAZON* is a cultural journal or a newspaper is a moot point. With the special awareness of the need to develop a midwestern voice, recognizing the inherent strengths and problems of midwestern women, *AMAZON* is a forum for the opinions and art of all women. In *AMAZON* one reads a genuine dedication to honesty and openness, and the kind of commitment from a collective which has struggled to survive for five years and intends to survive and grow even more.

APHRA   Published quarterly
Box 893 $5.50 per year
Ansonia Station   6½ x 8½, 150 pages, perfect bound
New York, NY. 10023

There is a lot one can say about *APHRA*. For one thing, *APHRA* is a survivor, and that is rare enough. Publishing since 1969, *APHRA* almost succumbed to the "small magazine syndrome" once, but with a great deal of support from readers, *APHRA* managed to reorganize and revitalize. This is a good thing since *APHRA* goes a long way in contributing to feminist culture. Calling itself a literary magazine, *APHRA* beautifully balances poetry and fiction with articles on sociology, the visual arts, interviews and herstory.

One of the nicest things about *APHRA* is its weight. 150 pages provide a lot of reading—this is important because they can publish short fiction and critical articles as well as poetry, without interrupting the balance of the magazine. Consistently, the articles are intellectually provocative, and well written. Issues are frequently themed and articles in the past have dealt with sexism in language, women in religion, the family, daughters and fathers, etc.

Very formally presented, *APHRA*'s visual appearance complements the contents and contributes to its professional look. One feels that individual issues of *APHRA* will not become dated. As a touchstone of the new feminist culture, it makes an important addition to one's library.

BARE WIRES　　　　　　　　　　Published irregularly
P O Box 9779　　　　　　　　　　　$.10 per single issue
San Diego, CA. 92109　　　　　　8½ x 11, 6 pages, stapled

If *BARE WIRES* is not quite like any other publication in this chapter, it is quite unlike any publication I have ever seen. A newsletter of communication, *BARE WIRES* contents are not easily classified. Produced now and then by writer/editor Helen McKenna, *BARE WIRES* is a personal view of the world by a woman who takes her humor dead seriously.

(See Press II: A Harmless Flirtation With Wealth.)

BEST FRIENDS　　　　　　　Published less than quarterly
c/o Nancy Gage Staley　　　　　Price: Send for info with SASE
800 Carlisle NE　　　　　　　　7 x 9½, 80 pages, perfect bound
Albuquerque, NM. 87106

Published by the Best Friends Poetry Collective, *BEST FRIENDS* is an engaging women's poetry magazine. There is a variety of form, style and subject matter in the poetry, rounded out with exceptional art reproductions. The aim of the magazine is to provide ". . . a forum, an esthetic process and a dialogue of American poetry by women. This is a sense that often becomes lost in the fractioned publishing system of American poetry— but it is a living body of expression to be shared and nurtured in all its forms and excellences. . . . "

A large editorial collective adds to the diversity of the publication. In their consideration policies, they exemplify a direction of many magazines. "We first assume the responsibility of understanding as well as possible what the writer is doing and aiming for before making any judgment on the quality of the expression and its suitability for each particular issue. For instance, on first readings, some of our editors prefer the highly-crafted, allusive and introspective poem, and fail to see what other editors admire in a more straight-forward, prosey approach to externally-oriented subjects and social conflicts. . . In some instances we decided that the style and content were not synonymous, and

14

that the content is sufficiently compelling to override some weakness in technique. . . In some other cases, we felt the highly crafted style was memorable and was the most interesting aspect of the poem, rather than ostensible subject matter." The result of their process is a magazine well worth reading.

BLACK BOX   Published on cassette tapes
P O Box 4174   6 issues/12 tapes
Washington, D.C. 20015 $22.50 per year
                           2 cassette tapes per issue, 2-3 hours long, boxed

BLACK BOX is "the first literary magazine to be published in cassette format. No texts, no paper—only the poet's voice cradling, caressing, sharing the poems which it uniquely holds." After a 400 year detour into the Guttenberg era, *BLACK BOX* offers a return to the tradition of oral poetry—where the distinctions between songs, chants, theatre, and poetry are broken down.

Any work that lends itself to oral interpretation is welcome to *BLACK BOX*. However, there are a few areas in which they are especially interested. As a literary magazine, *BLACK BOX* is concerned with literary interviews which are genuine discussions, not the interviews that are conducted by mail as is common to many magazines. Tape poetry using electronic hardware, songs, theatre pieces, and international poetry in binaural translation are other possibilities which *BLACK BOX* is interested in exploring. Black poetry and women's poetry are special areas of emphasis for *BLACK BOX*.

Women's poetry (like Black poetry) is so carefully tuned to the ear, so expressive when read aloud. Tape recording the voices of women's poetry is such an excellent idea!

To submit work to *BLACK BOX*, one should send at least ten minutes of work on tape. Any tape format is acceptable. No printed manuscripts will be considered. For interviews and dramatic material, query first.

BLACK BOX distributes literary tapes by other producers. Included in their collection are tapes of Denise Levertov, Adrienne Rich and Anne Sexton. Write for their catalog.

BLACK MARIA   Published quarterly
815 W. Wrightwood Ave. $5.50 per year
Chicago, IL. 60614   6 x 9, 70 pages, saddle stitched

Art and politics harmonize in *BLACK MARIA*, a politically oriented literary/cultural journal. A feminist perspective and an emphasis on strong women's images characterize the finely wrought literary pieces. Punctuating the short fiction, poetry and drawings are herstorical sketches of famous women and analytical articles on political topics.

BLACK MARIA has been publishing since 1971. A grant from CCLM has enabled the staff to spend more time doing community outreach programs. *BLACK MARIA* is published by Metis Press, making it an all-woman publication.

(See Press II: *METIS PRESS*

BOOKLEGGER/THE FEMINIST REVIEW OF BOOKS
555 29th Street
San Francisco, CA. 94131
                    For more information, send inquiry with SASE

In the cyclic way that Feminist magazines come and go, *BOOKLEGGER* has gone leaving behind the seeds for another magazine: *THE FEMINIST REVIEW OF BOOKS*. As Celeste West wrote, "Re *BOOKLEGGER*: flower bent but not broken!"

BOOKLEGGER magazine was made "by/for library workers" but provided valuable information, interesting discussions, and reviews for everyone who works with books. From a radical feminist perspective, *BOOKLEGGER* promoted small press books. Each issue contained short essays with bibliographies organized around specific topics. The topics varied extensively and included: "Do-It-Yourself Law," "Hotels," "Homosexuals," "Films—

Women," "Houses—Homemade," "Native Americans," "Radical Magazines," "Senior Power," etc. In addition to the bibliographies, there is always a larger section of small press book reviews, as well as an occasional article on a political topic such as "Class and Professionalism."

A complete index to *BOOKLEGGER* is available from Booklegger Press at the above address for $1. Back issues are available for $1.50 (Nos. 1-12), and $2.00 (Nos. 13-16) prepaid. Although *BOOKLEGGER* magazine is no longer publishing, each issue is an undated reference. Also from Booklegger Press is *POSITIVE IMAGES*: An Evaluative Guide to 400 Non-Sexist Films For Young People ($5.00) and *WOMEN'S FILMS IN PRINT*: An Annotated Guide to 800 Films Made by Women ($4.00).

Hopefully, *THE FEMINIST REVIEW OF BOOKS* will begin in 1978. Look for it!

BRANCHING OUT   Published bi-monthly
Box 4098 $6 per year, $7 foreign
Edmonton, Alberta T6E 4T1   8½ x 11, 50 pages, saddle stitched
Canada

A Canadian magazine by women, for women, *BRANCHING OUT* is a general interest feminist culture magazine—and a pure delight. Published on glossy paper with plenty of art and photographs, one is content to just leaf through this magazine at first —afraid that the contents won't justify the graphics, but they do—amply.

From a feminist perspective, *BRANCHING OUT* explores everyday life with feature articles and personal testimony. They have dealt with such issues as sexual politics, Canadian literature, strategies for law reform and spiritual identity. Each issue is themed; their treatment of their subjects is extremely imaginative. A recent issue on (of all things!) fashion was done with unusual sensitivity—from admitting that even feminists care about how they look, to exploring in depth the working conditions of women textile workers. They included that particular section with a hilarious photo essay of a woman in jeans and T-shirt, describing her look and accessories in true fashion-journalese ("This morning she has chosen a subtle mud-hued lace" for her work boots. . .). Native women, working-class women, as well as students and professionals are all included in the scope of *BRANCHING OUT*.

In addition to the feature articles and a regular column on law, *BRANCHING OUT* contains book and film reviews, poetry, fiction, art and photographs.

BRANCHING OUT pays all contributors with a subscription and a nominal sum. Increased payment to contributors is a high priority in their financial planning.

THE BRIGHT MEDUSA	Published quarterly
P O Box 9321	$6.50 per year
Berkeley, CA. 94709	6½ x 8½,, 40 pages, saddle stitched

A feminist literary journal, *THE BRIGHT MEDUSA* features poetry, drama, novel excerpts, short stories and occasional theoretical articles. A high priority is given to reviews of small press books, women's film and music. *THE BRIGHT MEDUSA* is a publication that proves that art and politics can be well blended.

CALYX	Published three times per year
Route 2, Box 118	$5 per year
Corvallis, OR. 97330	7 x 8, 60 pages, saddle stitched

A "calyx" is a part of a flower; the magazine *CALYX* is a part of the flowering of feminist literature. Devoted to publishing the voices of women in the Northwest, *CALYX* is a literary and art magazine. Tightly crafted poetry and fiction characterize this publication where art ranks higher than politics. Book reviews, interviews, essays and outstanding art work complete *CALYX*.

CAMERA OBSCURA Published three times per year
P O Box 4517 $6 per year
Berkeley, CA. 94704 5½ x 8½, 150 pages, perfect bound

A journal of film making and theory, *CAMERA OBSCURA* tackles its subject with a feminist and socialist perspective. Not for ordinary film buffs, *CAMERA OBSCURA* use semiology, textual analysis and psychoanalysis to study film from a theoretical point of view. The language is sometimes technical, sometimes very abstract. The magazine is one which requires slow, careful reading.

Recognizing that women are oppressed by the symbols used to represent them, *CAMERA OBSCURA* employs a feminist perspective in analyzing films. As an example of *CAMERA OBSCURA*'s style, here is an explanation of feminist film analysis:

> "A feminist film analysis recognizes that film is a specific cultural product, and attempts to examine the way in which bourgeois and patriarchal ideology is inscribed in film. This involves a process of investigation and theoretical reflection on the mechanisms by which meaning is produced in film. . . The study of film as signifying practice (through rigorous analysis of film as texts) contributes to an understanding of how ideology determines and is determined by the mode of representation."
> (Vol. 1, No. 1, pg. 1)

CHOMO-URI Published three times per year
506 Goddell Hall $4 per year
University of Massachusetts 5½ x 8½, 50 pages, saddle stitched
Amherst, MA. 01002

Translated literally, *CHOMO-URI* means "Mother of the Tourquoise Peak," the Tibetan name of a mountain which the English named after a man: Mt. Everest. The title was chosen to represent universal sisterhood in a world where "sexism transcends race and nationality. . . taking different forms from culture to culture." *CHOMO-URI* is offered as "an outlet for women's creative expressions and perspectives in a changing society, ... presenting the positive as well as the negative sides of women's experiences."

Emphasizing visual art as well as poetry and prose, *CHOMO-URI* is a "women's multi-art magazine." Black and white art reproductions are given as much weight and significance as the written word in this publication, resulting in a beautiful looking volume.

Learning to work as a collective, the entire *CHOMO-URI* staff reviews each submission. "To encourage each woman to continue working in her medium, we write to those whose work we do not publish, explaining the reasons and offering suggestions on strengthening her work. The responses we receive indicate that the process is mutually rewarding. This process takes about four months." They prefer to receive no more than five poems, no longer than twenty pages typed. Slides of art are considered, but the originals are needed for publication.

CHRYSALIS   Published quarterly
1727 N. Spring St. $10 per year
Los Angeles, CA. 90012 8½ x 11, 146 pages, perfect bound

Growing out of the *NEW WOMAN'S SURVIVAL SOURCE-BOOK, CHRYSALIS* has been a long time coming and well worth waiting for. With its first issue arriving in February 1977, *CHYRSALIS* is an eminently satisfying intellectual magazine of women's culture.

In their first issue, the editors explain: *CHRYSALIS*

"... takes its form and content from the women's movement itself. Feminism is not a monolithic movement, but rather includes the experiences, values, priorities, agendas of women of all lifestyles, ages and cultural and economic backgrounds. Women building practical alternatives to patriarchal institutions, women developing new theories and feminist perspectives on events and ideas, women expressing their visions in verbal or visual art forms—women's culture includes all of this, and *CHYRSALIS* exists to give expression to the spectrum of opinion and creativity that originates in this diversity."

The content, or at least the topics chosen, reflect the editors' commitment to presenting the diversity of women's culture. The first issue of *CHRYSALIS* contained articles and bibliographies on a variety of topics, including: health, psychology, herstory, politics and art. Articles which are both theoretical and practical are often accompanied by bibliographies and catalogues (in keeping with the *NEW WOMEN'S SURVIVAL SOURCEBOOK* format), to enable the reader to seek out additional information. There is also a wealth of art work, poetry, fiction and reviews.

The format of *CHRYSALIS* is dense; one gets one's money's worth. On most pages the format includes three typeset columns of fine print, representing anywhere from 600-800 words. Article lengths vary, but tend to be long, with illustrations that subtly enhance, never distract from the text. Where art work is presented alone, it is allowed more space.

CHRYSALIS has the potential for a very large audience. Undoubtedly, it will be passed around from woman to woman. It is equally likely that many will want to keep their own copies as a feminist reference in their library, supplementing dated catalogues, and as a treasure to be re-read for favorite works.

Poetry submissions should be sent to: Audre Lorde, 207 St. Paul Ave., Staten Island, NY., 10304. All other submissions should be sent to the Los Angeles address.

CONDITIONS   Published three times per year
P O Box 56 $6.50 per year ($5 to students and unemployed).
Van Brunt Station   5¼ x 8¼, 150 pages, perfect bound
Brooklyn, NY. 11215

"A magazine of writing by women, with an emphasis on writing by lesbians," *CONDITIONS* is a cultural journal of poetry, fiction and reviews. Special features explore the direction of women writing through interviews and in-depth articles of literary criticism. Because of the tight craft, the political awareness in the content, the careful layout and design, one is hard pressed to isolate any one feature of *CONDITIONS* as outstanding. But in the first issue of *CONDITIONS* there were 50 pages of well-written, thoughtful book reviews, most of them feminist press books. With these book reviews, *CONDITIONS* moves gracefully beyond the simple category of literary magazine and into the realm of the literary/cultural journal where all aspects of women writing are explored, supported and seeded.

CONDITIONS encourages the submissions of manuscripts of poetry, short fiction, novel excerpts, drama and other creative forms such as journal entries and excerpts from correspondence. Critical articles on women's/lesbian movements and institutions, issues involving race, class, age and aspects of lesbian relationships are also welcome. "We want *CONDITIONS* to include work in a variety of styles of both published and unpublished writers of different backgrounds. We welcome submissions from all women who feel that a commitment to other women is an integral part of their lives."

CONNECTIONS MAGAZINE   Published bi-annually
Bell Hollow Road $3.50 per year
Putnam Valley, NY. 10579   5½ x 8½, 70 pages, saddle stitched

CONNECTIONS specializes in a tight collection of poems, primarily, though not exclusively, by women. It is the policy of *CONNECTIONS* to print more than one poem by a contributor, giving the magazine the feel of an anthology. Both political and personal poems are well represented. *CONNECTIONS* occasionally prints line drawings and photographs.

COUNTRY WOMEN   Published bi-monthly
Box 51 $4 per year
Albion, CA. 95410   8½ x 11, 60 pages, saddle stitched

What is particularly appealing about *COUNTRY WOMEN* is its broad perspective. While essentially country-oriented, *COUNTRY WOMEN* offers enough in each issue to interest the city-dweller. The orientation is clearly feminist, but the range of articles runs the whole gamut of a woman's experience, and that includes activities that are not particularly or exclusively feminist.

The underlying perspective of *COUNTRY WOMEN* seems to grow out of that awareness of natural process that living in the country can put one in touch with. *COUNTRY WOMEN* is also one of the few women's magazines consciously attempting to integrate a "spiritual" and "political" perspective.

Each issue of *COUNTRY WOMEN* centers on a particular theme such as: Sexuality, Women and Work, Older Women, and presents articles, poems, and graphics on the theme. In addition, there is always a section of "practical" articles. Some, like cutting wood or veterinary medicine, are specifically for women living in the country. Others, on techniques of self-defense, auto mechanics, or food poisoning, are applicable to anyone. The emphasis is always the same: learning to be self-sufficient as women.

Poetry, journal extracts, short sketches, calligraphy, drawings and photographs grace *COUNTRY WOMEN*, breaking down those categories which divide the cultural journal from the literary and art journal.

DARK HORSE	Published quarterly
c/o Barnes	$3 per year
47 Stearns Street	Newspaper format, 10 pages
Cambridge, MA. 02138	

Biased in favor of New England artists, and dedicated to promoting the small press, *DARK HORSE* is "Boston's first poetry and fiction newspaper." A staff of mostly women rotate the editorial positions in recognition that editing is an art—and *DARK HORSE* is edited artfully. Each issue is themed, designed to build to a positive statement, but never overshadowing the statements of the individual works. Some recent themes have been "Metamorphosis," "Six Senses" and "Dramatic Monologues." Occasionally the themes are provided by the contributors, as in special issues of work by the very young and the very old, and another one (planned) of poetry from prison inmates. The graphics, drawings and photographs, are beautiful: *DARK HORSE* is not just another tabloid.

DARK HORSE features short poetry (rarely longer than 60 lines), short fiction (10 pages, double-spaced), drawings, photographs, reviews of small press books, and a regular communication column of news of the literary world, announcing readings, publications, grants, etc. The editors urge that potential contributors order a sample copy ($1) before submitting work.

Unlike most publications in this book, *DARK HORSE* avoids the label "feminist." They do not usually list themselves in feminist catalogues and publications (my usual places for discovering feminist publications). In fact, I had never seen a copy of *DARK HORSE* until I met two of the editors at a *COSMEP* conference. There we immediately fell into a conversation on what it means to call a publication "feminist." And in the hectic manner of conferences, we never did reach any understanding. The women at *DARK HORSE* feel that labels are not necessary and serve to put people off, to eliminate potential readers and contributors. Thus, despite the obvious feminism of the staff, the obvious feminist policies that underlie editorial choices, *DARK HORSE* wishes to remain free of labels, a sentiment that characterizes many small press publications. Whatever the label, *DARK HORSE* is open to art which presents positive, strong, sensitive images of women. They will not print anything degrading to women, or for that matter, degrading to anyone (sexist, racist, etc.). Women are published in *DARK HORSE* somewhat more frequently than men. And in an editorial policy more characteristic of the feminist press than the small press in general, *DARK HORSE* returns work with a personal note—emphasizing communication rather than the making of judgment.

DYKE, A QUARTERLY   Published quarterly
Tomato Publications, LTD. $8 per year
70 Barrow St.   Free to women in prisons and mental hospitals
New York, NY. 10014   8½ x 11, 50 pages, saddle stitched

"For Womyn Only" reads a notice on the cover of *DYKE*, a magazine produced by and for lesbian separatists. Covering a wide range of ideas and topics, *DYKE* editors believe that "almost every and any aspect of live can be looked at and analyzed through a lesbian vision."

Many of the articles in *DYKE* are informative. They have presented work on anything from preventative dentistry to how-to-build-a-backpack. Still, the magazine seems to function mainly as a network of communication for the lesbian separatist culture. Reviews of books, music, and theatre, and pages of letters from the readers and responses from the editors contribute to the sense of *DYKE*'s network function. As a whole, the magazine tends to reinforce a concept of separatism without contributing significantly to the development of a supporting ideology.

"We want to publish a magazine that fulfills our need for analysis, communication and news of our Lesbian culture. We believe that Lesbian culture presumes a separatist analysis. If Lesbian culture is intermixed with straight culture, it is no longer Lesbian, it is heterosexual and heterosocial, because energy and time are going to men. Lesbian community, Lesbian culture. . . means Lesbian only. *DYKE* is a magazines for Dykes only!"

Handsomely produced with articles, photographs and drawings, *DYKE* is typeset by OBU typesetters and printed by Tower Press, making it an all woman publication. Dyke pays all contibutors.

EARTH'S DAUGHTERS   Published irregularly
944 Kensington Ave. $2.50/4 issues
Buffalo, NY. 14215   Issues vary in size and format

There is no one phrase, not even a short paragraph, that can capture the essence of *EARTH'S DAUGHTERS*, a feminist literary and art periodical. It comes in all shapes, contains all manner of art, and is published at all times. Issue No. 4 was a little anthology of one woman "Robinson on the Woman Question": short poems in a 6 x 4 format. Double issue No. 5/6 was a heady collection of poetry and some rather interesting art work, which featured xerox reproductions of common household objects. *EARTH'S DAUGHTERS* specializes in surprise and unusual formats.

THE FEMINIST ART JOURNAL   Published quarterly
41 Montgomery Place $7 per year
Brooklyn, NY. 11215   8½ x 11, 56 pages, saddle stitched

Primarily for visual artists, THE FEMINIST ART JOURNAL is a handsome publication of critical articles, beautiful reproductions and photographs, interviews and reviews.

The editors describe THE FEMINIST ART JOURNAL as a forum for discussion of the following vital issues:

"Is there a recognizable women's sensitivity in art?

How have past and present attitudes toward the so-called decorative arts and the crafts affected women's status in the arts?

How to structure women artists' organizations.

The Collective vs the Hierarchy vs the Individual.

How artists (both men and women) can bypass the art establishment to bring art to a larger buying public?"

Occasionally, THE FEMINIST ART JOURNAL goes outside its visual art orientation to focus discussion on literature, dance and film-making.

THE FEMINIST ART JOURNAL pays all contributors and submissions are welcome.

FOCUS   Published monthly
Boston Daughters of Bilitis $6 per year
Room 323   5½ x 8½, 18 pages, unbound
419 Boylston Street
Boston, MA. 02116

FOCUS is literary review for gay women. Arriving in a discreet, unmarked envelope, FOCUS contains poetry, fiction, essays and reviews. All aspects of gay women's lives ar included, with an emphasis on dignified, positive literature by and for lesbians.

GILT EDGE   Published annually
c/o Women's Resource Center $3.50 in 1977
University of Montana   8½ x 10, 122 pages, perfect bound
Missoula, MT. 59812

Sometimes that which glitters is gold. Take for example, *GILT EDGE*, an exquisitely produced literary and art magazine where exceptional artwork and poetry and fiction are carefully married, each enhancing the other to produce the greatest total effect.

With a motto "a magazine of artists who are women," *GILT EDGE* is defiantly apolitical. There is no writing on the theme of social justice or any issue directly related to feminism. There is also no writing offensive to women—no portrayals of women as victims or shrews. What there is is a poetry of landscapes, of brief awakenings, of people encountered, of "gilt edges." Photogrpahs, drawings, and other reproductions breathe life into this magazine. Tending to wonderously feminine images, the visual artistry of *GILT EDGE* is its finest feature.

GOLD FLOWER   Published bi-monthly
P O Box 8341 $4/12 issues
Lake Street Station   8½ x 11, 16 pages, unbound
Minneapolis, MN. 55408

For women in the Twin Cities area, *GOLD FLOWER* is an excellent resource, combining community news with broadbased cultural analysis. Strictly for local women, *GOLD FLOWER* has the first "gossip" column I've seen in a long time. This column reports name changes, divorces, births, and rituals. Without the maliciousness associated with "gossip" columns, this feature may be a place where new rituals for a feminist society can be shared and developed. Reviews of local happenings, a calendar of community events and interviews with local women give *GOLD FLOWER* its basically regional appeal.

However, there are features of general interest as well. These include articles on spirituality, herbal remedies, and poetry. An unusual and interesting feature is a series of articles done by a local feminist theatre company which documents aspects of the artistic group process, and the political and emotional energy that collectivity requires.

GRAVIDA   Published quarterly
P O Box 76 $4 per year
Hartsdale, NY. 10530   5½ x 8½, 44 pages, saddle stitched

Published by the Women's Poetry Collective, *GRAVIDA* is a literary journal. "Our bias is excellence of craft, fresh imagery." The group functions as a collective with editorship that rotates for each issue, and as a weekly workshop for members. The result of their work is a fine, all poetry magazine which work on a variety of subjects, including gay and straight love. *GRAVIDA*'s contributors include men.

THE GREATER GOLDEN HILL POETRY EXPRESS
c/o The Feminist Poetry and Graphics Center
2829 Broadway   Published irregularly
San Diego, CA. 92102   Price varies from $1.25-$2.25 per copy
                                                      Format varies

THE GREATER GOLDEN HILL POETRY EXPRESS comes in different shapes and sizes. An issue containing the works of poets from all over the country costs $2.25; an issue of local poets is available at $1.25.

THE GREATER GOLDEN HILL POETRY EXPRESS is fun: fun to look at, but serious in content. The poems are both political and personal. The graphics, which are busy without being distracting, keep one turning the pages—express-fashion.

HERESIES   Published quarterly
P O Box 766 $10 per year
Canal Street Station   Format varies
New York, NY. 10013

"*HERESIES* is an idea-oriented journal devoted to the exam-
ination of art and politics from a feminist perspective. We believe
that what is commonly called art can have a political impact, and
that in the making of art and of all cultural artifacts our identities as women play a distinct role." Despite a liberal sprinkling of
poetry, art here refers mainly to visual art. This visual art is not
used as something to illustrate the texts; both the art and the
articles are reaching toward the development of a polictical
strategy.

HERESIES' structure reveals a great deal about their politics:
". . . a collective of feminists, some of whom are also socialists,
Marxists, lesbian feminists or anarchists; our fields include
painting, sculpture, writing, anthropology, literature, perfor-
mance, art history, architecture, and film-making. While the
themes of the individual issues will be determined by the collective, each issue will have a different editorial staff made up of
contributors as well as members of the collective. Each issue will
try to be accountable to and in touch with the international
feminist community."

Drawing together such a wide variation in backgrounds,
HERESIES is a collage of ideas and expressions. There is much
to read, and much to think about.

Unlike other magazines which use art as a stepping stone to
politics, *HERESIES* considers political topics on their own
merits—with or without accompanying art work. Thus, the first
issue contains articles which discuss wages for housework or
attempt to define socialist feminism along with some rather
erudite art criticism. *HERESIES* is not easily defined; they are
attempting to reach a very broad audience. The women who
read *HERESIES* will be artists, political activists, or both; they
will be intellectuals and they will be women who shun intellect-

ualizations. In *HERESIES* one can find theoretical articles along-side deeply involving personal testimony and fiction—in Spanish and in English. Along with the representational, such as posters of Chinese women at work, there are reproductions of abstract art.

HERESIES isn't striving to ridgidly define the materials they are working with: "As a step toward a demystification of art, we reject the standard relationship of criticism to art within the present system, which has often become the relationship of advertiser to product. We will not advertise a new set of genius-products just because they are made by women. We are not committed to any particular style or esthetic, nor to the com-petitive mentality that pervades the art world. Our view of femin-ism is one of process and change, and we feel that in the process of this dialogue we can foster a change in the meaning of art."

HERESIES announces all themes in advance and solicits manuscripts of 1000-5000 words in length. They will consider finished manuscripts or outlines. Visual artists should send photographs or reproductions. *HERESIES* pays all contributors a fee of $5-$50.

LADY-UNIQUE-INCLINATION-OF-THE-NIGHT
P O Box 803   Published irregularly
New Brunswick, NJ. 08903   Price varies: $2.00-$2.75
                                    7 x 8¼, 86 pages, perfect bound

"Lady-Unique-Inclination-of-the-Night is an American Moon Goddess. Her origins are in the Mayan culture of Mexico and Central America. We have taken her name as a way of identifying our deepest desire, the evolution of the meaning and truth of the goddess. She who is our most powerful projection of feminine consciousness, the source of understanding our limits and our limitlessness. . . Women have been denied their right to images which define and promote female power and independence. To reclaim images of the feminine, to share them with each other, and especially, to bring them to the world (i.e. to discover and

30

release the political potential of the spiritual) is a serious task which will continue to involve many women. *LADY-UNIQUE-INCLINATION-OF-THE-NIGHT* sees its specific work in providing a place for research and reinterpretation of the history of the feminine spirits."

LADY-UNIQUE is the thinking woman's spiritual journal, attempting a dialogue between theorists of political power and theorists of spiritual power. Sometimes the reading is tough as it delves into the disciplines of anthropology, history, literature, folklore, archaeology, and psychology, seeking to explore theories of the goddess.

Much work goes into the production of *LADY-UNIQUE*. The articles are uniformly well-written and amply documented with footnotes. Illustrated with images from Mayan folk art, the publication is beautifully printed and produced by an all woman staff.

Contributions for *LADY-UNIQUE* are eagerly sought. Especially welcome are essays (5-15 pages double-spaced) containing theory and information about the goddess. Relevant fiction, poetry, and experimental writing will be considered. Graphics are not solicited unless the artist has a series which might be used throughout an entire issue.

LESBIAN CONNECTION   Published monthly
P O Box 811 Free on request by Lesbians, $8 suggested donation
East Lansing, MI. 48823   8½ x 11, 30 pages, stapled

Put out by some very Ambition Amazons, *LESBIAN CONNECTION* is primarily a communication network. It is also a cultural journal, although not in the same sense as the other cultural journals in this book. It is the lack of ambition and cultural pretention that sets *LESBIAN CONNECTION* apart. But in so far as it reveals the lives and thoughts of American lesbians and shares new ideas and information, it is definitely an important cultural work.

In *LESBIAN CONNECTION* one finds articles, reviews,

letters, short statements of opinion. reponses, announcements and ads. It is a "nationwide forum of ideas by, for and about Lesbians." Ideas are flown like balloons and women who would never call themselves writers, or aspire to publication elsewhere, have a chance to communicate in this publication. Single spaced with one "connection" flowing into the next, *LESBIAN CONNECTION* is literally jam-packed with information.

THE LESBIAN FEMINIST   Published bi-monthly
c/o The Women's Center   Free, donations requested
243 West 20th Street   8½ x 11, 16 pages, folded
New York, NY. 10011

Published by a group known as The Lesbian Feminist Liberation, *THE LESBIAN FEMINIST* is both a newsletter of that organization and a political journal. Although there is a strong New York City orientation, *THE LESBIAN FEMINIST* publishes both personal and political analyses of lesbian feminist experience. Intermixed with photographs, local news blurbs and calendars, are articles on movement news, personal testimony and opinion, reviews, poetry, herstory pieces, journal entries, letters and dreams.

THE LESBIAN TIDE   Published bi-monthly
c/o Tide Publications $6.00 per year
8855 Cattaragus Avenue   8½ x 11, 40 pages, saddle stitched
Los Angeles, CA. 90034

Printed on newspaper, but folded like a magazine, *THE LESBIAN TIDE* breaks boundaries in content and graphics between a cultural journal and a newspaper. Through profiles of local women and articles on community news and issues, the women's community of Los Angeles is the primary focus of *THE LESBIAN TIDE*. It is a very reader-oriented magazine, with many pages devoted to letters from readers and responses. However, ample space is devoted to national news and cultural analysis, as well as reviews, photographs and graphics.

TIDE is produced by a radical-feminist collective whose

members believe that "basic change in this society is a prerequisite for real liberation for women and lesbians." Their own particular viewpoint is explored and developed on an editorial page. (Interestingly, the editorial page is a rare feature in feminist publications. Most publications will either present a narrow but integrated viewpoint, consistent throughout the publication, or they will present a variety of opinions, espousing none publically.) The *TIDE* collective is very honest about their politics, but open to other points of view. These differing points of view are often presented as news stories covering other social change movements, or reviews of local cultural events.

The resultant publication is highly eclectic—both in the politically diverse viewpoints it presents and in the tone of the articles which vary from the impassioned to the intellectual, from the journalistic to the personal.

THE LESBIAN TIDE pays contributors a nominal sum.

LESBIAN VOICES   Published quarterly
53 W. San Fernando $5 per year
San Jose, CA. 95116   7 x 8½, 60 pages, saddle stitched

What is relevant to lesbians is relevant to *LESBIAN VOICES* a literary/cultural journal. No two issues are exactly alike, as *LESBIAN VOICES* presents a variety of poetry, art, short stories, herstory, reviews, letters to the editor and responses, political opinion, and personal essays about everything from capitalism to feminist spirituality.

Editor Rosalie Nichols freely professes a personal bias in favor of "individualism, anarchism, lesbian separatism, feminist capitalism, atheism, and romantic literature." Many differing opinions are heard in *LESBIAN VOICES* as long as they are "rational" and presented with "a dignified format and construtive sense of life, in keeping with our belief that lesbianism can be, and should be, wholesome, fulfilling, and joyful."

There is an energy in *LESBIAN VOICES* that almost vibrates off the page. The crowded graphics contribute to this sense, but does not explain it, because this energy is totally positive. It must have something to do with the fact that *LESBIAN VOICES* is produced by the same crew that runs Ms Atlas Press and Ms Atlas Bookstore—and with three grand projects such as that, a great deal of women-energy is always generated.

(See Print Shops: *MS ATLAS PRESS*)

LETTERS   Published three times yearly
The Country Press $6 per year
P O Box 614   5½ x 8½, 60 pages, perfect bound
Saratoga Springs, NY. 12866

More collage than review, more experience than expression, *LETTERS* invites readers to share in the lives of the writers in unusual ways. Emphasizing personal points of view, *LETTERS* not only publishes correspondence along with other literary forms, but frequently prints these expressions in the author's own handwriting. Historically, letter writing was one of the few literary expressions open to women. *LETTERS* is a delightful extension of that old tradition.

"*LETTERS* enjoys sharing ideas, feelings, and experiences through the publication of poetry, fiction, facts, graphics and particularly letters, which are of special interest to their creators." A variety of type faces and handwriting styles enhance the personal touch. "Each contributor makes her own statement, becoming in a sense an editor and an intergral part of the concept of *LETTERS*."

LETTERS is an international literary forum for women (and occasionally prints men). "We are of many different colors, nationalities and persuasions. We are mothers and grandmothers. We are daughters, sisters, friends and lovers. We are, of course, more than any of these words can convey." As a publication, *LETTERS* is also more than words can convey.

LIGHT
Box 1105
Stuyvesant Station
New York, NY. 10009

Publishes 4 issues/volume
$4.50/volume
5½ x 8½, 60 pages, perfect bound

Editor Roberta Gould compiles an ecletic assortment of poetry in *LIGHT*. The first criterion that is applied to material is craft. After that, all points of view are welcome—except material that is racist, sexist, or fascist. Personal, political and aesthetic poetry are all included. What distinguishes *LIGHT* from other literary reviews is an outstanding international collection of political poems, translations and originals, which are always poems first, polemics second. A special translation issue featured political poems by women from Greece and Chile.

Lovely line drawings and photographs enhance the texts, frequently making wry commentary on the poetry, and always contributing to the vitality of the publication.

LIGHT publishes men, although not as frequently as women.

LILITH
Box 16c, 500 East 63rd St.
New York, NY. 10021

Published quarterly
$6 per year
8½ x 11, 50 pages, saddle stitched

LILITH is "the Jewish Women's Quarterly." To women who have examined Judaism and found it to be extremely patriarchal, yet cannot shake their religious and ethnic background, *LILITH* will come as a pleasant surprise. In *LILITH* one finds a real intellectual honesty and readiness to deal with the contradictions of Jewish Feminism. For example, *LILITH* admits to the problem that the Jewish community will not accept lesbians, but that there *are* Jewish lesbians. Contradictions are questioned, analyzed and solutions are sometimes offered. There is a commitment to change within the context of the religion which has a real Feminist integrity.

LILITH welcomes articles about Jewish women and analyses of news and events inside and outside the Movement. They also publish fiction, poetry, biography, children's stories, drama, literary criticism, photographs and original art. *LILITH* is rather sleek looking—appropriate for anyone's coffee table.

MAKARA   Published bi-monthly
1001 Commercial Drive $6 per year Canada, $7.50 foreign
Vancouver, B.C. V5L 3X1   8½ x 11, 50 pages, saddle stitched
Canada

MAKARA bills itself as "The Canadian Magazine by Women for People." It is an exquisite magazine. Produced by the Pacific Women's Graphic Arts Co-Operative and printed by Press Gang Publishers, the graphics alone make this magazine outstanding; the covers are so magnificient one might want to hang them on the wall. (*MAKARA* offers a poster series of cover reproductions.)

However, there is more than just visual appeal to recommend this publication. *MAKARA* features Canadian art and photography; articles by and about unusual people with unconventional approaches to social issues, sports, politics, entertainment, survival, work and health. Whatever the subject, *MAKARA*'s policy is to emphasize a positive outlook, reflecting their belief that real dialogue and a willingness to explore alternatives is an avenue to social change. In keeping with this approach, *MAKARA* is one of the very few publications to explore Native American culture, as well as Native American's political struggles. Poetry, fiction, children's stories, history, criticism, music, satire and reviews complete *MAKARA*.

There is a little something for everyone in *MAKARA*. The strong Canadian nationalism which runs steadily through the magazine makes it rather educational for Americans not familiar with the concept and the struggles associated with Canadian nationalism. Obviously, it is a magazine in which Canadians would take a great deal of pride.

MAKARA announces all themes in advance and pays all contributors.

(See Press I: *PRESS GANG PUBLISHERS*)

MEDIA REPORT TO WOMEN   Published monthly
3306 Ross Place NW $10 per year
Washington, D.C. 20008   8½ x 11, 16 pages, saddle stitched

"What women are doing and thinking about Communications Media" is an accurate description of the *MEDIA REPORT TO WOMEN*. Information, ideas and philosophy blend to form a mosaic of feminist press media, news services, radio/TV, film, art, graphics, speaker's bureaus, libraries, distribution companies and bookstores. There is an enormous amount of information in each issue, attesting to the strength of women's media.

To the *MEDIA REPORT* "female journalism is something different." They are as concerned with ethics as they are with information. *MEDIA REPORT* seeks to overturn the bias against women in the media.

THE MEDIA REPORT TO WOMEN publishes an annual Index/Directory. The Index covers media activities and research and the Directory covers women's media groups and individual media women.

(See Additional Resources: *WOMEN'S INSTITUTE FOR FREEDOM OF THE PRESS*)

MOUNTAIN MOVING   Published 2-3 times per year
c/o NU Women's Center $3 per year
619 Emerson   8 x 10, 30 pages, saddle stitched
Evanston, IL 60201

MOUNTAIN MOVING, "a feminist quarterly," is a cross between a cultural journal and a newspaper. The straight reportage which characterizes most of the articles, as well as the newsprint it is printed on, conspire to make *MOUNTAIN MOVING* resemble a newspaper. However, the conception is magazine-oriented with articles clustered around the topics "Lifestyles," "Prominent Women," "Literary," and "Images of Women." There is also poetry, short fiction and book reviews. Photographs, beautifully feminine art work and careful layout give *MOUNTAIN MOVING* a very attractive appearance.

MOUNTAIN MOVING is designed as a forum for feminist thought in the Chicago/Evanston area, with an end goal of helping to "knock down some of the barriers that keep women and men from reaching their full potential as human beings." Therefore, there are. occasional articles by men, as well as an assortment of articles on various feminist issues, such as battered women, feminist socialism, liberating sexuality, language usage.

MOVING OUT   Published bi-annually
4866 Third St. $2 per year
Wayne State University   8½ x 11, 58 pages, saddle stitched
Detroit, MI. 48202

Since 1971, *MOVING OUT* has continued to publish an exciting, polished, feminist literary and arts journal. A consistent core collective has worked on *MOVING OUT*, contributing to the rare maturity which is most evident in yearly improvements, particularly in graphics. Each issue is rich with essays, articles, reviews, poetry, fiction, photographs and drawings. All of the material has a feminist perspective which emphasizes a commitment to social change above any restrictions on sexuality or lifestyle. This means that one may read in *MOVING OUT* an awesome account of a homebirth, preceded by an equally moving lesbian love story. The emphasis is always on emotional honesty. *MOVING OUT* shies away from both academic and journalistic styles.

MOVING OUT will accept only previously unpublished materials. Their maxium length for acceptable manuscripts is 20 pages. They are open to all forms of writing and art on all subjects.

The best of five years of *MOVING OUT* has been collected in a book: *MOVING TO ANTARTICA*, edited by Margaret Kaminski (Dustbooks, $3.95/paper, $7.95). *MOVING TO ANTARTICA* features fifty different women writers with poetry, novel excerpts, short stories, diary excerpts, drama, articles, interviews and reviews.

(See Press I: *DUSTBOOKS*)

MS.   Published monthly
370 Lexington Avenue $10 per year
New York, NY. 10017   8½ x 11, 120 pages, saddle stitched

The best known of any feminist publication, *MS.* has come to define mainstream feminism. Sold on magazine stand everywhere in America, *MS.*'s availability has resulted in their dubious position of being the voice of American feminism. Obviously, with a movement as disparate as the Feminist Movement, no one publication can possibly define it. *MS.* does try to have a little something for everyone.

MS. is a national magazine "dealing with women's changing lives." They are as likely to write on battered wives as they are about men's oppression in a sexist society. *MS.* covers news, the arts, fiction, poetry, and stories for children. Each month they feature critical articles on issues ranging from Affirmative Action to Health to Consumer Affairs. They emphasize famous women, frequently doing cover stories on "stars" of the movement.

MS. is the most known, most controversial, most praised and most condemned publication in the women's movement. That must say something.

NEW AMERICA   Published three times per year
Department of American Studies $4 per year
University of New Mexico   9 x 9, 40-80 pages, perfect bound
Albuquerque, NM. 87131

NEW AMERICA: A REVIEW is published by graduate students of the American Studies Department at the University of New Mexico. With none of the alienating, fashionable anger that abounds in most university literary productions, *NEW AMERICA* is purely refreshing. Although not exclusively female, they have produced a very special all women's issue and should be considered a good non-sexist resource. Each issue has a central theme around which the materials center. Work has been presented by and about Native Americans and the Fall 1976 edition was a photographic study of the Southwest.

NEW AMERICA takes great care to publish a fine looking volume and invites submissions of articles, fiction, reviews, photographs and graphics.

OUT THERE MAGAZINE   Published quarterly
6944 W. George Street $5 per year
Chicago, IL. 60634   8½ x 11, 100 pages, plastic spine

OUT THERE MAGAZINE is a poetry journal publishing men and women. One all women's issue has been published; editor Rose Lesniak feels a lack of publicity has prevented her from receiving poetry from women she would like to hear from. *OUT THERE* publishes experimental poems, long poems, and art, and welcome more submissions from women.

PAID MY DUES   Published 4 times/volume
c/o Women's Soul Publishing $4 per volume
P O Box 11646   8½ x 11, 60 pages, saddle stitched
Milwaukee, WI. 53211

PAID MY DUES, A Journal of Women and Music, is made to order for women who take music seriously—as performers or members of the audience. The only feminist publication devoted entirely to woman-made music, *PAID MY DUES* publishes original songs, articles about the women in music, interviews, reviews, photographs, drawings, cartoons, satire and criticism. Music herstory is effectively presented, covering a wide range of thought and new information, from the works of Fanny Mendelssohn (Felix's sister) to the music of the 50's.

Behind the philosophy of *PAID MY DUES* is the recognition of the difficulty women face in the music world. Putting theory into practice, *PAID MY DUES* actively protects the rights of artists associated with the magazine. Written agreements made with contributors to *PAID MY DUES* before publication include a token payment and arrangement concerning how the work will be used. *PAID MY DUES* believes that it is the exclusive right of the artist to determine the fate of her work. They use and protect copyright laws.

Like many other feminist publications, *PAID MY DUES* is forced into an irregular publication schedule while the staff works full time to support themselves.

In addition to producing *PAID MY DUES*, Women's Soul Publishing has two other ventures. A pamphlet called "Producing Concerts ($.50) contains "a years worth of woman-sense" on concert production. *MY SISTER'S SONG* is a 28 page discography of over 2,000 entries of music recorded by women from Tammy Wynette to Meg Christian ($.90 includes postage).

THE PAINTED BRIDE QUARTERLY Published quarterly
527 South Street $5 per year
Philadelphia, PA. 19147 6 x 9, 72 pages, perfect bound

Louise Simons and R. Daniel Evans co-edit this distinguished literary review which publishes both men and women. *THE PAINTED BRIDE QUARTERLY* is in the best tradition of the "small magazine," open to experimental as well as traditional work. Many women are published in *PAINTED BRIDE*, and not just token women; it is apparent from the content that the editors share a genuine commitment to publishing not only feminist art by women, but non-sexist art by men as well. Music, poetry, photographs, art, reviews, but no fiction, can all be found in *THE PAINTED BRIDE QUARTERLY*.

THE PASSAGE   Published quarterly
Institute for the Study of Women in Transition $12 per year
40 Pleasant St.   8½ x 11, 20 pages, saddle stitched
Portsmouth, NH. 03801

Specially designed as a "magazine for the expression of women's transitional issues," *THE PASSAGE* publishes poetry, short stories, plays, sketches, cartoons, literary and art criticism, photographs and black and white ink graphics. Although not explicitly defined, it seems that "women's transitional issues" refer to the problems women face as they shed their traditional roles as wives and mothers and take on the challenge (and difficulties) of living as whole people. *THE PASSAGE* is especially receptive to the work of older women.

Other periodicals of the Institute for the Study of Women in Transition include *THE JOURNAL OF TRANSITIONAL ISSUES CONCERNING WOMEN* (4 issues/$18) and *THE IN-STITUTE NEWSLETTER* (6 issues, $6).

(See Press I: *THE INSTITUTE PRESS*)

PRIMAPARA   Published bi-annually
P O Box 171 $3 per year
Oconto, WI. 54153   5½ x 8½, 48 pages, saddle stitched

PRIMAPARA is more than a literary magazine, more than its pages of poetry, drawings and reviews. *PRIMAPARA* is a support network for Wisconsin women writers, providing both a market-place for their writing and a medium for exchange between readers and writers. As the editors explain, *PRIMAPARA* is "our reaffirmation that the writing talent of Wisconsin women equals that of other areas. We continue to focus only on our state's residents... (and have) gained a personal rapport with many contributors and subscribers that doesn't seem possible if we were attempting a nation-wide journal." The editors aim to create a viable writing community in their state.

PRIMAPARA's example can be a useful model for other re-gionally based publications. The need for support between writers is as great as the need for markets. *PRIMPARA* provides a nec-essary service in an intelligent, open way.

PRIMAVERA   Published 1-2 times per year
Ida Noyes Hall $.3.50 per issue
University of Chicago   8½ x 11, 90 pages, perfect bound
1212 East 59th Street
Chicago, IL 60637

PRIMAVERA is a handsome literary journal which provides

a market primarily for Chicago based writers and artists. Decidedly apolitical in editorial policy, though not necessarily in content, *PRIMAVERA* strives to present a mix of feminine sensibilities. Each issue includes short stories, poetry, essays and art. The full size format enables them to reproduce large drawings without losing detail or impact.

PRIMAVERA is another example of a literary journal whose staff members view their function as more than the placing of the written work on the page. Unlike most readers of material submitted to literary magazines, the staff of *PRIMAVERA* not only selects material for publication but also attempts to pinpoint strengths and weaknesses of the manuscripts. As a result of meetings and correspondence with contributors, a widening circle of women have become aware of other writers in the greater Chicago area.

PRIME TIME   Published bi-monthly
420 West 46th Street $7 per year
New York, NY. 10036
     Special rates if unemployed or subsisting on Social Security
8½ x 11, 24 pages, saddle stitched

PRIME TIME is an unequivocally politicized feminist cultural /political journal, "by and for old." With interviews, personal essays, political analysis, and news briefs, *PRIME TIME* seeks to "1) analyze our situation as older women, 2) vent our problems and 3) find ways to solve them."

The mood of this journal is one of considerable warmth, support and concern. All problems of older women are compassionately (and passionately) discussed—whether the problems are those of displaced homemakers, discriminatory factory policies, the forced retirement of professionals, or physical health. With the issues of Aging, Ageism, and older Role Models well-recognized concerns of all women, *PRIME TIME* is a valuable resource for the young and old alike.

QUEST: A FEMINIST QUARTERLY   Published quarterly
P O Box 8843 $9 per year
Washington, D.C. 20003   6 x 8½, 80 pages, perfect bound

QUEST is the rarest of political journals: one that analyzes the future, as well as the present that, balances theory with well-researched factual articles, that is promoting an active search for strategies of change. Each issue of *QUEST* covers a specific theme in-depth. The treatment of each theme suggests that *QUEST* is designed as an educational tool, as well as a forum for social, political and economic theory.

A statement from the editors explains *QUEST*'s orientation:

> "*QUEST* wishes to explore the differences and similarities in ideal-ogies and strategies among various segments of the women's movement . . . (reaching) those who are creating and teaching political, social or economic change. . . *QUEST* wishes to contribute to the evolution of better strategies and tactics, to be a process for evaluating previous theory and practice. . . The time has come to expand feminist ideology. Improved ideology and strategies will give feminist and other organizers a basis from which they can work with a clearer sense of direction."

QUEST's emphasis is on theory, most of which is presented in intellectual language. Although *QUEST* is open to printing poetry, interviews, cartoons, satire, etc., much of their previous content has been in the form of theoretical essays.

Topics of recent issues have been "Communication and Control," "Work, Work, Work," "Race, Class and Culture," and "Women and Spirituality."

Beautifully designed and amply illustrated, *QUEST*'s timeless content make it a fine addition to one's library. *QUEST* accepts only original, unpublished materials and pays all contributors.

ROOM   Published irregularly
P O Box 40610 $2 per single copy
San Francisco, CA. 94140   5½ x 8½, 64 pages, perfect bound

The herstory of *ROOM* is the herstory of many publications

in this book. "The concept for *ROOM* grew out of an ongoing women's writing workshop. The excitement of sharing our work each week made us aware of the need for more dialogue among women who write."

Publishing prose, poetry, and graphics by known and new writers and artists, *ROOM* contains a wide range of artistic styles. Open to both experimental and tradional work *ROOM* presents a picture of what "literary women" are writing these days. *ROOM* also presents interviews with women writers, articles and book reviews.

ROOM OF ONE'S OWN   Published quarterly
1918 Waterloo Street $6 per year, $7 foreign
Vancouver, B.C. V6R 3G6   5½ x 8, 80 pages, perfect bound
Canada

Published by the Growing Room Collective, *ROOM OF ONE'S OWN* is a "Feminist Journal of Literature and Criticism." Fiction and poetry are given the highest priority with a liberal sprinkling of criticism, book reviews, and art intermixed.

An occasional all Canadian issue and a predominance of Canadian writers is strong proof of *ROOM OF ONE'S OWN*'s nationalism, a characteristic of most Canadian publications. Because it is Canadian, there are some real differences between *ROOM OF ONE'S OWN* and sister literature journals in America. For one thing, Canadian Feminism is more closely aligned with left politics, hence there is a very strong working class consciousness. This linkage with the left also results in the publishing of work by men once in a while. Because Canada has not become the melting pot which America has, awareness of ethnic cultures continually surfaces. In *ROOM OF ONE'S OWN*, one can read of different Native American cultures and about French and English Canadians, with poetry in both languages.

A *ROOM OF ONE'S OWN* has a professional appearance and a serious approach to literature. All of the writing in a *ROOM OF ONE'S OWN*, and particularly the fiction, evidences a great emphasis on control of craft by the writers.

RUBYFRUIT READER   Published monthly
P O Box 949
Felton, CA. 95018
    Send inquiry with SASE for price and format information

Few enthusiasts of feminist culture will miss that the title of this publication is inspired by Rita Mae Brown's book *RUBY-FRUIT JUNGLE* by Daughters Press (See Press I), a lesbian novel. *THE RUBYFRUIT READER* is a "lesbian communique." It contains news items gleaned from national feminist newspapers as well as notices of local events. Although preference is given to publishing the work of Santa Cruz women, *THE RUBYFRUIT READER* will consider general interest articles, poetry, fairy tales, reviews, and "vignettes of lesbian lives and loves" by other women as well.

At the time of writing, *THE RUBYFRUIT READER* has a mimeographed format and a local orientation. However, the *RUBYFRUIT* collective would like to start printing the publication as soon as the money can be raised. And many a successful, national feminist publications has followed the very same path.

THE SECOND WAVE   Published quarterly
Box 344 $4 per year
Cambridge A   8½ x 11, 52 pages, saddle stitched
Cambridge, MA. 02139

THE SECOND WAVE, "a magazine of the new Feminism," is perhaps the most literate of the political journals, or perhaps the most political of the literary journals. The Second Wave Collective sees it as a political journal"'. . . defined and active through content, structure and process. *SECOND WAVE* is both an alternative to and a confrontation with the political and cultural violence that descends on our heads every day; it is a tool with which we hammer at existing social and economic structures to open up new directions for a woman's revolution. . . What we have printed reflects a spectrum of issues which affect women's lives: violence, rape, spirituality, motherhood and daughterhood, lesbianism, herstory and myth, and revolutionary feminist vision."

The spectrum of issues presented is indeed political. But the packaging of *THE SECOND WAVE* transcends the traditional formats of political journals. In addition to articles and analysis, there are many pages of poetry, fiction, book reviews and art.

SECOND WAVE is handsomely produced and visually accessible with large print and typeset columns. Megaera prints *THE SECOND WAVE*, making it an all-woman publication.

(See Print Shops: *MEGAERA PRESS*)

SYBYL-CHILD   Published three times per year
6909 West Park Drive $8 per year
Hyattsville, MD. 20793   5½ x 8½, 60 pages, saddle stitched

SIBYL-CHILD is a "women's arts and culture journal" where cultural analysis weighs as heavily as art with a vast array of reviews, articles, short stories, poetry, fiction, art, and even (in Vol. 2, No. 1), a board game called "A Tub of One's own." The editors describe *SIBYL-CHILD* as "the voices of women's diversities in lifestyles, feelings, politics, and personal myths, both those that need destruction and those that need creation. . . Our goal is to present the reality of women's participation in all the arts and to explore the variety of women's impact on culture."

The importance of emerging feminist culture to *SIBYL-CHILD* can be measured by the space given to it. In *SIBYL-CHILD* one finds pages of book reviews, film reviews, art analysis. These reviews are frequently presented in the beginning of the publication, holding a prominent place. Most literary publications keep the book reviews in the back pages. As part of their commitment to increased communication among women, *SIBYL-CHILD* will publish information about organizations or projects that are of interest to other women. They also provide a listing of books received, and exchange publications, with addresses and descriptive blurbs.

The content of *SIBYL-CHILD* varies from issue to issue. Certain editions contain more cultural analysis, other more literature and art. Vol. 2, No. 3 was a special fiction issue. In one respect, *SIBYL-CHILD* is always consistent: they only publish writing that evidences a great control of craft. Unsolicited manuscripts accompanied by an SASE are always welcome.

SINISTER WISDOM	Published three times per year
3116 Country Club Drive	$4.50 per year
Charlotte, NC. 28205	6 x 9, pages and bindings vary

In a serious attempt to create "an Amazon Culture Center," *SINISTER WISDOM* is a lesbian/feminist cultural journal. The consciousness of *SINISTER WISDOM* is that of the "lesbian or lunatic who embraces her boundary/criminal status, with the aim of creating a new species in time/space;" or said another way: "the creation of a revolutionary lesbian imagination in politics and art."

Publishing essays, herstory, fiction, poetry and political and cultural analysis, in fact, everything except straight journalism and how-to articles, *SINISTER WISDOM* is not simply a magazine about lesbians. It is an attempt to create a culture—and this necessitates a self-conscious awareness in the effort to deal with language and art in new, experimental ways.

If this sounds vague or exotic, discussing a special edition on lesbian publishing (Vol. 1, No. 2) may make it clearer. In this issue, a 135 page, perfect bound edition ($2.50), lesbian writing and publishing was reviewed and analyzed. The sections dealt with aesthetics, politics, information, and projections into the future. Bertha Harris, one of the contributors to that issue of *SINISTER WISDOM* explains what it is all about: "We are peeling off layers—of inhibition and of what we've learned—and trying to recapture that which is the source of literature, which is intuition totally engaged with intellectuality, with a sense of arrogance about it."

SO'S YOUR OLD LADY
3149 Fremont Avenue S
Minneapolis, MN. 55408

Publishes six issues/volume
$7.50 per volume
8½ x 11, 22 pages, saddle stitched

SO'S YOUR OLD LADY is a "lesbian/feminist journal" with the emphasis on lesbian. A literary and art journal, *SO'S YOUR OLD LADY* publishes short fiction, poetry, drawings, photographs, and reviews that leave the reader with a warm feeling, a sense of shared intimacy with the writers. The work is pointedly personal, with political overtones. And communication ranks higher than control of craft; new writers appear alongside polished and published writers.

The full size format allows for lovely integration of words and drawings.

SPEAKOUT
P O Box 6165
Albany, NY. 12206

Published monthly
$3.50 per year
8½ x 11, 20 pages, stapled

In its sixth year, *SPEAKOUT* retains its mimeographed newsletter format. Other publications, proving their will to survive will frequently aspire to a more "professional" or slick appearance. But *SPEAKOUT* has continued to conscientiously place their collective energy into writing and community outreach instead of fund raising for an up-graded appearance.

With articles, book reviews, and poetry, *SPEAKOUT* seeks to provide upstate New York with a consistent source of news about local feminist activities, and to supply a forum for readers to explore internal and external feminist development.

SQUEEZEBOX
334 North Vassar
Witchita, KS. 67208

Published three times yearly
$3.50 per year
5½ x 8½, 45 pages, saddle stitched

SQUEEZEBOX, A MAGAZINE OF PRESSING SOUNDS contains a variety of styles. Despite its title, *SQUEEZEBOX* is confined to the written word; it does not make any sounds. But

49

with the energy contained in its pages, *SQUEEZEBOX* does not need to add another dimension to its credits. Restricting the content only by a one-page limit on poetry and prose, *SQUEEZE-BOX* presents prose poems, concrete poems, imagist poems, political poems, any and all kinds of poems and short fiction. The overall effect is not chaotic at all; *SQUEEZEBOX* brings fresh air. There is a genuine openness to new forms, a tolerance lacking in more narrowly defined publications.

Publishing out of Kansas, *SQUEEZEBOX* is especially concerned with developing local and regional talent. Partial to publishing women, editor Mardy Murphy will also publish work by men.

(See Press II: *PAPER TIGER PRESS*)

SUNBURY   Published three times per year
Box 274 $5 per year
Jerome Avenue Station   5½ x 8½, 80 pages, perfect bound
New York, NY. 10468

In labeling *SUNBURY*, one meets many of the contradictions that arise from applying a system of strict categories. First of all, *SUNBURY* is a poetry journal. The poems collected from an anthology of feminist poetry. These are poems which escape the label "political rhetoric," yet are political; poems that are written by Third World women, lesbians, mothers, and women whose labels are unimportant since they write as representative women. The poetry is feminist in the affirmation of the poets' woman-selves, feminist in the clear and lyrical language, feminist in he true things they say about women. With this emphasis on the political nature of the poetry, *SUNBURY* belongs to the ranks of magazines actively creating feminist culture.

The contradictions surface when one mentions that they also publish men on occasion. (Does this mean that *SUNBURY* is non-sexist—meaning not feminist, but not offensive to women? *SUNBURY* is feminist in my mind.) The second contradiction is that *SUNBURY* is marketed both as a magazine with subscriptions and as an anthology/book.

The format of *SUNBURY* is austere. With no photographs or drawings, the poems lie flat on the page, letting the words carry the entire message. This is reminiscent of the classic literary review.

SUNBURY is obviously appealing to many people; the subscription list numbers over 1500—which is very rare for any poetry journal.

(See Press I: *SUNBURY PRESS*)

SYZYGY   Published bi-annually
3901 Ledgewood Drive $5 per year
Cincinnati, OH. 45229   6 x 8½, 70 pages, perfect bound

SYZYGY specializes in publishing short fiction and sketches. The word "syzygy" means yoking together, especially of opposites. The editors of *SYZYGY* have chosen that name with care. The describe themselves as "a group of women of uncommon backgrounds yoked together by common gender, common geographical location and common respect for the written word." They are "under thirty and over seventy, and every age in between. . . Jewish, Chicano, and White Anglo-Saxon. . . from New York brownstones and Colorado barrios, Texas ranches and homes in Cincinnati's West End."

It is a pleasure to read in *SYZYGY* the work of Black and Chicano women. It is a pleasure to read the work of women outside the New York City/California circuit. *SYZYGY* has my respect for producing a wonderful magazine, representing many points of view, including the male point of view on occasion, and many different prose styles.

SYZYGY is a new publication and promises to play an important role in publishing serious fiction by women (and men). There are all too few publications like it; and *SYZYGY* is most welcome.

(See Press II: *CINCINNATI WOMEN'S PRESS*)

13TH MOON   Published bi-annually
P O Box 3 $4.50 per year
Inwood Station   6 x 9, 128 pages, perfect bound
New York, NY. 10034

With the motto "A literary magazine publishing women who-ever we choose to be," *13TH MOON* is an intensely feminine exploitation of contemporary women's literature and art. Editor Ellen Marie Bissert states: "The goal of the *13TH MOON* is not a feminist magazine per se. It is feminist in the general sense of being concerned exclusively with the work and viewpoint women. *13TH MOON* is involved with the writing of women rather than political issues, despite the feminism of the staff."

Without a pre-determined political bias, each contribution to *13TH MOON* is judged on its own merits. Thus *13TH MOON* presents a remarkably accurate picture of women today representing Amazons and victims.

Two aspects of the content of *13TH MOON* are particularly striking. First, the length enables the publication of longer pieces of fiction, novel excerpts, herstory, biography, interviews and poems of varying lengths. The second aspect that is characteristic of *13TH MOON* is the physical sensuality of much of the work. After reading this magazine from cover to cover, one sees, smells, feels,—lovers entwined, blood running down one's legs, lying in freshly cut grass.

THROUGH THE LOOKING GLASS   Published monthly
P O Box 22061 $5 per year
Seattle, WA. 98122   Or free to prisoners and poor people
                                        8½ x 14, 16 pages, stapled

THROUGH THE LOOKING GLASS is a political news-letter, "a women's and children's prison newsletter." Articles, interviews, news items, and poetry are written by, or focused on, women and children incarcerated in prisons and jails, mental hospitals, juvenile detention and foster homes, halfway houses, poverty, and destructive family homes. Their purpose is to encourage analysis of the American justice system, and to remind people of the different forms of prisons and the consequences for the prisoners and their families. Information is provided about pending legislation and court cases, with addresses provided when letters of support or protest are solicited.

VELVET WINGS   Published three times per year
1228 Oxford Street $4 per year
Berkeley, CA. 94709   5½ x 9, 60 pages, saddle stitched

VELVET WINGS features poetry, short prose and artwork by both men and women. There is a great variety of styles in this publication, a blend of political and non-political content. Editor Sarah Kennedy is actively seeking more submissions. "Send a SASE (or else you won't get it back!) and don't be impatient. . . I'll get to you. Send a contributor's note too."

Issue No. 1 of *VELVET WINGS* was printed by Sarah Kennedy at Shameless Hussy Press.

(See Press 1: *SHAMELESS HUSSY PRESS*)

WEST END   Published quarterly
Box 354 $5 per year
Jerome Ave Station   7 x 8½, 50 pages, saddle stitched
Bronx, NY. 10468

WEST END, A MAGAZINE OF POETRY AND POLITICS, contains prose as well as poetry, photographs and an occasional interview. Published out of New York, the underlying perspective is clearly urban. Both men and women are equally represented. *WEST END* specializes in "Poetry and other writings that support the movement for social change in this time, in this America, under these conditions."

Without the sustaining vision of building a feminist, women-oriented future, *WEST END* presents a more dismal picture of the world than many woman-only publications. Editor Gail Darrow Kaliss writes: ". . . and still there is a part of the picture missing: the sense of struggle; along with all the description of what is wrong, what is missing in our lives, there needs to be some sense that this is not unending. Perhaps many of the writers who would be sending us such work are too involved with the struggles they're in to put them into poetry—but we need their view."

For those interested in what politically-oriented male writers, especially Black male writers, are producing, *WEST END* is an excellent resourse.

(See Press I: *WEST END PRESS*)

THE WILD IRIS   Published irregularly
c/o Marty Moatz-Austin $2 per issue
1732 Cedar Street   7 x 8½, 78 pages, saddle stitched
Berkeley, CA. 94703

Taking their name and inspiration from Susan Griffin's poem: "Love should grow up like a wild iris in the fields," this *WILD IRIS* is a feminist literary magazine. The editors of *THE WILD IRIS* met at a writing class led by Susan Griffin. Out of the class grew an on-going writing workshop. Most of the editors are still a part of that workshop, though the magazine has an independent existence. Meeting in a class gave these women a chance to collaborate which might not have occured otherwise; their ages vary from 31 to 73—reflecting a range still rare in collectives these days.

Publishing a balance of poetry and prose, the editors welcome submissions from feminists everywhere. Because the editors are (with one exception) women with family and/or job obligations, it is not possible for them to adhere to a publication schedule. Therefore, they do not have subscrition rates, and rely soley on bookstores for distribution. They hope to have a fourth issue out in the Fall of 1977.

THE WITCH AND THE CHAMELEON

c/o Amanda Bankier　　　　　Published three times per year
Apt. 6　　　　　　　　　　　　　　　　　　　　　$4 per year
2 Paisley Ave S　　　　　8½ x 11, 30 pages, saddle stitched
Hamilton, Ontario
Canada

THE WITCH AND THE CHAMELEON is the first of its kind: a feminist, science fiction magazine (or fanzine, as some would call it). Questions of politics and philosopy are deeply emeshed in the science-fiction related criticism one finds in *THE WITCH AND THE CHAMELEON*. In addition, there are letters, fiction, poetry and reviews. There is an intimacy to the writing—almost as though these were personal letters, essays, exchanges with friends. And there is a feeling that important exchanges are taking place, especially in the area of feminist literary criticism. This is a publication of interest to anyone interested in literature, especially fiction. Starting with science fiction and fantasy, a tremendous wealth of ideas and information about the craft of writing are shared.

WOMENSPIRIT

WOMENSPIRIT　　　　　　　　　　　Published quarterly
Box 263　　　　　　　　　　　　　　　　　$6 per year
Wolf Creek, OR.　97497　　　8½ x 11, 70 pages, bindings vary

Anyone fascinated by the subject of women's spirituality will find *WOMENSPIRIT* an invaluable resource, and a delightful addition to their library. With no ultimate definition of a tremendous range of philosophies, presenting articles on witchcraft, healing, herbal remedies, concepts of animism, goddesses, matriarchies and much more. Their purpose is to foster a growing inquiry into and deeper exploration of the nature of the spiritual. This material is presented in poetry, essays, personal testimony, art, reviews, songs and photographs.

A statement of purpose from an early issue explains more of *WOMENSPIRITS'S* goals: ". . . to illuminate our former confus-

ions, to heal our wounds, to end our isolations—to bring acceptance and insight into all of our experiences: the crazy wild terror
ones, the weird places, and the black ones, as well as the ecstatic
and serene ones. Our intention is to put women in touch—in
communion—with each other and ourselves. The impact we hope
for is. . . the risky, daring step into authentic sight. . . we always
want to look at the consciousness: it must be pro-woman,
woman-proud, aware of the potential of women. *WOMENSPIRIT*
is a magazine to make space for sharing the deepest questions of
women now." (Spring, Vol. 1, No. 3)

WOMEN: A JOURNAL OF LIBERATION

3028 Greenmount Avenue   Published 4 issues/volume
Baltimore, MD. 21218 $5 per volume
                                      8½ x 11, 60 pages, saddle stitched

Since 1969, *WOMEN* has been producing a political/cultural
journal where photographs of anonymous women, poetry and
artwork give the magazine a warmth, the sense of reality and
centeredness in daily life.

Each issue center on a specific theme as it relates to women—
ordinary women, anonymous women, women of all classes, races,
political definition and lifestyle choices. Their purpose in developing these themes is to make women from differing backgrounds
interesting to one another, and to provide a space where communication that crosses age/class/race barriers can take place.
This is done through interviews with outstanding, though not
famous women. Articles are written by women who may not be
professional writers, but who have something to say. Most importantly, when *WOMEN* is exploring a particular theme, they
take special care to go directly to the source. An exceptionally
well done issue on Aging (Vol. 4 No. 4) contained articles by and
about specific older women. Other themes that have been explored include: The Cost of Living, Sexuality, Women as Workers
Under Capitalism, The Power and Scope of the Women's Movement, and Androgeny.

In making a genuine commitment to communicate with as

many women as possible, not just women with academic or movement backgrounds, WOMEN goes one step further than most women's publication. WOMEN is skillfully edited so that all the materials are clear and concise—accessible to most reading skill levels—without diluting the power of the materials presented. And the materials *are* powerful—and moving—they are about women as we truly are.

WOMEN/POEMS   Published irregularly
107 Upland Road $1.75 single copy
Cambridge, MA. 02140   5½ x 8½, 36 pages, saddle stitched

WOMEN/POEMS presents an unusually tight collection of poems. Many voices and styles are represented, including prose poems. What unifies these poems is the sense that each is a complete entity and does not hinge on commonly assumed politics, or any preconceived notion of good and bad poetry.

WOMEN/POEMS is published irregularly; the editors will return submissions if they do not plan to put together a magazine in the near future.

WOMEN TALKING, WOMEN LISTENING
P O Box 2055   Published annually
Dublin, CA. 94566 $2.25 per single copy
                        7 x 8¼, 42 pages, saddle stitched

"WOMEN TALKING, WOMEN LISTENING II has no particular philosophy or direction other than representing the various views and themes of the contributors' poetry, with an aim to encourage more women to write about women and how women view their life experience."

WOMEN TALKING, WOMEN LISTENING is a warm collection of women's voices building upon each other. A great many of the poets are publishing their work for the first time in this collection. There are many different styles and themes explored, with the greatest recurrence of poetry from women with families and children.

In Vol. II, Joyce Erwin-Jensen commented, "Yes, sisterhood is powerful; for over the coffee cups in suburbia there is poetry, there are biographies, there are novels, and there is history in the making. Just listen."

WOMEN'S AGENDA   Published monthly
c/o Women's Action Alliance $10 per year
370 Lexington Avenue   8½ x 11, 16 pages, saddle stitched
New York, NY. 10017

A national resource magazine for women activists, the WOMEN'S AGENDA is a politically radical publication, bent on breaking down the sterotypes that separate one woman activist from another. Editions are themed, and focus on different issues each month. Particular emphasis is placed on information about legislative reform. Regular columns include information of women's groups, fund raising, and grass root activities.

(See Press I: *WOMEN'S ACTION ALLIANCE*)

WORD WEAVINGS   Published annually
Matria Press Collective $2 single copy
816 Hazen   8½ x 11, 30 pages, unbound
Grand Rapids, MI. 49507

WORD WEAVINGS is an unbound anthology of graphics and poetry. Printed on heavy matt paper in four shades of earthtones, it is a beautiful collection that can be hung on a wall, given page by page to friends, or hoarded in its plain manila envelope. The lay-out has been done with an exquisite care that offsets a splendid mosaic of words and drawings.

WREE-VIEW   Published bi-monthly
156 Fifth Avenue, Room 537 $3 per year
New York, NY. 10010   Format varies

WREE-VIEW is the newsletter of Women for Radical and Economic Equality, an organization affiliated with Women's International Democratic Federation. *WREE* is a coalition of

Black, white, Chicano, Puerto Rican, Asian and American women —housewives, workers, trade unionists, unemployed, students, senior citizens, professionals—all demanding a say in the future of America and an end to all forms of male supremacy—of which racism is a major aspect. The newsletter provides interesting articles on the issues around which *WREE* is organizing: A proposal for a Women's Bill of Rights, better public education and day care, guaranteed health care. And noting that we do not live by bread alone—there is sometimes a section called: Bread and Roses—poetry by women in keeping with the politics of the newsletter.

WOMEN'S STUDIES PUBLICATIONS
A WELL KEPT SECRET

Exciting, creative work is being done in the area of Women's Studies. Women are revising history, reclaiming biology, transforming psychology, destroying myths of sociology, and discovering lost literature, art and music.

We know of some of this work. Under the old tradition of "publish or perish" in the universities, certain works of original research and thinking by women researchers has found its way into university press books. In more recent years, the market for information on women has been exploited by the establishment press, and more women scholars have published via that route. Much more original work has found its way into the fruitful grounds of women's studies publications.

Unfortunately, the fertility of women's studies publications is a well-kept secret. This chapter introduces women's studies publications to the general non-university reader with the belief that they are an important aspect of women publishing, and an under-appreciated arm of the women's movement. For women scholars who work outside of universities, for women hungry for knowledge of our heritage, for women concerned with building a Feminist future, women's studies publications are a thirst-quenching well of information and inspiration.

****

There are certain problems inherent in reviewing women's studies publications. Personally, I place a great value on a publication's accessibility. I value writing which is easily understood because it is not obscured by academic jargon. I also feel that a publication should strive for an attractive format. Most women's studies publications fall short on at least one criterion. However, the content of all of these publications are unusually valuable intrinsically, so I will raise my objections and move on.

Professors in the field of women's studies often find themselves in a gratuitous position at best. Because they are associated with a male-run university, they are mistrusted by many feminists. (Perhaps this explains why women's studies publications are so under-reviewed in the feminist press.) Meanwhile, a woman's position in the university is usually insecure. Most universities do not embrace the idea of women's studies willingly. In a brilliant article, Marilyn Frye explores the dilemna of the feminist professor:

"Sometimes I catch a glimpse of myself in a classroom, in a university building, clothed and fed by the university, before an audience brought there by the university; and I am very seriously spelling out and explaining for them as persuasively as I can a radical feminist perception of the world and coaching them in the arts of right reason and clear vision so they will be able to discover for themselves what is going on in this sexist culture. And the better I am at teaching these things, the more truth I find and communicate, the more good I do the institution. The fact that it allows someone to stand in it and say those things, gives credit in the eyes of the students and the wider public. That I am saying truths makes the whole thing more tolerable for the women. The better I am, the better they feel about being in the university, the more they are inclined to believe that professors know what they are talking about, the more they feel that the university really is a place where knowledge will bring them freedom. And the stronger is the institution. But among the truths is the truth that the institution is male-dominated and directed to serve the ends of a male-dominated society, economy and culture. As such, its existence, not to mention its strength and vigor, is inimical to the welfare of women, and probably to the survival of the species. . . The university is in the business of authority, by bestowing its authority on selected token representatives of non-standard views, it enhances its own authority, which is used and designed to be used in the maintenance and justification of male hegemony over knowledge."
(*QUEST*, Vol. 3, No. 3, pg 30)

Real truths are communicated in women's studies publications. But the fact remains that these truths are usually presented under the auspices of the male university, whether or not the university owns the publication. There are independent women's studies publications, but they differ little in content or style from the journals actually owned or financed by a university. There is a reason for the academic language and style of the women's studies journals—women professors need to have their writing recognized as scholarly by the university. Many professors are required to publish a certain number of articles per year. These articles must be published by a "credible" publication. Universities judge credibility on the degree to which a publication conforms to male-defined standards of scholarship. A professor who ignores the biases of the university runs the risk of failing to secure tenure. Without tenure she cannot teach her truths; she cannot use the universities research facilities; she cannot continue her valuable research. Therefore women's studies publications cater to the dictates of male standards and fascinating reading is often obscured by academic jargon.

Fortunately, this isn't always the case. Some publications have a genuine commitment to reaching non-university women. *FRONTIERS* is one such journal:

> "We noted that our sister journals were largely either scholarly or popularized. We wanted to find a balance between these poles which seem unnecessarily to divide women, because after all, university women lead real lives in the 'real world' and women outside the university make valuable contributions to learning. We wanted to create a journal in which we could all share our experiences and expertise, which would publish articles that were both substantive and readable, and which would allow us to learn from each other."
> (*FRONTIERS*, Vol. 1, No. 1, pg iv)

Unfortunately, *FRONTIERS* has a very dull-looking format: pages and pages of type, unbroken by graphics or photographs. It looks intimidating. (Very likely, women studies publications operate on a financial shoestring and money for graphics is scarce.)

Whether or not women's studies publications recognize the political impact of language and format, they do operate from a political context. Rooted quite firmly in the women's movement, women's studies publications are in the unique position of being able to answer the question: Where have we come from and where are we going? Embracing so many different disciplines, women's studies publication are an integral part of a movement which is exploding the myths that have held women down under the guise of "scientific truth." Women's studies publications are one more aspect of women's publishing, one more way of stretching toward a new Feminist future.

In the following chapter, I list and review women's studies publications. Part I catalogues Women Studies Journals—those publications which contain research and theoretical articles. Part II contains additional resources for women scholars, newsletters and information sources.

ATLANTIS   Published bi-annually
Box 294 $5 per year
Acadia University   8 x 10, 170 pages, perfect bound
Wolfville, Nova Scotia
Canada

By far and away the most attractive Women's Studies Journal, *ATLANTIS* combines creative writing and visual art with academic articles and studies for an informal touch. The very title "Atlantis" reflects a difference from the other, more austere, journals. Atlantis refers to the ancient mythical kingdom which disappeared in an earthquake. For this publication Atlantis represents the lost kingdom of women which women are striving to rediscover by discovering themselves.

An interdisciplinary journal, *ATLANTIS* publishes critical and creative writing on all subjects related to women. They emphasize Canadian scholarship and articles appear both in French and English. Although the focus is primarily academic, the articles are readable and interesting. *ATLANTIS* also publishes reviews of books and films, photographs and drawings.

FEMINIST STUDIES   Published bi-annually
417 Riverside Drive $8 per year
New York, NY. 10025   6 x 9, 230 pages, perfect bound

"*FEMINIST STUDIES* is an indepentdent interdisciplinary journal founded for the purpose of encouraging scholarly and other analytic treatments of issues related to the status and conditon of women." "Other analytic treatment" refers to political analysis. Thus, an article called "Creating a Feminist Alliance: Sisterhood and Class Conflict in the New York Women's Trade Union League" appears side by side with "Dinah Murlock Craik and the Tactics of Sentiment: A Case Study in Victorian Female Authorship."

The title of this publication is aptly chosen. *FEMINIST STUDIES* is about women. It is also about feminism as a mode of analysis and a strategy for change. Emphasizing history, literature, and politics, *FEMINIST STUDIES* is a refreshing change of pace, rounding out the weighty material with an occasional poem. Unfortunately, *FEMINIST STUDIES'* valuable contribution to feminist culture will only be found by the devoted reader—the language is frequently difficult to read and the print is the smallest size imaginable.

FRONTIERS: A JOURNAL OF WOMEN'S STUDIES
Women's Studies Program   Published three times per year
Hillside Court 104   8½ x 11, 160 pages, perfect bound
University of Colorado
Boulder, CO. 80309

This journal makes the attempt to "begin to bridge the gaps between university and community women." Noting that "our sister journals were largely either scholarly or popularized," *FRONTIERS* collective strives to "find a balance between those poles which seem unnecessarily to divide women, because after all, university women lead real lives in the 'real world' and women outside the university make valuable contributions to learning."

Written in language unobscured by an academic filter, *FRONTIERS* presents a heterogeneous collection of essays, reviews, speeches, occasional poetry, and studies on just about anything. Issues are themed and articles cluster around such topics as "Women and Work," "Women and Violence," "Therapy from a Feminist Perspective" and "Women's Oral History."

In both approach and focus, *FRONTIERS* holds true to its goal of providing a bridge between academic and non-academic women. *FRONTIERS* seeks articles from all people concerned with women's issues. "We especially encourage interdisciplinary and collaborative articles. Academic articles should be original and useful contributions to scholarship. We also welcome short notes concerning personal experiences, reviews, and criticism. Publication will be based on interest to the general readership, clarity, and academic soundness." The themes chosen represent a commitment to developing dialogue on issues of concern to all feminists. Articles are frequently written from a radical feminist perspective.

FRONTIERS has no formal affiliation with any university, although it is partially funded through a Colorado University agency. The journal is produced collectively by a staff made up of women living in Boulder, some of whom are students, faculty and staff of the university.

HECATE   Published bi-annually
G.P.O. Box 99 $4 per year
St. Lucia, Queensland   4 x 6½, 112 pages, perfect bound
Australia 4067

Coming out of Australia, *HECATE* is a women's interdisciplinary journal designed to provide a "forum for discussing, at a fairly theoretical level, issues relating to the liberation of women. The title is significant: "We have named our journal

'Hecate,' a symbolic gesture to all that is proud, untameable, autonomus, compassionate, angry, strong, creative, intelligent and brave in women that, although repressed and denied for thousands of years has never been crushed, and now pushes toward the light like shooting blades of barley. Hecate is mythologically represented as a bitch and as the witches would have said 'So mote it be'."

Unlike most women's studies publications, *HECATE* publishes original poems, stories, plays and art, as well as criticism about art and literature. In addition, there are research findings in many different academic disciplines—herstory, psychology, sociology, etc. Programs of women's studies courses are another occasional feature of *HECATE*.

The openness to non-academic forms as well as the politically based articles allows *HECATE* to stand on equal footing with feminist political journals. However, *HECATE*'s uniqueness is derived from its special understanding of the relationship between the women's movement and women's studies:

> ". . . What is feminism? Are there contradictions between our short-term and long-term goals? If so, how do we cope with these contradiction? Are there new ways to define power, authority, leadership, and initiative which do not lead to a "structureless tyranny"? Where have we come from and where are we going? These questions exist and must be answered. Can we afford to limit ourselves to action without reflection guided by the acquisition of new thought and knowledge?

> In this context, women's studies can be seen, not as sterile intellectualization, but rather, as an integral part of an ongoing movement helping to explode myths which contain and limit the scope for women to change the material and psychological basis of their existence. . .

> It is in this light we should see women's studies. . . as political commitment which offers viable alternatives and strategies—a new praxis."

(*HECATE*, Vol. 1, No. 2, pg 5)

THE KATE CHOPIN NEWSLETTER

c/o Emily Toth   Published three times per year
Department of English   8½ x 11, 40 pages, stapled
University of North Dakota
Grand Forks, ND. 58201

Readers of literature might recognize Kate Chopin as the author of *THE AWAKENING*, an author recently re-discovered by feminist researchers. Chopin is known as a "regionalist"—a writer who writes with a strong sense of place, or with a sensibility which derives from a specific geographic area. Kate Chopin has thus been chosen as namesake and muse for a feminist literary journal devoted to sharing information about women regionalists, especially "lost" women regionalists.

Articles on both well known and forgotten writers and their books appear in the *KATE CHOPIN NEWSLETTER*. In addition, there are theoretical articles "defining the powers and limits of regionalism." The *NEWSLETTER* also publishes announcements and calls for papers in related areas of research.

SIGNS: A JOURNAL OF WOMEN IN CULTURE AND SOCIETY

The University of Chicago Press   Published quarterly
11030 Langley Avenue $12 per year
Chicago, IL. 60628   6 x 9, 300 pages, perfect bound

Sometimes reading *SIGNS* is tough going, but the rewards are there for those who work for it. *SIGNS* is an interdisciplinary journal publishing compelling articles and tantalizing insights about women in social science, humanities and natural science. Each issue contains a brief editorial which provides a focus for viewing the articles. Additionally, there are a group of review essays which suggest new directions for study. All of the work is from an international perspective. One of their most interesting issues contained articles about women in China.

"We want *SIGNS* to represent the originality and rigor of the new thinking about women, sexuality, sex roles, the social institutions in which the sexes have participated, the culture men and women have inherited, inhabited and created. We also want *SIGNS* to point to directions modern scholarship and policy can take."

One aspect of this originality in thinking is to present original historical documents for the reader to judge on her own. Thus, *SIGNS* liberally mixes some fascinating personal testimonies that read as well as any novel or short story in a literary journal, along with the analytic, technical essays.

UNIVERSITY OF MICHIGAN PAPERS IN WOMEN'S STUDIES

1058 LSA Building	Published 2-3 times per year
The University of Michigan	$10 per year
Ann Arbor, MI. 48109	8½ x 11, 190 pages, perfect bound

Published by students and faculty at the Women's Studies Program at Ann Arbor, *PAPERS IN WOMEN'S STUDIES* is an interdisciplinary journal which focuses on original research articles, monographs, dissertations, annotated bibliographies and reviews. There is much valuable information in each issue, particularly in the bibliographies, but one must wade through a great deal of academic language.

PAPERS IN WOMEN'S STUDIES accepts manuscripts in photo-ready form. This save them the expense of typesetting (which would increase the subscription cost), but the result is a very uneven appearance.

WOMEN AND LITERATURE

WOMEN AND LITERATURE	Published bi-annually
Department of English	$7 per year
Douglass College	6 x 9, 66 pages, saddle stitched
Rutgers University	
New Brunswick, NJ. 08903	

WOMEN AND LITERATURE seeks to be a forum for the "scholarly treatment of women and literature and a small part of the effort to reconstruct our forgotten heritage."

Originally a modest, mimeographed venture called *THE MARY WOLLSTONECRAFT JOURNAL, WOMEN AND LITERATURE* has increased its scope. Encompassing known and unknown women, they present erudite articles documenting the writing of eighteenth century novelists whose work chronicles their age and the development of the novel. Their coverage of literature extends into the nineteenth century to commentators on that century's economic and social scene. Mary Wollstonecraft, writer and feminist, remains a primary focus. *WOMEN AND LITERATURE* is also concerned with the literary treatment of women by male and female authors. They publish book reviews and descriptions of work in progress.

Each year with their fall edition, *WOMEN IN LITERATURE* presents an annual bibliography of literature in English by and about women. Covering all historical periods from 600-1960, the bibliography contains 2500 entries. It also indexes over 500 periodicals, including feminist journals. "The bibliography, sent to all subscribers, is designed to suggest the range of scholarship on women and literature, indicate unusual ideas for study in a new area, help avoid duplication of effort, and offer a comprehensive view of changes in the field."

WOMEN AND LITERATURE emphasizes a scholarly approach to its subject, but as a resource for women interested in literature, its contents are invaluable.

WOMEN'S STUDIES   Published three times per year
Gordon and Breach Science Publishers, Inc. $14.50 per year
One Park Avenue   6 x 9, 120 pages, perfect bound
New York, NY. 10016

"*WOMEN'S STUDIES* provides a forum for the presentation of scholarship and criticism about women in the fields of literature, history, art, sociology, law, political science, economics, anthropology and the sciences." It differs from most other women's studies publications in that it also publishes some poetry, short fiction, and film and book reviews.

Manuscripts should be submitted in triplicate to Editor, Wendy Martin, Department of English, Queens College, CUNY, Flushing, NY., 11367.

INFORMATION RESOURCES FOR WOMEN'S STUDIES

INERNATIONAL CANADIAN NEWSLETTER OF
RESEARCH ON WOMEN   Published three times per year
Department of Sociology of Education $7 per year, $8 foreign
Ontario Institute for Studies in Education
252 Bloor Street W   8½ x 11, 168 pages, perfect bound
Toronto, Ontario M5S 1V6
Canada

THE INTERNATIONAL CANADIAN NEWSLETTER OF RESEARCH ON WOMEN is so full of information it is undoubtedly the first publication to look at when beginning a research project. As an interdisciplinary, academic reference periodical, the CANADIAN NEWSLETTER promotes communication between researchers in women's studies. Abstracts of recent research reports and publications make up a large section of the NEWSLETTER, along with notes on ongoing research. Limited by size, the NEWSLETTER emphasizes the work of Canadian scholars, but as the title indicates, includes work by researchers the world over. Bibliographies, book reviews, commentary and announcements complete the NEWSLETTER.

WOMEN STUDIES ABSTRACTS   Published quarterly
P O Box 1 $20 per year
Rush, NY. 14543   5½ x 9, 100 pages, saddle stitched

WOMEN STUDIES ABSTRACTS is a quarterly publication covering research on women in history, media, medicine, religion, work, women's liberation and other topics. An abstract is a very brief summary of an article or book. Each issue contains about 150 abstracts plus additional bibliographies, and articles.

Cost of a subscription is high, but readers are encouraged to submit eight abstracts in exchange for a year's subscription. An abstract should be written for articles which are the result of original research. "Helping to write abstracts will increase coverage of the field, and allow for a more careful selection of the material; abstractors are especially needed in the fields of law, economics, psychology, literature, religion, and of materials published in languages other than English."

Writers who wish to insure an abstract of their article in *WOMEN STUDIES ABSTRACTS* should submit a copy of the article with an abstract they have written. "It should be important to you that your work become known, so you have every reason to want to take advantage of this offer." Unlike other abstract journals, *WOMEN STUDIES ABSTRACT* does not require a fee from the author; listings are free. Any periodical wishing to be abstracted should write and send some sample copies.

WOMEN'S STUDIES NEWSLETTER   Published quarterly
The Feminist Press $7 per year
Box 344   8½ x 11, 30 pages, saddle stitched
Old Westbury, NY. 11568

In 1972, The Clearinghouse on Women's Studies began publishing the *WOMEN'S STUDIES NEWSLETTER*, a publication which would spread information and contribute to the growth of women's studies on college campuses. By 1977, women's studies had spread to hundreds of campuses and had begun to make an impact on academia; and the *WOMEN'S STUDIES NEWS-LETTER* became the official publication of the newly formed National Women's Studies Association.

Continuing to disseminate information on the development and direction of women's programs, the *WOMEN'S STUDIES*

NEWSLETTER has extended its coverage to include issues in elementary, secondary, and community education. They also cover all the news and announcements of the Women's Studies Association. In addition to feature articles and newsbriefs, the NEWSLETTER also contains information on conferences, workshops, jobs, media, and publications.

In addition to publishing the WOMEN'S STUDIES NEWS-LETTER, the Clearinghouse on Women's Studies maintains a small library and resource center. They welcome the opportunity to exchange with other feminist publications.

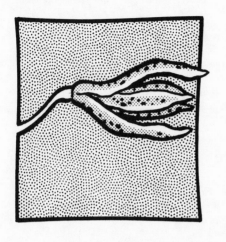

women's
newspapers

WHY READ A WOMEN'S NEWSPAPER?

Behind every women's newspaper is a belief that the male news establishment does not cover women's news and issues adequately. As Susan B. Anthony suggested: "Just as long as newspapers and magazines are controlled by men, every woman upon them must write articles which are reflective of man's ideas. As long as that continues, women's ideas and deepest convictions will never get before the public." (*NEW WOMEN'S TIMES*, Vol. 3, No. 2). Women's newspapers seek to remedy this.

Basically, there are two types of news that women's newspapers incorporate. The first has to do with women's rights. With women as powerless as they are in this society, much of the news about women is about their oppression, about the routine and systematic deprivation of rights they experience. Court battles receive prime coverage in women's newspapers. These legal disputes encompass everything from custody suits involving lesbian mothers to wrestling matches with local officials to keep health facilities open despite funding cuts. Women's newspapers are leading resources in the coverage of the trials of women activists and women-victims named criminals—i.e. prostitutes and women who have killed rapists in self-defense. Many newspapers sprang into being around the struggle to have individual states ratify the ERA. Legislation like the ERA, abortion laws, and displaced homemaker protection laws are all important topics in women's newspapers.

The second type of news, systematically ignored in establishment papers, is news features on women's contributions to society. This includes news of outstanding women who are making it in the male world, such as legislators and professionals, as well as women who are making vital contributions to all women and are doing so outside the patriarchy, sometimes even outside the law. Women are making a space for themselves in the world, but only women's newspapers follow the progress of women's businesses, credit unions, theatre groups, land trusts, communities, presses and record companies. The existence of these women-spaces is a vital sign that the women's movement is alive and well. Yet somehow, the male presses choose to ignore all this. Instead they publish editorials and features, written by men or women, which proclaim: "The Women's Movement is Dead."

In a way, one can read women's newspapers for "the rest of the news": what the male presses don't cover, or what they don't cover with their much vaunted "impartiality." With tongue in cheek, *MAJORITY REPORT* chose their newspaper's name to convey the fact that while women make up the largest segment of the population, they are under-represented in the male press.

One of the greatest deficiencies of the male press is the profit orientation. News is defined by what sells. Many times when the public could benefit by a responsible press, the male presses are silent. For example, the feminist press has published health news for years. Their reportage has included studies done by establishment medical researchers and reports by women with personal experience. Thus, long before the FDA acted, the feminist presses were warning women of the dangers of the Dalkan Shield. (Pity the woman without access to a responsible feminist press because the profit-oriented press has never served, nor will it ever serve her needs!)

Sensational stories sell in the male press, non-sensational do not. When the male press chooses to cover a court case in depth it will usually opt for a case involving a famous person. Thus, unremarkable Claudine Longet, movie star and wife of a famous singer, convicted of manslaughter, received more coverage in the male press than did Inez Garcia. Garcia, tried twice and acquitted, had been charged with murdering a man who had raped her. Garcia's acquittal establishes a real precedent for self-defense against rape. Garcia's act (of bravery? of survival?) is a powerful example to women who no longer wish to be victims. Is it any surprise that the male press did not choose to cover this case extensively?

When the male press does record women's events it is frequently with a negative perspective. For example, the male press provided ample coverage of the International Women's Year Conference sponsored by the U.N. and held in Mexico in 1976. The conference was an organization fiasco, and the male press made a great fuss over it, dwelling on the bad aspects and ignoring any of the good. Later, when the International Tribunal of Crimes Against Women occurred in Brussels it was virtually ignored. Yet at this Tribunal *real news* was made. Not only did women from all over the world set down and record their common oppression, but especially, Arab and Israeli women sat down together and jointly affirmed their common sisterhood.

Culture and politics are inextricably woven together in women's newspapers. Whereas the male press is concerned with upholding the status quo (owned as it is by large corporations and maintained through advertising), feminist newspapers are concerned with building a whole new society. Culture, that is: art, literature, psychology, music, etc., is a vital part of the new society. With the philosophy threaded through the women's movement that "the personal is political," culture takes on even greater significance for feminists. Telling the truths of women's lives through the art they create is the basis of the current feminist culture. In a society where images of women have been distorted over centuries by male-defined art, science and religion, telling the truth about who and what women are is very political. It is as important an ingredient of the feminist vision as the development of political power.

Almost all women's newspapers publish reviews of books, films, music and theatre. Usually they review the work of women. In addition, many newspapers feature herstory, poetry and art.

Science and spirituality are other aspects of culture reported on in women's newspapers. Under the general topic of "Health News," scientific myths about women are examined. Thus Freud is demystified and his misogyny explained. Biology as destiny is re-examined as women introduce masturbation, lesbianism, motherhood, and violence as topics for open discussion and revelation. Promoting self-help and feminist therapy, independence from the male medical establishment is supported. Meanwhile, science and spirituality meet in discussion of herbal remedies and methods of self-healing. Chants and rituals are also featured as aspects of the new women's spirituality.

The fact that the male press doesn't cover women's news adequately or even accurately is the reason that many women's newspapers began. It is one reason to read women's newspapers, but by no means is it the only reason. Women's newspapers are an active, vital part of the women's movement. At worst, they are a passive process through which news is filtered in a manner sympathetic to women. At best, they are at the vanguard of the movement, providing a forum for the development of political theory and art. Recording our present conditions, women's newspapers insure our past against distortions, our future against oblivion. Control of the press is an integral and dynamic necessity.

LOOKING AT THE DIFFERENCES

Women's newspapers are as diverse as the women's movement itself. They represent a wide, wide range of ideologies. At one end, the radical feminist newspapers represent more than half the newspapers in this book, sharing a common purpose: to challenge racism, sexism, classism, and heterosexism. At the other end is an eclectic assortment of newspapers with at least one common goal: passage of the ERA.

Radical Feminist Newspapers

The radical feminist newspapers are concerned with basic social change. A key phrase of these newspapers is "confronting patriarchal capitalism." This means that much space is devoted to criticism of the American government and economy, while positive support is extended to those who live outside approved white, male-oriented, middle class arenas.

Radical feminist newspapers are organizing tools, disseminating information on political prisoners at home and abroad, on pending legislation and how it will affect women, on court cases which may have broad results or which may need broad support. Radical newspapers do more than filter the news: they make a call to action, describing how and when lobbying should be done, what letters should be written, where defense money should be sent, how to gain entry into a court to support the defense. With concerned, and frequently partial journalism, radical newspapers function to raise consciousness, defense money, and also to educate. Thus, as the trial of Susan Saxe continued, and numerous women were approached for information to be used against Saxe, many newspapers ran articles on what to do if accosted by the FBI—don't talk.

The struggles and needs of working women are amply documented, as are those of minority women. In this way, radical feminist newspapers differ the most from the other women's newspapers. "Struggle" is a key word. The women writing these newspapers see surviving with dignity as difficult at best, requiring constant vigilance against the criminal justice system, health professions, pharmaceutical companies, banks, etc. Whether they are advocating a lesbian separatist nation, or a feminist socialist revolution, radical newspapers are all seeking radical change. Thus they share a multi-purpose: spreading information, organizing their readership, and developing political/ social theory and strategies.

The politics of radical feminist newspapers include a commitment to women in other countries, particularly third world women. With a concern for the plight of women which extends beyond the rare international conference, the radical feminist newspapers record the forced sterilization of women in Puerto Rico, the mistreatment of rape victims in Australia, the changing conditions of women in Cuba, the malnutrition of babies in developing countries where U.S. baby food companies urge women to buy expensive formulas rather than breast feed. The Canadian newspaper, *THE OTHER WOMAN*, deserves special mention for its extensive coverage of women all over the world.

Radical newspapers place the greatest emphasis on woman-defined culture. No one really knows what a feminist culture is. Women, as scientists, as musicians, as writers, as artists, as spiritual beings have been defined by men and male standards for centuries. Feminists are asking the question: What is feminist art? What is woman-defined, woman-oriented culture? Radical feminist newspapers perform an essential role in laying the boundaries of feminist culture.

An entire field of feminist criticism is emerging to evaluate feminist arts, and newspapers are playing a vital role in its development. Unlike the feminist criticism in the scholarly journals, this critiscism is more concerned with personal reactions than the theory behind it. Thus, it is grass roots theory, criticism in practice written by non-experts; someday the theory will catch up to it and modify it. What the radical newspapers do is to print the poem, as well as the review; to record the art show, and to discuss the origins of the art; to review the record and to talk about the politics of the record company. These newspapers are a forum for a great wealth of ideas—and that includes new thinking about history and science as well as art.

Other Woman-Oriented Newspapers

Whereas the radical newspapers form a cohesive group sharing a common commitment to building a unique women's culture, directly confronting cherished American values, other kinds of women-oriented newspapers do not lend themselves to categories so easily. Although a few broad statements apply, what is most true about these other newspapers is they vary greatly.

The one unifying bond of all of these newspapers is that they are concerned with sexism in this country. All of the newspapers support the ERA. Few are concerned with the political struggles of women in other countries. Their main thrust is support for legislative reform on the state and federal level. Education reform, job training, and affirmative action are issues which are frequently addressed.

Meanwhile, these newspapers vary greatly in the degree to which race and class are seen to have an impact on feminism. Like the SPOKESWOMAN and THE HOUSTON BREAK-THROUGH, many of these newspapers are directed toward middle class women. The visual format of THE SPOKESWOMAN would be intimidating to women who never read intellectual journals. THE HOUSTON BREAKTHROUGH imitates the male press with an advertisement profiling the kind of woman who reads BREAKTHROUGH—invariably a professional woman. Both of these newspapers promote radical ideas about race, class and government reform, yet address a middle class community.

There are mañy such contradictions among these newspapers. Men often make token appearances. One paper even features a cooking column by a male senator! Romantic, heterosexual love is also explored. Articles such as "New Ideas for Brides" appeared in *NEW DIRECTION FOR WOMEN* (Summer 1976) and "Marriage and Your Mate" was featured in *SHE* (February 1977). Although many other newspapers do not directly address men, or male-oriented women, none address lesbians directly. This means that they do not review most feminist press books, nor do they promote most woman-made records. There is little emphasis on building a unique women's culture. However, women's contributions to, and images in, the general culture are examined in depth through a feminist perspective.

What these women-oriented newspapers demonstrate is that there are many different ways of expressing Feminism, and many different ways of combatting sexism. It is best to consider these newspapers as individual identities, each carving its own space in a movement broad enough to hold them all.

As Debra Susan Abbott of *THE BLUE LANTERN* has pointed out to me: "The (*BLUE LANTERN*) group has decided as a collective to do things this way—slowly opening the doors to more radical issues, and moderate those by having simple human interest stories and things not blatantly feminist but of interest to the community. We are not trying to do an *OFF OUR BACKS* because we don't have the feminist community here to support that, or advertisers who would understand. This is limiting in many ways but for us it generally means survival."

****

As a body of writing, all of the women's newspapers taken together represent the most accurate reflection of the women's movement available. If I have covered the radical newspapers in greater depth and with greater sympathy it is because they conform to my own beliefs. While I am unable to eliminate my own personal prejudices, I recognize that the feminist movement is broad enough to hold many different philosophies. After all, legislative reform such as the non-radical newspapers seek can improve our present conditions while freeing the energies of more radical women to quest for long-term change.

Radical or not, women's newspapers are changing women's lives and are themselves always changing. But don't take my word for it; I have admitted to allowing myself personal prejudices. I encourage women to pursue their own truths about women's newspapers. I want women to write for, subscribe to, and support women's newspapers. And that, after all, is one of the reasons for this book.

CHOOSING A WOMEN'S NEWSPAPER

On the following pages, I list women's newspapers with very brief descriptions of each. Assuming that anyone still reading is a writer looking for a market for her work, or a subscriber looking for the newspaper she will appreciate most, this section is designed to point out certain things to look for when choosing a women's newspaper.

Writers will be happy to know that all newspapers consider unsolicited materials. Many of the nationally oriented newspapers would be glad to extend their coverage by hearing from reporters from all over the country. Feature writers also have an open market with women's newspapers. Many will publish poetry, short essays, personal opinion, reviews, interviews, and herstory. (Be sure to always include a SASE.)

There are two advantages to the writer who submits work to women's newspapers instead of literature/cultural journals. One is that newspapers are published more frequently and have larger staffs. Therefore, one can hope to hear of an acceptance or rejection quickly. The greatest advantage of publishing in a newspaper is that one's work is assured of the widest possible circulation. Most newspapers pay with contributor's copies.

When considering subscribing to women's newspapers, the first decision one should make is whether one wants a radical perspective or not. After that, the most pertinent consideration is that all newspapers, whether or not they claim a national audience, contain geographic biases. *OFF OUR BACKS*, out of Washington, D.C. has the smallest geographic bent, possibly because events which occur in Washington tend to have national impact. *MAJORITY REPORT* seems to operate under the assumption that New York City is the capital of the feminist movement. To the extent that that belief is true, theirs is nationally oriented. However, *MAJORITY REPORT* is the only feminist newspaper published bi-weekly and many will overlook their tendency toward provincialism in favor of their ability to get the *news* out. Since all women's newspapers provide extensive coverage of how the state legislatures deal with women's issues, reading a newspaper from within one's own state can be crucially important during election times.

Geographic consideration aside, there are personal reasons why women will prefer one newspaper over another. One may read a certain newspaper because one appreciates the over-all writing or graphic style. Or one may especially enjoy the writing of a particular staff person. For example, one may want to read *BIG MAMA RAG* for Chocolate Waters' frequent contributions of poetry and a humorous dyke-view of the world. Or one may want to read Alta's regular column "Mothers Milk" in *PLEXSUS.*

Most newspapers cover one particular area better than others. Although all of the radical feminist newspapers follow the situation of women in prison and women fighting in the courts, *THE WOMEN'S PRESS* does an outstanding job in that area. Likewise, *THE NEW WOMEN'S TIMES* does an excellent job with health news. *HERA* and *SISTER COURAGE* are particularly concerned with confronting urban racism and classism.

However, the difference between newspapers tend to be subtle; newspapers, particularly the radical ones, tend to be more alike than different. For this reason I have limited my remarks about each one. My suggestion to potential subscribers is to order a single issue at a time until the right newspaper is found.

Researching this book, I have had the fortune of reading many, many women's newspapers. The experience has been radicalizing and educational. It is an experience I highly recommend.

BIG MAMA RAG   Monthly
1724 Gaylord Street $5 per year, free to prisoners
Denver, CO. 80206 $.55 single issue

Radical/feminist news journal with a national orientation and
a somewhat socialist perspective. Provides excellent coverage of
women's/lesbian culture with poetry, herstory and analysis. In-
depth political analysis and feature articles. Circulation: 9,000.

THE BLUE LANTERN   Monthly
P O Box 3343 $3 per year
Charlottesville, VA. 22903 $.25 single issue

Locally oriented for a community without a strong feminist
community. Low-keyed profiles of local women and analysis of
women's issues.

EQUINOX   Monthly
Box 133 $4 per year
Newton, MA. 02159 $.30 single issue

"A grass-roots, suburban newspaper publicizing the achieve-
ments of women in the western suburbs of Boston." Specializes
in feature articles, interviews, poetry and art. Very little political content, other than the political nature of the topics chosen
—such as wife beating.

FEMINIST COMMUNICATIONS   Monthly
4003 Wabash Avenue $3 per year
San Diego, CA. 92104

Radical feminist newspaper covering local, state, national and
international news. Also publishes poetry, reviews, health. Local
monthly calendar included.

HERA
2041 Walnut Street
Philadephia, PA. 19103

Monthly
$6 per year
$.50 single issue
Free to prisoners in jail and mental hospitals

Radical feminist newspaper covering local, national and international news. Event oriented political analysis directly confronts issues like racism and classism. Publishes some poetry, reviews, letters.

HOUSTON BREAKTHROUGH
P O Box 88072
Houston, TX. 77004

Monthly
$5 per year
$.50 single issue

Unlike any other newspaper in this chapter, *THE HOUSTON BREAKTHROUGH* covers the entire range of news about women in one city exclusively. Where other newspapers might cover the news of the lesbian/feminist community, *THE HOUSTON BREAKTHROUGH* extends their coverage outside the feminist community, but always through a feminist perspective. Their radical outlook is somewhat diluted by a middle class/professional women's approach but their ability to reach out into the entire community for news of women is an important model. Circulation: 10,000.

KINESIS
Vancouver Status of Women
2029 West 4th Avenue
Vancouver, B.C. V6J 1N3

Monthly
Inquire for price
$.35 single issue

Radical feminist leftist perspective. Extensive coverage of Canadian and international news. In-depth analysis of issues affecting all women regardless of nationality, such as family violence, cultural pornography, child care and abortion. Presents a great wealth of information and resources.

MAJORITY REPORT
74 Grove Street
New York, NY. 10014

Bi-weekly
$5 per year
$.25 single issue

Radical feminist newspaper with national and international news and a New York City bias. Also publishes articles, interviews, criticism, reviews of books, poetry, drama, film, media. Lists galleries and women's businesses. Only bi-weekly feminist newspaper. Circulation: 10,000 plus.

NEW DIRECTIONS FOR WOMEN
P O Box 27
Dover, NJ. 07801

Quarterly
$3 per year
$.75 single issue

A news quarterly "for women, not just for feminist." Emphasizes health, arts, legislation, family, equal rights, books, religion.

NEW WOMEN'S TIMES
1357 Monroe Avenue
Rochester, NY. 14618

Monthly
$5 per year
$.40 single issue

Western New York's only radical feminist newspaper contains everything one looks for in a feminist newspaper: local, national, international news and analysis, reviews, herstory, poetry, cultural analysis. Particularly good coverage of health news.

THE NORTHERN WOMAN
316 Bay Street
Thunder Bay P, Ontario

Monthly
$3 per year
$.50 single issue

Free to single parent families and senior citizens

Radical feminist newspaper with a local perspective. Like most feminist newspaper in Canada THE NORTHERN WOMAN has a leftist orientation and covers the concerns of working women most extensively. Also features poetry, herstory and personal testimony.

OFF OUR BACKS
1724 20th Street
Washington, D.C. 20009

Monthly
$6 per year
$.45 single issue
Free to prisoners

Nationally oriented radical feminist newspaper. Extensive coverage of national and international news and analysis, health, survival, culture, poetry, prisons, letters. The collective has a branch in Chicago to extend their coverage of national news. Pages of commentary present various viewpoints.

THE OKLAHOMA NEW WOMAN
P O Box 60729
Oklahoma City, OK. 73106

Monthly
$6 per year
$.50 single issue

Locally oriented, focused on passage of the ERA and similar legislative reform. Espouses a social/political commitment to equal rights for men and women. Circulation: 800.

THE OTHER WOMAN
P O Box 928
Station Q
Toronto, Ontario
Canada

Bi-monthly
$4 per year
$5 per year America
$.50 single issue
Free to prisoners and native women

International radical feminist newspaper with nationalistic perspective. Coverage of international news as extensive as coverage related to the building of a strong Canadian women's movement. Also examines culture, lifestyles, health, education, environment, art.

PANDORA
P O Box 5094
Seattle, WA.

Monthly
$8 per year
$.50 single issue
Free to low income persons

Politically aware news journal covering news of interest to Washington State women, including some national news. Excellent coverage of women in the arts.

PLEXSUS   Monthly
2600 Dwight Way $5 per year
Room 209 $.55 single issue
Berkeley, CA. 94704

Nationally oriented, radical feminist newspaper covering local, national and international news. Outstanding coverage of culture and the relationships between culture and politics. Articles have dealt with lesbian separatism in relationship to Olivia Record policies, relationships between the feminist press and publishing choices made by writers, etc. Also: book reviews, films, personal essays.

SHE   Monthly
3256 Robincrest Drive $6 per year
Northbrook, IL. 60062 $.50 single issue

SHE stands for "Serving Human Equality" and publishes men as well as women. Nationally oriented, their policy is oriented to raising men's consciousness about women's roles, as well as women's. Publishes more essay and opinion than news.

SISTER   Monthly
P O Box 597 $5 per year
Venice, CA. 90291 $.50 single issue

Radical feminist newspaper. Publishes national, international and local news, plus features. Also poetry, cartoons and reviews.

SISTER COURAGE   Monthly
P O Box 296 $4 per year
Allston, MA. 02134 $.35 single issue

Radical feminist newspaper. Regionally oriented, although excellent coverage of national political issues such as legislation, health, housing, employment, day care, unions, extends beyond regionalism. Relevant to third world, working class and elderly women as well as those affiliated with the lesbian/feminist community. Adresses political issues more frequently than cultural, however occasionally produces a special supplement to regular editions which discusses and reviews books, writers and artists. Circulation: 10,000.

SOJOURNER   Monthly
P O Box 138 $4 per year
Cambridge, MA. 02141 $.50 single issue

Regionally oriented, broad-based feminist newspaper: "The New England Women's Journal of News, Opinions, and the Arts." Poetry, reviews, national and local news and news analysis, local calendar.

THE SPOKEWOMAN   Monthly
53 West Jackson Street, Suite 525 $12 per year
Chicago, IL. 60604 $1 single issue

Nationally oriented, *THE SPOKEWOMAN* is a news digest, filtering the news from a feminist perspective. Covers legislation, health, employment, education and politics. Also book reviews and professional job listings. Follows a newsletter format and addresses professional, educated women. Circulation: 12,000.

UPSTREAM   Monthly
227 Laurier Avenue West $6 per year
Suite 207 $.25 single issue
Ottawa, Ontario K1P 5J7
Canada

A nationally oriented radical feminist newspaper with enough general information and political analysis on topics affecting all women that it transcends national boundaries. Like most Canadian women's newspapers, *UPSTREAM*'s leftist sensitivities emerge in the emphasis placed on the economic aspects of survival. The most complete women's newspaper available, *UPSTREAM* covers news of interest to working and middle class and native women. Also sports, a separate culture section with poetry, reviews, interviews.

WHAT SHE WANTS   Monthly
c/o Womenspace $6 per year
3201 Euclid Avenue $.50 single issue
Cleveland, OH. 44115

Radical news journal blending articles of local and general interest. Covers everything from poetry to politics: mechanics, unions, health education, motherhood. Special letter column called: "Off My Breast."

WOMANEWS   Monthly
c/o Women Unlimited $3.50 per year
12 NW 8th Street $.30 single issue
Gainseville, FL. 32601

A low-keyed, issue oriented newspaper. Editions are themed; recent topics have been celibacy, literary arts, Black women. Circulation: 4,000.

WOMANSONG   Monthly
P O Box 3264 $3 per year
Columbus, OH. 43210   Free on request

A radical feminist newspaper with a socialist perspective. Nationally oriented. Special resources section. Poetry. Emphasized anaylsis of political issues over straight news.

WOMEN: A BERKSHIRE FEMINIST NEWS JOURNAL
P O Box 685   Bi-monthly
Lenox, MA. 01240 $3 per year
                                $.50 single issue

Follows a newsletter format to provide news and cultural analysis to women in the Berkshires: regionally oriented. Radical feminst perspective. Serves mainly as a communication network for area feminist groups.

WOMEN RISING   Monthly
P O Box 1209 $2.50 per year
Phoenix, AZ. 85001 $.25 single issue

Locally oriented news journal featuring news of the Arizona women's community.

WOMEN'S PRESS   Monthly
P O Box 562 $4 per year
Eugene, OR. 97401 $.25 single issue
                         Free to prisoners in jails and mental hospitals

Radical feminist newspaper covering international, national, state news and cultural analysis. Outstanding coverage of women's prision and Native American struggles.

NEWS SERVICES

Without the resources to send reporters all over the world, many feminist newspapers rely on news services to supply news items. Most news services operate on a subscription system: for a set price, the news service will send a regular packet of news items to tapes. Here is a brief sampling of some:

FEMINIST NEWS SERVICE
P O Box 18417
Denver, CO. 80218

To be operational in January 1978. To be involved send $5 for a newsletter and a report on its current status.

HER SAY
Zodiac News Service
950 Howard Street
San Francisco, CA. 94103

A weekly dispatch of news of special interest to women designed especially for radio. Items are brief, to the point, taking sharp and sometimes humorous swipes at the patriarchy. Inquire for price.

LIBERATION NEWS SERVICE
17 W 17th Street, 8th Floor
New York, NY. 10011

Used by many radical feminist newspapers, the Liberation News Service publishes weekly packets of news copy and graphics, plus a monthly graphics bundle. LNS is set up as a male/female collective. Cost: $20 per month.

Dorothy Allison, an Editor of Quest: A Feminist Quarterly.

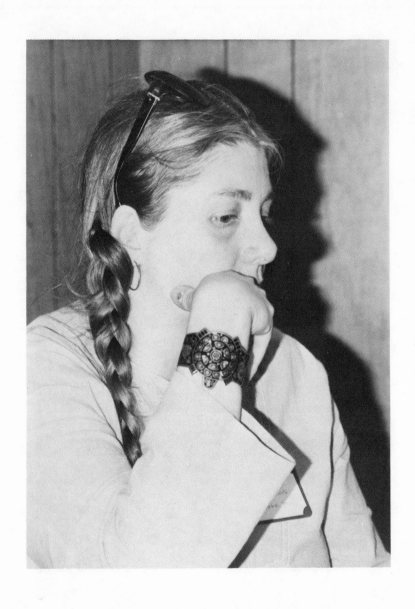

Anne Pride, Co-publisher of Motheroot Publications.

Virginia Scott, poet; publisher of Sunbury Press and Literary Journal.

Joan Larkin, poet; publisher for Out & Out Books.

Elaine Gill, Co-publisher of The Crossing Press.

Camille Tischler, Smedley's Bookshop Collective

presses

"THE FEMINIST SMALL PRESS PUBLISHING"

In putting together this part of *GUIDE* which deals with small press publishing houses I have been trying to understand the intricate webbing that is women's publishing. I have dealt in depth with the women's presses in the United States. The Canadian press scene is less complete. Part of the reason for this is that Canadians prefer to publish Canadians and rarely solicit manuscripts from American women. Therefore it has been harder to track down their press information. Sometimes, this sleuthing process has become extraordinarily confusing. One letter has led to another contact which has meant writing still another person and so on. . . .

However, this very confusion is wonderful! Back in 1967 there was nothing to get confused about. Women's presses existed in dreams if they existed at all. Ten years later we have a profusion of women's presses and this marvelous confusion. Happily and proudly, we can now progress to Stage II, clarifying the outlines of what exists. More and more women want to publish and realize that an increasing variety of options is available. Unraveling these options is important and is where most of the lack of clarity lies. Feminist writers and publishers can become an effective power base. Without communication with each other, however, we have very little change of effecting the real changes women in publishing deserve. Hopefully, this *GUIDE* will make clear how extensive and strong women in publishing have become.

In order to fill the void in women's publishing one courageous and flamboyant route has been self publishing, a route I strongly supported myself when I published my first book with *NO APOLOGIES*. Self publishing has been a defiant woman's *I AM*.

Valuable, legitimate, creative, we did not want to wait around for society's token crumbs. However negative the associations, a "vanity press" was often the only option for women writing the truth of being woman. "Vanity, thy name is woman" was a clay phrase women of the 70's have had to reshape into a new vessel, tough, beautiful, and above all, *enduring*.

However, even most self-published work carries a press label. With the growing number of individuals or groups of women developing their own press labels for self-financed work, the confusion expands. Which of these presses define themselves as enough of a business to want to deal with the woman "out there" with a manuscript? Which of these press labels represents an individual or a group with a vision for doing beyond self-financed books if they had support? Which ones may be vaguely planning to phase out their press when the writer or writers are well known enough to publish elsewhere? Which of these "presses" owns a press?

There is no question when one is talking about Daughters, Diana, The Feminist Press, Shameless Hussy or the Women's Press Collective that one is talking about real, viable women's presses. Whatever the organizational or political differences between them (and there are always some), these presses, and others share a commonality in longevity and number of books sold that institutionalizes them in women's cultural herstory. Some of the smaller presses have been somewhat harder to define.

My criteria for inclusion has been based on that vague and abused term "Feminist-oriented." It has seemed to me that presses, even if run by women, that simply mirror society's traditional image of women, that seemed to support social intolerence and inequality, classism, sexism, or racism did not reflect the spirit or reason behind the explosion of women's publishing. As such, I did not feel they were appropriate for this book. For the most part that type of press does not wish to identify with women's publishing anyway.

In a few cases I made a choice not to include a press which proclaimed itself Feminist. In one instance this happened to be a

106

male publisher who said he had published eight books by "Feminist" men and two books by women. In addition to the obvious disparity between the number of books published by men and the few by women, the books I read from the press seemed to confuse free love with Feminism, a not uncommon mistake made by men who dub themselves "Feminists." Men, who interpret Feminism as some kind of license to take more open advantage of women's sexuality, have completely missed the point. This kind of press attitude I also felt was outside the spirit and purpose of this book.

However, I have included some presses where men, as well as women, are very involved. Perhaps a note is appropriate at this point as to why I have included these non-sexist presses in a *GUIDE TO WOMEN'S PUBLISHING*. To my way of thinking it would be prejudicial and incomplete to leave out those presses which are working out non-hierarchical organizational structures and attitudes that include both men and women. It makes no sense to me to ignore strong feminist who run presses with men. By the same token it would be equally unfair to leave our feminist women who are willing to print books by men.

There may be other non-sexist presses that would fall into my guidelines than the few in this book. However, they are not very visible, or else not responsive. While I feel it is important to document those presses which are attempting to bridge the gap between male and female publishing, the rate of response from non-sexist presses has been very poor. I have taken the position that, if a so-called non-sexist press by other criteria did not take queries about being listed in a *GUIDE TO WOMEN'S PUBLISHING* seriously enough to answer my letters, they subtley reinforced a sexist stance regarding women writers. Under those circumstance I have felt very comfortable with excluding them.

Once I decided that a press fit my criterion as "Feminist-oriented," I tried to deal with each one as unique. Whenever possible I have tried to include guidelines I knew about. Does a press define itself through what it publishes? Is the sexuality of the writer (whether she needs to be lesbian, straight, or bisexual) important? Does the writer's politics (anarchist, socialist, mainstream or whatever) make a difference? Is the spirituality of the writer relevant? Are her religious views express in her writing a criterion for making her work acceptable to particular presses?

I asked the same questions over and over again, but I got many different answers: How did you begin? How many women work with your press? Do you survive financially? Do you need other jobs? Do you have a particular philosophical or political base? Do you solicit manuscripts? What kind of writing are you looking for? Do you have a policy for paying your authors? Do you own a press or do you farm out work to a press shop? How do you distrubute your work? What is your sales volume as far as you can figure? What are your dreams for the future? Any other comments. . . . ?

Questions and criteria, while useful for helping the reader to know where I'm coming from, do little to minimize some confusions. The criteria for inclusion, do not eliminate the variations in "Feminist-oriented" presses. I debated long and hard about how to separate these presses into useful categories. The most suggestive distinctions are between lesbian, women only, and non-sexist presses. However, the more books I read and the more letters I received, the more simplistic and inadequate this seemed. One characteristic of women's publishing is a tendency to blur images, to defy being divided into neat little boxes.

For instance, while it clearly is important to know whether a press is only looking for works from lesbians, the definition of "lesbian" is blurred. Also, to divide women's publishing into divisions artificially underscoring sexual preference seems to me to ignore the fact that a lesbian press deals with the whole woman. While a woman's art is obviously affected by her sexuality, it is not limited to it. It seems to me more important to emphasize that, whether a press is lesbian-oriented or not, the full range of woman's creativity is supported by a woman's press, not just her sexuality.

Secondly, women's presses are committed to change and they frequently disregard their own self-prescribed boundaries. A women's press set up to print poetry may suddenly publish a novel. A press begun as a self publishing venture unexpectedly may begin to solicit manuscripts. A print shop may try publishing and distributing books under their own press signature. A press set up exclusively to print women may surprisingly decide to take on work from a male contributor.

This penchant to change, to move in a different direction is delightful to me, but may mystify those who are used to stable systems. Frankly, I think the fact that women's publishing is constantly changing is one of its biggest strengths. What some would negatively term "erratic," I would applaud as the enviable ability to grow.

This growth is reflected in the presses' experimentation with organizational forms. The vast majority operate with some variety of collectivity. Women have been on the bottom of too many hierarchical structures. Because of this there has been a strong desire to make non-hierarchal structures work. All of us were trained in a competitive society. In the beginning few of us had any real experience with how to work cooperatively. The resulting trial and error has been both joyous and painful. The glow of sisterhood sometimes fragmented into angry flashes from women determined to work, thereafter, as loners. The *loner* does not necessarily reject non-hierarchical structures. What the term usually means is that a woman prefers being a loner, to being part of a hierarchy. Despite the frustrations involved, the turbulent collective experimentation of the early 70's is now providing us with a seasoned body of creative organizational models and experience that seem to work.

In the final analysis I divided this collage of women's press publishing into four categories:

> *PRESS I:* Presses with four or more titles
> *PRESS II:* Presses with one to three titles
> *ALL-WOMEN PRINT SHOPS*
> *NON-SEXIST CHILDREN'S PRESSES*

Each responding women's press, while having its own peculiar integrity, voiced (either explicitly or implicitly) strong ties to the *whole* of women's publishing. On this level, whether a press has published one or fifty books, published books either for adults or children, is a print shop, or even if it has ceased to exist, it is an organic part of the full and exciting herstory of women's publishing. It is this pervasive spirit which made me unhappy with divisions like lesbian, women only, and non-sexist. These divisions seemed more like separations destructive of the whole. There are differences, yes, and important ones, but my vision of the world encompasses these differences as complementary, not as divisive components. I weary of intolerance and inequality in any form. I believe in radical change and healing.

My first two categories are not intended to be hierarchical even though Group I presses have published more books than those in Group II. For instance, Shire Press is in the Press II category. As a self publishing press label for Helen Garvy, the press has only two titles on the market, but it has the highest batting average in the whole women's publishing scene for number of volumes sold. Helen Garvy's $1.00 manual on *HOW TO FIX YOUR BICYCLE* has sold over 100,000 copies to date. Spreading the book around by herself and through small press distributors, she is a good example of how impossible it is to have hierarchies, even in the order of categories.

In that sense women's publishing has accomplished in a very short ten years what the male norm in publishing has always maintained couldn't be done. Whatever the differences between feminist women in publishing, this rejection of hierarchies is the strong thread that links all of us together.

And Feminist Consciousness. . . ? Women's publishing makes a statement affirming the *value* of being equal to the *power* of *BEING*. The crime of being "better than thou" will meet strong resistance. While woman's reality is the present, I doubt if she will ever again herself to be a silent spring, a rung on any ladder. She rises from the center of the earth bubbling hot in creation's cauldron or flowing wet on deserts dry of feeling. Wicked witch (wicked because of the power to change), nourishing mothers (enslaved because of her power to feel life), the woman of colors (whose blood was supposedly inferior), the sensual goddess (prostituted if aggressive and wanting). . . We embrace all of her into the *whole woman.*

> Power w/no hate
> no tyranny
>
> Just Power

"ONE STORY"

While doing this book I became aware of certain threads lacing publisher to publisher, press to press. These recurring fragments became more and more familiar. I began to see that all the presses in this book shared a certain common herstory/ history, even while the details in each case imprint their own brand of uniqueness. Reasons for beginning, trying to stay alive, efforts to remain loving, supportive, honest, political, non-profit, this story of struggle repeats and repeats. It is the story behind feminist publishing, and the story behind non-sexist wrestling.

When I received the twelve page hand-written letter which is *"ONE STORY,"* I realized that it was re-telling a publishing herstory that related *in spirit* to all of us. *"ONE STORY"* is Susan Shaw Weatherup's account of Before We Are Six, a Canadian women's publishing house for non-sexist children's books:

Hello. . .
. . . Please, please accept my apologies for my delay in responding to your first letter. I did want to take a moment to sit down & have a cup of something & jot off a page to you, but somehow, in the midst of the confusion which currently surrounds me, the opportunities to do so were quite limited. I had every intention of replying & I really am sorry a second request on your part was necessary. . . .

I am alone at BWA6 at this time. Not a very terrific feeling, to say the least, one woman attempting to run a publishing house is pure "madness."

Enough of my tale of woe. Ah, where to start, well the logical place being the beginning, I will make an attempt to find some sanity in all this "madness."

We started in 1972, the result of an Opportunities for Youth

112

(OFY) grant (federal aid for employment of students during the summer months). I will spare you & not delve into the long-winded description of the events that took place that summer. Both men & women were employed on that grant. We felt a certain degree of accomplishment when the grant ended.

During the summers of 1973 & 1974 we were fortunate to receive 2 more OFY grants, to continue our research, to update our bibliography & the final summer to concentrate soley on publishing non-sexist/stereotype books. On the final grant only one male was hired. It was obvious that women were into this a lot more.

We had been receiving quite a lot of correspondence, people requesting any material etc. related to the whole notion of sexism, & also wanting copies of our books (looking back on them, I can now say: "as bad as they were"). So, from September 1973 to May 1974 (between grants) myself and another woman handled all correspondence, distribution of our bibliography & books etc. from my kitchen. It was due to the response, that we received our 3rd grant. That summer we made an attempt to organize—to sell the books to cover mailing cost, rent of office, etc. That summer was quite productive. The grant was to end in August. Three of us decided to continue operations of BWA6 for 6 more months, to determine if there was any future for us all. It became apparent at that time that we should establish ourselves as a women's publishing house.

Those first six months were crazy. I was a full-time university student, fortunately I was setting up my own program (self-motivated study thing), so I could devote a fair amount of time to BWA6. Also, I had a one year old son.

The other woman had saved some money from working on the grant, so she was able to devote most of her time to BWA6. The third woman popped in & out. Of course—no one received a salary. We were lucky to cover expenses & perhaps put a few $$$ away per month.

Good old 1975—International Women's Year. Our secretary of state had 2.5 million dollars to give away to all us terrific women, to do our thing. We figured (as did some others) that we were sure to get a thin slice of the pie. After all, a women's publishing house publishing non-sexist/stereotype children's books! Perfect! We applied for three different grants but to no avail.

We did not get a penny. Rumors circulated that perhaps we were too political or whatever. Well, things started to look very bad. We were so angry, because we were broke & the whole thing was bullshit. Francis had used up all her savings, everything, & had to move in with us. And I was in the horrible position of being "kept" by my husband. I had contributed *no* money into our family for nearly a year. By the end of the summer, we had had it, had lost every battle we set out to win.

Our books were selling (slowly), covering (barely) our monthly expenses, but there was nothing for minimal salaries, any type of promotion to increase sales, let alone the purchase & printing of new manuscripts. So, we decided to fold. Francis took off to the Yukon, where she still is today. I had made arrangements to sell our remaining stock to The Women's Press in Toronto.

For the last few weeks depression was my only motivation. Fortunately, my depression turned into anger, & anger I can deal with a lot more effectively so I got on the phone & called some friends & suggested to them, that as women it was their duty to pitch in & get BWA6 moving. And we all know how terrific women can be. The following week, two new women joined our forces.

In September 1975 we applied for a Local Initiatives Program (L.I.P.) grant. Another federal program to employ people during the winter. We got it & hired three other women. BWA6 operated as a co-operative (good & bad). There was not the same degree of dedication & love for BWA6 on everyone's part, but for the most of it, the grant proved quite successful.

It was necessary to move to a larger office (complete with lots of windows & fresh air). We printed 20,000 books. Reprinted three of our original five titles (revised editions) & two new titles. The grant allowed only $600,00 for printing. Our bill was over $7,000.00. During that time we learnt as much as we could about typesetting, layout, etc., etc., Previously, we would collate, saddle stitch & trim all our books to cut costs.

The grant ended in May 1976. Everyone left except myself & another woman. It was a long summer. Once again, no salaries. We had the printing debt to pay off. In October 1976 we received some funding from the Ministry of Education to publish two new books. At that time my daughter Jessica was born. She was in the office from eight days old on. Everything was running very smoothly until December,

1976. Our two books were coming along, perhaps ready for the printer by middle January. Unfortunately, January through March 1977 went down the tube. . . .

The other woman involved in BWA6 was not only my "business partner" (for lack of a better description) but a very close friend. Her life quite suddenly fell apart, & with it so did she. I shudder just to think of those times. I was torn in my support. I wanted to be with & help her through her ordeal, but in order to do that BWA6 would lose. There was no one else to keep it going. Fool that I am, I attempted to do both & let me say it was sheer "madness." For three months I waited to see if she would come back & continue at BWA6, but suddenly without warning , she decided to leave town.

I now find myself months behind in getting our new books & catalogue out & in a financial bind. The grant is over. The two of us took out a bank loan which I am now responsible for alone.

I realize, in re-reading what I have just written that I sound like the voice of doom. I am sorry. I didn't intend to get into it. Let me get a fresh cup of tea, clear my head & continue on. . . .

Hello! My head is now clear (whatever that might mean. . .)

This may be hard to believe, but I do feel optimistic about BWA6's future. I have no doubts about the next few months & how rough they will be. We are very dependent on educational sales & summer certainly dampens the market. I will have to give up our office to cut down on the monthly expenses, helping to pay back the loan, & move BWA6 into my home. I'll miss the office. Fortunately, we have space in our home. We bought an old run-down general store in a small town a couple of years ago, which we have been rebuilding.

Our two new titles & catalogue should be ready in approximately six weeks.

Financially speaking. . . Like other Canadian publishing house in competition with American publishers for the North American market (forget the world!) we are still dependent on financial assistance. Our government recognizes our (all Canadian publishers) dilemma & does come to our rescue (in their own small way). Hopefully in a year or so with the addition of new titles, BWA6 can be self sufficient. That is my goal. Trying to run a business with only five titles (with the majority being sold at a 50-60 percent discount) does not generate enough income to pay salaries plus expand BWA6. It will take time & effort to close the gap.

I'm hoping in the fall to be able to hire one other woman. Gone are the days of volunteer labor. . . .

We are incorporated as a non-profit organization. I'm currently getting a strong Board of Directors together. I need input & advice.

Realizing I have not limited myself to one page, I will close by briefly saying that BWA6 has been motivated by Feminist beliefs and dedication to a co-operative working structure, although the latter has not always proved successful.

Please bear with me, as I write this at 3 a.m. I am somewhat hazy in my thoughts. Those involved in BWA6 have always felt, that, as women, we have much to gain if BWA6 can be successful. It has been hard, as our political beliefs have often brought us together, but once there we have found that attempting to run a business & survive with many of those beliefs takes twice as much work. Yes, I often feel discouraged. How much easier it would be to view BWA6 strictly as a business with the only motive being profit. . . .

Let's keep in touch,

Susan Shaw Weatherup

Presses Publishing Four or More Titles

AKWESASNE NOTES
Mohawk Nation
via Roosevelt Town
New York, 13683

AKWESASNE NOTES is a Native American newspaper but as a major publishing source for Native American voices in this country, it falls into the press category. With a circulation of 84,000 it is a resounding voice. Concerned with supporting a culture which dominant white society has consistently suppressed, the paper treats Indian art and philosophy as inseparable parts of life. The careful lines between living and art which the white man has so studiously drawn have not been, and art not relevant to Native Americans. Even as Blacks, Chicano, and Native Americans have had to fight this separation, so many white women must do the same. The symbols and images of an oppressed people are an essential and sustaining part of everyday life. Indian prose reads with the wisdom and flow of poetry and song.

Set against the common reality of white male oppression of Indian rights and suppression of an extraordinary democratic culture, the female rights issue has less relevance. Respect for women, as well as children has always been as integral a part of Native American culture as respect for men. This is not to say that there are no women's rights issues in Indian society, but the denigration of female mind, which is so much a part of the white male oppression of white women, does not have the same overtones in the male Native American view of women. The Western white woman, reclaiming herstory, can find strong role models in Native American culture.

Respect and reverence for life includes all of the earth as a mother and the sky as a father. As such, Native Americans are as concerned about rape of the land as the rape of souls. *AKWE-SASNE NOTES* brings the best of its Indian writers and activities to its seasoned pages. Their arguments for ecology action, combining reverence for freedom and life in all its forms, are basic. However, Native Americans are more than logical, practical and angry. The philosophy that undergirds their call for action reaches into the place where our souls live, stifled by Western greed and repression.

In addition to the newspaper *AKWESASE NOTES* has published over thirteen books (brochure available upon request), poetry, and non-fiction (historical, cultural, political). They carry a significant number of beautiful posters (17 x 22), a calendar, wholesale crafts and Indian tobacco. Their printing is done by Glad Day Press, a Movement printer in Ithaca, New York, distribution is handled directly.

There is no fixed subscription rate for receiving *AKWE-SASNE NOTES*. Their subscribers come from a wide spectrum of the population with varying incomes. They suggest sending your name and address with anywhere from $1-$5-$10 plus, whatever you can pay for five issues.

The fact that *AKWESASNE NOTES* is one of very few Native American presses in this country is further indication of the generally oppressed financial state of Native Americans. Grant monies to support Native American presses seem to be non-existent. Although the small presses are beginning to print Native American writing, the fact remains that the presses getting funds to do this are still white.

Hopefully, the demand for funds to start more Native American presses, to launch *AKWESASNE NOTES* further into the book business (to make the paper itself solvent) will grow so that words like these of Buffy St. Marie's can resound across the canyons of any oppressed heart, woman or man:

118

We'll celebrate each other. We'll encourage each other, and paint each other's pictures in a thousand masterpieces. The bitterness that burned our hearts will die down when we need it to, and it will become embers and coals, and we'll cook over it, and love each other in its light, and tell each other funny stories beside its glow, and warm each other with songs of the beauty of our relatives, songs of our ancestors and our grandchildren, our Indian past.

We won't forget—and we won't be victims anymore.

ALICE JAMES BOOKS
138 Mt. Auburn Street
Cambridge, MA. 02138

Many women's presses are founded in recognition of a woman writer ignored during her own lifetime simply because whe was a woman. As one of the founding visionaries behind Alice James Books, poet Marjory Fletcher has finally brought to Alice James (1848-1892), brilliant, overshadowed sister of the famous James brothers, William and Henry, the belated credibility she so richly deserved. Though she was unpublished during her lifetime, in her name, many contemporary women poets will be read and recognized as writers.

Alice James is a book publishing cooperative emphasizing poetry of women. In order to publish with them, the writer must become an active member of the cooperative, which means a writer needs to live in the Boston area. When a manuscript is accepted, the writer automatically becomes a member of the cooperative and is expected to put in a certain amount of time in the office learning typesetting, layout and production. The aim of the press is for each author to make design, layout and promotion decisions on her own book. This keeps control of production in the hands of the writer and means that the writers are not subject to the powerlessness of having someone else making all the decisions on their book.

Publishing six books a year since 1974, Alice James has over twenty titles on the market with an excellent record in distribution and sales. In two years they sold over 4,000 books to libraries alone. They are clearly one of the most successful poetry cooperatives in the country. In addition to publishing single works by members, each book series for the current year publishes a book containing the work of two or more women. In series III Robin Becker, Helena Minton and Marilyn Zuckerman join in one book, *PERSONAL EFFECTS* (perfect bound, $3.50). In series IV, Alice James combines two books in one with *THIRSTY JAY* by Kathleen Aguero and *PERMANENT WAVE*, by Miriam Goodman inside the same covers (perfect bound, $3.50).

ARACHNE PUBLISHING
P O Box 4100
Mountain View, CA. 94040

The hard work of getting (and keeping) women's herstory in print is serious business. Those stories of pain, struggles, repression and violence need to be written, need to be read. However, after a normal day of feminist toil with your vaginal infection, and the gynecologist, your honors degree and the welfare department, your headache and the "COPE" commercials, most of us could use a good laugh. There is very little humor in the Women's Movement. Arachne's cartoon books are welcome relief.

Created by feminist artist, Bülbül, each of four books in print presents in cartoon form the kind of political satire women have been waiting for. Instead of women's being the usual butt of jokes, men are. *"I'M FOR WOMEN'S LIB. . . BUT"* ($1.25) came out in 1973, *"DISSECTING DOCTOR MEDI-CORPSE"* ($1.25) followed in 1974. More recent books are *"EVERY-BODY'S STUDYING US"* (the ironies of aging in the Pepsi generation) and *"SUGAR DADDY'S A STICKY MYTH!"* (a collection of cartoons on men and power). All of the books are saddle stitched and professionally printed by Up Press, a women's print shop. Up Press also prints the books for New Seed Press (non-sexist books for children). Bülbül printed her first two cartoon books in association with New Seed, but later took on

120

her own label: Arachne Publishing.

Good cartooning, although appreciated by most of us, does not have a very high priority in feminist publishing. Bülbül wrote, "Arachne was set up to publish feminist cartoons. . . because no other media was interested." Arachne is not soliciting but talented cartoonists might want to query about possibilities. Three of Bulbul's books are distrituted through *WIND*, or can be ordered directly.

"We break even, have outside jobs and are learning a lot about the politics of cartooning in the process. My dream is to do a book of cartoons and writing that would set the world on end. Coming soon. . . of course!"

(See Print Shops: *UP PRESS*. Children's Presses: *NEW SEED*. Distributors: *WIND*).

CATALYST
Blantyre Avenue
Scarborough, Ontario
Canada

Catalyst is a Canadian press, a cooperative publishing house devoted to the work of lesbians and gay men. Production of each book is author-controlled, with the writer having as much or as little to say in the making of the final product as she/he wishes.

Catalyst was founded in 1967, but only began publishing books in 1970. They are financed largely out of personal resources, though they have received some grant money from the Canada Council and the Ontario Arts Council. They are able to publish three to five titles a year. Their most recent book is *THE ANCIENT AND OTHER POEMS* by Judith Crewe ($3.50). They did not mention what else they had published.

All of the printing at Catalyst is farmed out. Press runs are 500-1000 copies for a first printing. If the first edition sells out, they reprint. "We feel we have a pretty good distribution for a small press, selling to stores, libraries, mail order dealers and private customers all over the U.S. and Canada, plus some outlets in others countries."

Their standard royalty is 10 percent of the list price of each book sold. They are also interested in publishing author-subsidized books, "provided they meet our standards. We are not a vanity press." Inquiries should be sent directly to the publishers.

The name, Catalyst, aptly fits what, as a press, Catalyst is trying to accomplish. They are a group that initiates an energetic reaction that enables them to proceed, printing, that might not otherwise be printed, that might not be able to initiate that next reaction in a potential reader's mind.

CAROLINA WREN PRESS
Box 209
Carrboro, NC. 27510

Moving into a very special place in the South, Feminist publisher Judy Hogan says that she is one of the few publishers in the South who is really open to both women poets and Black writers. Putting her press into operation in 1976, Judy quickly published what she calls the "magic number of books" in order to be taken seriously in the Small Press. In addition to four books by individual poets. Carolina Wren has a fine women's anthology, BLACK SUN/NEW MOON, which features new writers from North Carolina. Up to this point books from the press have been saddle stitched, but future books will be perfect bound.

After five books of poetry, Carolina Wren is about to publish its sixth book and first novel. Sharon Ramirez's novel, BREAKDOWN, is the poignant story of the disruptive effect of World War II on a single American family. The pressures and fears involved in the family breakdown are told through the eyes of a seven year old child as she struggles to interpret what is happening around her.

Judy feels very strongly about creating a world that is equal and tolerant, spaces for all people to have a chance to grow in. Her publishing reflects these basic beliefs, three books by women, and three by men. "I'm convinced that everything I'm publishing is important, but I feel I'm treading on eggshells. Relationships with people I publish are very personal and become very important." One of the women poets she published included in her book a piece dedicated to Judy, which was a poem about Judy's death. "How can you measure anything by that? Being a publisher is so much more than just publishing books you believe in."

At the moment, Judy Hogan is not soliciting books, "I already have 12 books in the wings." However, she is open to hearing from people with manuscripts. She also has the possibility of serving writers and presses in another way. As director of *COSMEP/SOUTH DISTRIBUTION* and the *COSMEP* Van Project, she is interested in adding more books to her distribution service. (See Distributors).

THE CROSSING PRESS
Rd 2
Trumansburg, NY. 14886

In their own words, Elaine and John Gill are operating a press "where the word 'poetry' means life-giving and yielding." They publish new American and Canadian work with individual volumes of poetry (titles by women: Alta, *I'M NOT A PRACTISING ANGEL*; Lyn Lifshin, *BLACK APPLES, UPSTATE MADONNA*). They also print minority anthologies: a gay anthology, a women's anthology (*MOUNTAIN MOVING DAY*), an American Indian and a Soledad Prison anthology. They put out a basic Chinese cookbook written by a man and another on vegetarian cookery by a woman, *WINGS OF LIFE* by Julie Jordan. Currently they have a rapidly growing series of illustrated stories for children, which are non-sexist creations and delightfully readable. They have other ideas for the future. . . "in fact, whatever is food for the mind, the body and the soul. . . (to) make the crossing into new life."

Authors with The Crossing Press receive 10 percent of the net amount the press receives. Initially, they worked with their own presses, but press runs are now sufficiently large to warrant using independent printers in the area.

Leaving college teaching jobs (Elaine was fired; John quit), they started out with a literary journal, *NEW* (now defunct), an old mimeograph machine and faith. Now nine years latter, "We are growing bigger. We don't need other jobs to survive. We haven't held outside jobs since 1969. Philosophical and political base? Sure. . . to produce books we believe in, books that are solid, hopefully some books that will change people's consciousness." At Crossing Press workers are about evenly split between the sexes, three women and four men. "We are basically a mom and pop enterprise, but with lots of feed-through from people who work here."

The Crossing Press distributes in a variety of ways: salespeople, Women in Distribution, Bookpeople and others. They need a gross of $60,000 to $70,000 "just to keep rocking." They do not solicit work because they find enough that they want to publish on their own. However, nothing ventured, nothing gained and so. . . a letter of inquiry may have a place.

Moving far beyond their beginnings, Elaine and John Gill represent the grit, imagination and fearlessness that has turned The Crossing Press into a major success story in small press publication. Living around the corner from dairy and truck farms in rural upstate New York, they have splintered legends that say presses have to be in major cities in order to be successful.

DAUGHTERS, INC.
22 Charles Street
New York, NY. 10014

Daughters has broken many small press feminist myths by publishing excellently written novels with high quality production and effective distribution methods. With each year Daughters becomes more and more solid for women as a real alternative to the big press. We know how well they've done and take real pride in their success. *RUBYFRUIT JUNGLE* by

Rita Mae Brown was practically a best seller and *THE COOK AND THE CARPENTER* by June Arnold could well become a classic in American literature.

Works do not necessarily have to be lesbian in tone. This is an assumption often made by the public because Daughters has published a number of fine lesbian writers. Daughters solicits manuscripts from all voices of the Movement, but they are not interested in praise of Jesus, nuclear family, or personal journals, which lack the tension they prefer in the novels they publish. With publication of each Daughters book a new literary form seems to be launched. So far every novel from Daughters has been without literary precedent. We have grown to expect highly innovative literature, as well as good stories. At present, Daughters is distributing over 16 titles, including *SISTER GIN*, a second novel by June Arnold.

Two women provide the core structure of Daughters: Founders, novelist June Arnold, and lawyer/editor Parke Bowman. Bertha Harris, novelist/women studies teacher, works as an editor two days a week and shares in the on-going growth and work of Daughters.

Among feminist presses, Daughters is becoming one of the strongest voices to urge women-identified artists to assert their independence by publishing with women's publishing houses. They realize the immense difficulty of reaching such a state in an economically male-dominated society, but as June Arnold says, "Women have to learn they can afford to say no." A woman who publishes with a male press, no matter how much control she is given over her book, is still economically dependent. The reality still exists in that situation that since a man giveth, a man can still take away. The woman remains powerless.

Along with the Women's Press Collective and Diana Press now both in Oakland , Daughters depicts a strong political position for separatism in women's publishing. It would be inaccurate to simplify this policy of radical independence as simply feminist separatism. The term itself implies many things

125

even within the Women's Movement.

Broad use of the term as a catch-all phrase often negates or simplifies differing modes of operation or thought among feminist publishers. It accounts for a certain amount of mistrust and misunderstanding between women's presses. For Daughters the real issue of separatism is economic and is far more complicated than being or not being lesbian. Daughters maintains that it will be only when women can withstand the lure of immediate money, and at some personal cost, support all-women's businesses, that women will be able to build structures necessary for real economic independence. The women of Daughters do not see this as providing an alternative to present society. They feel they are building the real one.

In operation since 1973 and enlarging, Daughters is now in a position to offer solid royalty contracts to women novelists they publish. As such they provide a substantial financial option for women over against women publishing with commercial trade houses. That in itself should indicate to the skeptical that they know what they are about. The theories of Daughters and the Daughters realities have a powerful blending in the same brew.

DIANA PRESS, INC.
4400 Market Street
Oakland, CA. 94608

Lesbian-Feminist Diana Press has been a stable, vital cornerstone in women's publishing from the very beginning. What no one else would, they did—like Rita Mae Brown's *THE HAND THAT CRADLES THE ROCK; WOMEN REMEMBERED;* and *CLASS AND FEMINISM.*

Publishing non-fiction and poetry (18 titles at this writing), Diana continues to support both the development of solid

Socialist-Feminist theory and/or the work of lesbian writers. Recently, Coletta Reid of Diana joined forces with Barbara Grier in order to edit and publish an important Diana Press three book series. This new series is culled from work printed in *THE LADDER*, a pioneer journal of lesbian writers which is no longer publishing. The *LADDER ANTHOLOGIES* include: *THE LESBIAN HOME JOURNAL*, twenty-two stories by well-known lesbian writers; *LESBIAN LIVES*, biographies of over sixty women; and *THE LAVENDER HERRING*, lesbian essays. Taken together or separately, the three books provide vibrant tribute to historically unheard-of lesbian writers.

Diana Press does not farm out production work. It is well equipped to do its own printing, as well as binding on the premises. Almost as important as the publishing under its own imprint, Diana does a great deal of print work for other feminist publishers. A number of women's presses and publications regularly send their work to Diana to be printed, saddle stitched or perfect bound. Even if a press looking for a printer finally decides to send the work elsewhere, Diana Press women are very willing (as time allows) to do what they can to help a woman design and plan her book(s) or to provide whatever help they can to facilitate distribution. This kind of cooperation which is so much a part of women's presses, is simply unheard of in commercial trade houses. Can you imagine calling up Random House and saying. . . "I have this book and I wondered. . . ?"

While needing to survive financially, Diana still offers low cost printing services. These women do not base their own survival on what they feel is the destructive profit motive typical of commercial printers. Printing costs continue to spirial, but in 1976 publisher Margaret Kaminski contracted with Diana to print a 48 page book of poetry for her Glass Bell Press. Four hundred dollars included typesetting, paste-up, printing and perfect binding. The quality is superb and a publisher looking for a printer usually cannot match that. Diana seeks submissions from lesbian writers and encourages women publishers to send them material for printing estimate.

While their own label is exclusively for lesbian writers, the women of Diana Press are very happy to deal with any Feminist woman in their press shop activities. They believe women should do it themselves, rather than give in to a male who will reap most of the profits from sale of their work. Like Daughters (fiction), and the Women's Press Collective (poetry and non-fiction), Diana takes a strong position that women writers in order to gain real economic independence should work (if at all possible), through a feminist publisher or printer.

(See Press I: *NAID PRESS*)

DOWN THERE PRESS
3416 22nd Street
San Francisco, CA. 94110

With no prior design Joani Blank came into feminist publishing almost by accident. "I duplicated a sexual self-awareness work book I had put together for my clients (I do sexuality workshops and counseling for women) and people liked it so much I decided to publish it. I also learned calligraphy around that time and a do-it-myself job seemed to be most appropriate. I never considered getting someone else to publish my stuff. The men's sex playbook came next and then *GOOD VIBRATIONS*. I'm now finishing up a sex playbook for children (ages 8-12)."

Joani Blank's books are all hand lettered, which gives her sexuality books a more personal touch than if her information was antiseptically presented in formal type. *THE PLAYBOOK: FOR WOMEN/ABOUT SEX* (8½ x 11, saddle stitched, $3.00), is really a very non-threatening, useful work book of questions which a woman can ask herself about her own sexuality. Answers to many of the questions suggest that the reader make drawings instead of word responses. The other two playbooks are similiar. *GOOD VIBRATIONS* (5½ x 8½, saddle stitched, $1.85), is a guide to different models of vibrators, with pros and cons, financial and physical data.

"I've done virtually no advertising. *WIND* carries two of my books and Bookpeople carries one. The *DISTRIBUTORS* in Illinois carry all three. I have sold over 6,000 copies of *THE PLAYBOOK: FOR WOMEN/ABOUT SEX* and 2,000 each of the other two (very few through distributors). Yes, I could survive on my earnings from the books, but barely. I've not been doing much hustling lately 'cause I've started a vibrator store (catering to, but limited to women) in San Francisco. That really grew out of my doing the vibrator book. I carry 31 varieties of vibrators in my store. I still do counseling and I teach a human sexuality class in community college."

"I work alone in both my store and publishing. I farm out printing (to women printers). I'm not soliciting manuscripts since I only (so far) publish my own stuff. My plans for the future depend on how the store goes and how my books do."

(See Distributors: *WIND, BOOKPEOPLE*)

DRUID HEIGHTS BOOKS
685 Camino Del Canyon
Muir Woods
Mill Valley, CA. 94941

"I started this originally with the initial intention of bringing out my own work, mostly poetry, since longer manuscripts cost too much. I named it, at first, Druid Heights *Press* because I had long cherished a hope of having some sort of a press to bring out my own and perhaps other work ignored by the commercial publishers. This was long before the explosions of little presses of various sorts (my dream, this is). I never had enough money or enough time from lean freelance bread-winning. But in late autumn of 1970 a friend who had access to printing facilities offered to bring out a small collection of my poetry I had named *MOODS OF EROS*. I invented Druid Heights Press to carry that book of 999 copies out to friends and others who might be interested. The response was good though the distribution, bookkeeping and other chores were trying."

Three years later Elsa Gidlow brought out two more poetry

volumes of her own work, *MAKING FOR MEDITATION* and *WISE MAN'S GOLD*. In 1976 she published her fourth book, a prose pamphlet *ASK NO MAN PARDON: THE PHILOSO-PHICAL SIGNIFICANCE OF BEING LESBIAN*, which nearly sold out a 1000 copy press run in a single year. Well reviewed in women's publications, *ASK NO MAN PARDON* is clearly her best seller. Of the two other books in her series, one is a small run of her sister, Thea Singleton Gidlow's poetry, and a new book by Terry Ryan, self published through Druid Heights Books.

Having finally established her label and in a position to sell many more books, Elsa Gidlow is seriously considering phasing out except for providing the label occasionally for writers to self publish under. "I may do this with/for other women, a sort of diffused collective effort if you wish to regard it so. No one is likely to make any money, lucky if all investors break even."

Druid Heights Books can be ordered directly from Elsa or through *WIND*.

(See Distributors: *WIND*)

DUSTBOOKS
P O Box 1056
Paradise, CA. 95969

Somewhere back in 1963 Len Fulton was a biostatistician working for State Public Health, and also writing novels. Spending day after day drawing up column after column of numbers brought in bread, but wasn't exactly his vision of survival. On his own time he started a literary magazine called *DUST*. As editor and aspiring writer, he could begin to enlarge the known community of commiserating writing souls.

By sliding into publishing himself, Len Fulton also hoped to find out what was going on in the small press world. He discovered that nobody "out there" seemed to know what any body else was doing. The biostatistician head reared up and gradually Len Fulton sifted his "dust" into a *DIRECTORY OF*

LITTLE MAGAZINES AND SMALL PRESSES. Now in its thirteenth annual edition, the *DIRECTORY* has grown into an international handbook, listing over 2,000 magazines and small presses. Companion volumes are: *DIRECTORY OF SMALL MAGAZINE PRESS EDITORS AND PUBLISHERS, SMALL PRESS RECORD OF BOOKS,* two "How-to" manuals on publishing, and the *SMALL PRESS REVIEW (SPR),* a monthly newsletter with small press news and reviews and updates.

When Len Fulton got involved in a commitment to share small press publishing information, the small press was mostly a male domain. Now Dustbooks is an active supporter of small press publishing of women's writing. *GUIDE TO WOMEN'S PUBLISHING* will further expand this *DIRECTORY* series.

Dustbooks centers around its key Directory titles, but the press carries over 24 titles of poetry, fiction and non-fiction as well. "We are open to all ideas as far as manuscripts go, though anything that doesn't have some style in the literary sense won't get through here with our imprint. We are very open to small press and publishing info in book form simply because Dustbooks is founded in that, and tries to be the world's foremost expert in the subject. We look for a balance in our list between fiction and poetry, and non-fiction because otherewise we'd be insolvent in six weeks. . . We have to limit this gambling to what our resources can stand. We do 2-3 books of poetry a year, usually from unsolicited piles." Late in 1975 Dustbooks published *MOVING TO ANTARCTICA,* an anthology of literary works previously published in *MOVING OUT,* a Detroit based feminist literary magazine. Edited by Margaret Kaminski, one of the editors of *MOVING OUT,* the book has a strong appeal.

Since 1969 Dustbooks has been a full time operation for Len Fulton, and Ellen Ferber joined the press in 1972. "Right now working 'in house' we have (you're not going to believe it), three men and three women, all but Ellen and I part time (and Ellen holds a full time tenured faculty position in literature), so guess it's really just me; about 100 hours a week. . . The people who work for us are salaried and would not be interested in a 'collective' approach though I admire those who make it work. . . We do about 10,000 transactions a year and this ties up 3-5 person-days a week. . . Both Ellen and I are through-going loners who go at it 16-20 hours a day—no one else could stand to do that, and we couldn't stand to have them on our asses either!"

Other activities: Dustbooks recently took over operation of The Small Press Book Club, which is specifically Ellen Ferber's domain. Also, Len and Ellen did a cross-country book selling trip during the summer of 1974, becoming rather infamous in the process. The most immediate reason for the trip had been to get Len's novel, *THE GRASSMAN*, and the Dustbooks' Directories into a lot of bookstores through a personal contact approach. Two hundred and fifty bookstores and two months later, the two of them had "sold $1300 worth of books, spent $2000 in seven weeks and put 10,000 miles on our car." A book selling travelogue, *AMERICAN ODYSSEY*, came out of the experience plus solid promotion of "small independent publishing, do-it-yourselfism, contemporary literature, and non-corporate-giant endeavors of several kinds," all of it very supportive of small press publishing.

Ellen Ferber's comments about the experience of going into bookstores to sell their books is absolutely classic, and represents the kind of dedication-determination it takes to become a solvent in the small press business. The small press always faces the unenviable position of trying to *create* a public taste for new literature, rather than simply feeding into popular opinion. That has never been easy and, tried or untried, the thought is enough to send shivers down any writer's spine. One can easily imagine (even if one hasn't experienced it) standing in front of a book-shop door with one's own book grasped between two coldly-sweating palms. It isn't any easier, Ellen says in *AMERICAN ODYSSEY*, even if it isn't your own book. . . " I had never sold, not girl scout cookies, not anything, before. I was afraid of it, and was shamed at my relief when there was only one store in walking distance and I could sit and wait hopefully in the car.

I had no special talent for it, and I'm not much good at it even yet. It got easier, but I don't know now if it would be any easier if I started out to do it again. But it was worth doing, and, easier or not, it would be worth doing again. So long as Americans opt for the market place, people will have to get out there and keep the place clean."

(See Additional Resources: *INTERNATIONAL DIRECTORY OF LITTLE MAGAZINES AND SMALL PRESSES, DIRECTORY OF SMALL MAGAZINE PRESS EDITORS AND PUBLISHERS, SMALL PRESS RECORD OF BOOKS, SMALL PRESS REVIEW*. See Distributors: *THE SMALL PRESS BOOK CLUB*)

EFFIE'S PRESS
1420 45th Street
Studio 45
Everyville, CA. 94608

In these commercial days it is hard to find a printer/publisher who loves the look and feel of a book, who is willing to spend the hours required to design and letterpress the Beautiful Book. Usually printed in limited editions, such a book is sometimes almost worth buying for its looks, simply to hold it, to know what care went into its printing. However, to find a press that does all that and is still concerned about content is rare. Add to this the fact that Effie's Press is run by a woman who is printing feminist writers whose voice we want to hear, and you have *pure dynamite!* Yet despite this explosive combination, Bonnie Carpenter of Effie's Press still keeps a low profile.

I began Effies's Press in November of 1973 as Effie's Books. . . wanting to offer an independent woman edited small press alternative for women writers. (The Small Press in itself offers an alternative to big east coast publishing houses as well as a kind of quality book that only small letterpress shops are into producing).

The press publishes quality, first edition letterpress books of poetry, prose and short stories of unknown or unpublished women writers, as well as publishing new or experimental works of previously published women. The books are printed on turn-of-the-century (early 1900's) printing presses. . . using hand-set types and five rag papers. The shop has 3 presses, 2 platens and a Kelly B Flatbed. All printing, typesetting and design is done in the shop by yours truly. (The shop is located in a warehouse; have a painting studio upstairs above the presses.)

In 1974 I had received a NEA grant to publish 5 women's chapbooks. At present finances are basically hand-to-mouth in terms of production of new books. I am confident things will get better though. . . At present I am open to side jobs; such as designing books, typesetting, printing and/or designing of posters, stationery, bookcovers, title pages, etc.

I do consider manuscripts that come to the press via mail. Thus far however, most of the books I've done are of poets I have sought out. I usually publish an edition of 500 books and the author receives 10 percent of the edition as royalties.

My vision for the future of Effie's Press is to open it up to a partnership and take on an extra woman printer to step up production. At present production is slow because I'm doing the entire process. . . I am more interested in centering my energy around the design and layout and promotion of the books.

At the moment Effie's Press is carrying six titles, two of them are sold out: *TWENTY-ONE POEMS* by Adrianne Rich (first edition sold out, second edition in the planning stage) and *LETTERS* by Susan Griffin. The other four titles include *KEEPSAKE* by Barbar Granville ($2.00), *A LETTER AT EASTER* by Beverly Dahlen ($3.00), *ONE NIGHT STAND* by Mary Mackey ($4.00), and *ANY TIME NOW* by Francis Jaffer ($3.00). Effie's Press only distributes through Serendipity Books in California which requires exclusive distribution rights.

And, finally, Bonnie Carpenter says of her Effie, that she is "a feminist press creating books of quality for all of us to enjoy and take pleasure in."

EIDOLON EDITIONS
P O Box 629
Point Reyes Station, CA. 94956

Eidolon Editions is a second coming as a press for publsiher Diane diPrima. Her first foray was Poets Press which came into existence in 1964. At that time with financial support from painter friends and "a few other folks in NYC, I bought a Davidson 241 and put it in a store-front. . . I went to 'printing school' for a week and learned how to run the machine (I was the only woman in the class), and got on with it. Poets Press printed 29 books in 5 years—only a few of which were by women, but a great number of which were 'first books' by writers often third world people. It came to an abrupt end in 1969, after a series of unfortunate rip-offs. . . In 1972 I began to publish again, and have since done five books as Eidolon Editions."

Doing beautiful editions, Eidolon has completed three books by the publisher, *LOBA 2, FREDDIE POEMS,* and *CALCULUS OF VARIATION* ("I re-began to get some of my own stuff out"); and two other fine books, *BETWEEN OURSELVES* by Audre Lorde, and *ARCHES* by Jackson Allen. Diane does not see her press as exclusively a "women's press" though at the present time she is planning a great many more books from Eidolon written by women rather than men. "It all depends on what manuscripts come my way and look good. There's still of course a huge stockpile of women's writing to be 'gotten out' as soon as possible."

The four books being readied for publication reflect this spirit: *WATER WHEEL* by Betsy Ford, *QUICK ALCHEMY* by Jeanne diPrima (introduction by Anne Waldman), *A PAINTER'S POEMS* by Joan Thornton, and *DREAMS ARE ANOTHER SET OF MUSCLES* by David Shaddock.

At Eidolon "women & men work with the press, on a come-and-go kind of basis. I pay folks to come in when they can, and do some of the necessary work, but basically do the typesetting & production myself. The press has never made any money—if a book of mine sells well, or, say Audre's book, the money automatically goes into other books. The press at this point is located in an office in Point Reyes which is also a community center for graphics and layout: that is, my IBM composer serves many groups and needs and purposes; and occasionally I give folks instruction in layout, or self-publishing."

> My philosophical base is anarchist—the 'cooperative' kind. I haven't been soliciting mss. because I have more than enough commitments already: I often encounter someone in a writing workshop that I am teaching, who seems to me ready for publication & then I ask Her/him for a mss. In this way, I have THE WOMAN'S GUIDE TO MOUNTAIN CLIMBING by Jane Augustine, also waiting on future publication (This is a book of poems).

Eidolon usually pays authors with 10 percent of the copies of the book. Occasionally, if there is a need, and the publisher can find the funds, she will pay a 10 percent royalty in cash, or split between paying books and cash. "In any case, I pay on publication, rather than sending royalty statements & going thru all that elaborate bookkeeping. When doing Poets Press stuff I owned press, copy camera, platemaker, etc. But since starting again as Eidolon Editions, I have found it a lot more practical to keep it down to making camera copy in the office & farming the printing & binding out. I give my work to (usually) the cheapest bidder who can do a quality job."

Diane says that she has no real notion about the Eidolon sales volume, though she thinks that Eidolon's three most recent books (ARCHES, BETWEEN OURSELVES, & LOBA 2) will be sold out by the end of the year. As for future goals, Diane diPrima says with unbeatable poetic style. . . "No, No dreams for the future—just work as it comes, and stop when I've had it."

THE FEMINIST PRESS
Box 334
Old Westbury, NY. 11568

The Feminist Press is a non-profit, tax-exempt educational and publishing organization, founded in 1970. In their own words "What distinguishes The Feminist Press from other publishing houses is our pupose: We are engaged in educational change. From the beginning our work has been to reach people with stories of women's lives, to restore the heritage of women's writing and to bring to the classroom a new literature with a broader vision of human potential. This work has grown over the years in direct response to the needs of parents, teachers, students and community. We are now involved in a wide range of educational activities aimed at offering alternatives to sexual stereo-types in books and curriculum. At present there are thirty titles on our published list and our daily work is carried on by a small paid staff augmented by volunteers." In addition to books for adults The Feminist Press publishes a healthly number of non-sexist books for children.

More than a publishing house, The Feminist Press is a nation-wide source of information on women's education at all levels. They carry on a wide variety of educational programs and projects. They are a clearinghouse on women's studies programs. Their *WOMEN'S STUDIES NEWSLETTER* has been designated by the National Women's Studies Association as the official news organ of that organization. They also design and teach various in-service education courses for public school teachers, teach courses at the State University of New York on educational publishing and children's non-sexist literature, plus provide an on-the-job publishing internship at the press, which involves students in every aspect of publishing from editing, typesetting and printing through shipping book orders.

The press is organized as a collective. As a result sometimes things take a bit longer to process. "It normally takes us about two months to circulate proposals and mss. received which are not immediately rejected because of subject (outside our line) or treatment (sexist)." Proposals are read and commented on by the nine members of the Publications Committee and discussed. The publishing program focuses on reprints, biographies, children's books and educational curricula. "One of the members of the Committee undertakes to communicate with the authors of each proposal explaining our decision regarding their work."

We don't have a separate staff for any area of Press work, although we do have a children's book committee, a High School Project

Committee, an educational projects committee, etc. In fact, the Press is basically organized into these—and other—committees, which we call work committees. Of them all, only the High School project committee has a degree of separateness because of it's being a grant project—but only a degree of separateness. For example, everyone on that committee, even though several of its members were specifically hired for the grant, does Press work in areas other than the High School project. . . Whether or not we decide to publish a given book—either children's or any other—is determined by the entire Press staff, not just the particular committee involved.

Publication of *VOICES*, an original poem-play by Susan Griffin, seemed to represent a real departure from the carefully defined educational guidelines of The Feminist Press. The suggestion that *VOICES* meant The Feminist Press had made a radical departure in their publishing policy is erroneous. "*VOICES*, quite simply, was a gift to us from Susan Griffin. We were only allowed to print 1500 copies of the play, and she is not taking any royalties whatsoever. It's quite true that it doesn't fall into any of our publishing categories, and, as such, makes it difficult to announce that we do not publish plays. But our tax-exempt status limits us to works that can be defined strictly as 'educational,' and we could not have published *VOICES* if it had not been a gift."

Continuing to adhere closely to their educational policy, The Feminist Press has gone far beyond attempting to fill the void in availabililty of women's writing. They are *creating* a need for informed women everywhere to read the historical and present work of women in order to intelligently shape a powerful continuing herstory.

(See Children's Press: *THE FEMINIST PRESS*. Additional Resources: *WOMEN STUDIES NEWSLETTER*)

THE GREENFIELD REVIEW PRESS
Greenfield Center, NY. 12833

The Greenfield Review Press began in 1969 when Carol and Joe Bruchac returned from three years in Africa. In addition to

THE GREENFIELD REVIEW, a literature magazine, Joe and Carol run a substantial chapbook series (saddle stitched). At the moment they carry only two poetry books by women: *NEVER STOP DANCING* ($1.00) by Toni Ortner Zimmerman (editor of *CONNECTIONS*, see Feminist Publications); and *HOPI ROAD-RUNNER DANCING* ($2.25), a collection of poems by Wendy Rose, half-Hopi and former staff writer for *MANY SMOKES* magazine. The latter is one of the rare books on the market written by a Native American woman.

> Our first book was a collection of work smuggled out of Soledad Prison which we published in 1971. Since then we have brought 24 more chapbooks and received a grant from the NEA and a grant from CCLM for the press itself. Because of the emphasis in our press on the work of Third World people we have not published as many chapbooks by women as we would like to—although in proportion to the actual number of manuscripts we have received from women we have accepted a *much higher* percentage. If we are lucky enough to receive funding in the coming year from NEA or any other source, we will be open to unsolicited manuscripts after July 1977 and we hope to be able to accept at least as many manuscripts from women as from men.

Although Carol and Joe carry the bulk of the work done at Greenfield Review, and hold down jobs on the side, they have another man and woman who also give time to both their magazine and the press a number of times during the year. Carol says that the philosophical base behind their work is "The Earth, our Mother, a commitment to good writing, good poetry (according to our own subjective standards). . . With the Press we now pay authors $10.00 on acceptance of their manuscript, then give them a straight 10 percent of the retail price of every book sold plus 10 free copies. (We have a contract.). . . We print from 500-1000 copies of each chapbook and sell them out within 3 years after publication in most cases. But we send out a lot of free copies for review and so on. . . Our dreams for the future are to continue doing what we're doing and keep our sanity. Also to publish more books of poetry by Third World women in particular. We have at least two scheduled for 1977 (Sandra Esteves and Janet Campbell Hale)."

THE INDIAN HISTORIAN PRESS
1451 Masonic Avenue
San Francisco, CA. 94117

Jeannette Henry startled the publishing world with *TEXT-BOOKS AND THE AMERICAN INDIAN*. Very concerned with inaccuracies regarding Indians that were being taught in American schools, Jeannette Henry edited this textbook about Native Americans to be used as a model for teaching. "This is the book that at least one commercial publisher attempted to have suppressed." Although printed a number of years ago the book is "still current, still compelling, and will be extremely useful and revealing until the situation changes and falsification ends about the American Indian. Judging from conditions in 1976, the remedy is still years away."

With over 18 titles by Native Americans this unique press (unique in the sense that American publishing represents few books about Indians written by Indians). The Indian Historian Press books present accurate accounts of Indian culture and history, all non-fiction.

In addition, Jeannette Henry and her husband Rupert publish monthly a national Indian newspaper, *WASSAJA*. Annual subscription is $10.00 from the publishers. The newspaper is heavy with straight news reporting on issues of concern particularly to Indians such as water rights, litigation, treaties, tribal activities, land suits, education, fishing rights, federal awards, and the latest news of new books. The press also publishes a magazine of the Indian American for young people, *THE WEE-WISH TREE*. "The word "Weewish" is an Indian word meaning 'Acorn Food.' It is used by most Indians of Southern California. Acorn food, made from the meal of the acorn, has the same place in Native American economy as flour and wheat have in Western economy. From this word has been built a familarity with things Indian, suitable for (as one reader put it) all young people from 2 to 92. Published in 32 pages, two colors, small enough to carry anywhere, seven times during the school year, [it contains]

Indian games, traditions, customs, stories, legends and information about the tribes and peoples. Book reviews are not merely critical 'reviews.' They are recommended books titled 'Books to Read.' "

Like most of the presses in this *GUIDE*, The Indian Historian Press represents a multiplicity of interests and causes. Although not explicitly feminist, or with feminism as a noticeable thrust of their publishing, this is one of the few places where an Indian woman can publish. Oppression and suppression of truth was their reason for beginning. In that sense, all of the presses in this book share a cause.

THE INSTITUTE PRESS
40 Pleasant Street
Portsmouth, NY. 03801

The Institute for the Study of Women in Transition was started in 1974, achieved non-profit status in 1975 and celebrated two years in operation in June 1977. Their statement of purpose perhaps defines them best. . . "as a vehicle to promote the efforts of individuals and organizations concerned with women's issues, and to gather, coordinate, and disseminate information. In addition, we are dedicated to the advancement of research on women's issues, and to the fulfillment of the educational needs of all women in the process of transition."

With a staff of ten full and part time employees they are trying to focus on some of the needs of women in transition. Adequate employment for women is one major problem. Within their own organizational structure they have been providing employment where they feel it is most needed. Three of their employees were previously on welfare, three were long term unemployed and two low-income senior adults.

The Institute provides technical assistance to local and national agencies and organizations on such topics as proposal writing, resource development, management and program planning. They plan conferences and seminars on a national basis where such issues can be dealt with. They furnish training for low-income women in traditional and non-traditional skills, such as office management, printing, radio and television production. One specific area for training is The Institute Press. Through a CETA-sponsored program they have been able to hire and train several apprentices in the use of printing equipment, pricing, scheduling, sales procedures, graphics and camera work.

As an arm of the Institute, the press prints three publications: *THE PASSAGE*, a quarterly magazine of creative expressions of women's transitional issues (See Feminist Publications), *JOURNAL OF TRANSITIONAL ISSUES CONCERNING WOMEN* (4 issues per year, $18.00), and a bi-monthly *INSTITUTE NEWSLETTER* ($6.00 per year).

The press has published twelve booklets on a variety of topics relevent to women, such pamphlets as: "Notes on Biological & Physiological Aging" by Betty Daniel-Green ($1.50), "Widowhood: A Way Out of the Maze" by Helen May Bull ($2.50), "Employment Seekers Guide" by Nancy Gifford ($2.50). Also carried are Bibliographies (menopause, women's history, rape, etc.), Fact Sheets (blood pressure, hysterectomy, mastectomy, laproscopy, etc.), and Conference Summaries. They have one full length manual by Betty Daniel-Green, *RESOURCE DEVELOPMENT FOR WOMEN AND WOMEN'S ORGANIZATIONS* ($5.00), information on fundraising from a community, state, and national perspective.

In addition to training apprentices and publishing materials the Institute feels are relevant and important to women in transition, the press provides non-profit printing service organizations, and publishing facilities "for writers who want their work in print but cannot afford the high costs of printing."

The Institute provides a broad base of support for women, and their press is an integral part of their work. A publications brochure and additional information about the Institute are available on request. They handle their own distribution and are willing to deal with single orders.

KARMIC REVENGE LAUNDRY SHOP PRESS
P O Box 11
Guttenberg, NJ. 07093

Rita Karman, an editor for the press, says their name means "a sort of communism of the psyche." They started in business because they had a printer-friend. They now work with two to six people. Like many small presses, they don't really survive financially on their publishing activities alone. All of the members require outside jobs.

Books they have published underscore a mystical/cosmic/imagined world rather than an existing one. Rita Karman has a pamphlet on astrology and guidance, as well as an *ASTROLOGICAL PORN PHANTASY*. Lea Kavablum's work is called *CINDERELLA: RADICAL/FEMINIST/ALCHEMIST*. Their latest book is poetry by Zipora Delonsanhelis called *ON THE EVE OF GOD'S 40TH*. The brochure for 1977 includes eight saddle stitched publications ranging in price from $.75 to $3.00.

In response to the question as to whether they solicit manuscripts, Karmic Revenge answered "yes & no" but left unanswered exactly what that meant. Books can be ordered directly from KRLSP or from *WIND* distributors.

(See Distributors: *WIND*)

KELSEY ST. PRESS
2824 Kelsey Street
Berkeley, CA. 94705

Without a doubt Kelsey St. Press may have one of the funniest children's stories around. *A GIRL NAMED HERO*, written and illustrated by Kit Duane (saddle stitched, $2.95), has all of the zany imaginative features of a Dr. Suess but manages to come off as a very Feminist book. To produce such a book in these days of grim survival is no small feat. Along with *A GIRL NAMED HERO* Kelsey St. has four other titles, particularly for adults: *WORK WEEK* by Karen Brodine (poetry, $2.50); *MAKING THE*

PARK (a women's anthology, letterpress, $3.75); *HAIR-RAISING* (a women's anthology, $3.75); and *DREAMS IN HARRISON RAILROAD PARK* by Nellie, writing of growing up Chinese in America ($3.00).

Like most women's presses Kelsey St. operates as a collective. In this case there are five women. Their beginnings as a press grew out of a writers' group for women, a familiar route in women's publishing to starting a press. "We don't pay royalities. We're a feminist press. We're interested in translations of women, poetry, graphics, children's stories, a variety that reflects the fact that there are five of us. Some of us work full time. Some are married. Our politics vary, but we're all feminist; that is, we want to work with women to publish women."

> One of us has a letterpress. We design our offset books and make them camera-ready and then have them printed at a local print center. We distribute through local distributors (Bookpeople) and our own legwork and promotion. After a year and a half of ups and downs, we feel strong as a group and happy with what we're doing and the people in the community of men and women, most of them are women, that we're working with.

Patricia Dienstfrey, as spokeswoman for Kelsey St., said that as for the future "our dreams are to continue, I guess. . . Here I falter, and drop the 'we' I've been using so liberally." Sensitive to the need for women to speak for themselves, women's presses invariably find it difficult to talk about what they are doing collectively without qualifying their personal enthusiasm as an individual opinion. Such sensitivity is typical of women's publishing houses and is a welcome wind in the publishing field.

(See Distributors: *BOOKPEOPLE*).

KNOW, INC.
P O Box 86031
Pittsburgh, PA. 15221

> In 1969 the second wave of the feminist movement was a new idea. Small campus groups were appearing at colleges and universities.

NOW was a three-year-old reality, chapters springing up around the country. Not much was being written about the movement, only an occasional magazine article or perhaps a serious paper presented in a professional journal. The need to spread the word was obvious and the need to share what serious writing was available among those feminists working in the movement was vital. In Pittsburgh, 19 NOW members came together to try and fill that need. Their solution was the incorporation of a tax exempt, non-profit organization named *KNOW* in reference to the knowledge they planned to share. (*KNOW NEWS*, September 1975).

Since then *KNOW* has been publishing under the motto "Freedom of the press belong to those who own the press." They have printed literally hundreds of informative pamphlets, making valuable knowledge accessible to thousands of women. Reprints of essays, pertinent articles and research studies cover such wide-ranging topics as "mental & physical health, academe, employment, sexuality (lesbianism, sex role stereotyping, sexism), child care, law, justice, equal rights, feminism, etc. These pamphlets vary in price from $.10 to $1.00 with the median rate around forty cents. The politics of *KNOW*'s prices (low), as well as the politics of what they choose to print clearly show that *KNOW* truly owns their press and are making it the property of all women. Their newsprint catalogue is available upon request.

In the beginning as orders for *KNOW* increased, the success of the original volunteerism decreased. Volunteerism was not a philosophy with which the group was comfortable. They felt then, as now, that people should be paid for their work. By 1971 *KNOW* had hired five workers and the Collective was formed.

We knew from the beginning that our basic reason for working together was to change the oppressive society in which we lived. It was obvious that we did not want to model ourselves after the system we were trying to change in order to work toward change. The concept of a boss, or of one worker's labor having more value than another's was alien to our purpose. With the Collective structure we found a flexibility that suited us, and has continued to suit us through the years. It is not always an easy system in which to work. It demands a constant balance and personal attention from every member to maintain that balance. The members are responsible to themselves as well as to the

145

group. It has been a very successful and exciting experiment.' (*KNOW NEWS*, September 1975).

Besides *KNOW*'s huge selection of pamphlets, they publish a select number of books. All of them have a specific goal of raising the reader's feminist consciousness. *I'M RUNNING AWAY FROM HOME BUT I'M NOT ALLOWED TO CROSS THE STREET* by Gabriella Burton is still a delightful seller. One of their new books, *SHE SAID/HE SAID* by Nancy Henley and Barrie Thorne is an annotated bibliography of sex differences in language, speech, and non verbal communication. *KNOW* only publishes one or two books a year. In 1977 they are printing *MENOPAUSE*, and in the fall they plan to issue a volume of papers presented in New Jersey at a psychology of women conference as a volume in their Female Studies Series.

Speaking from the Collective, Flo Scardina writes:

Our article authors get no money; they get 10 copies of their work each time it is printed if they wish, up to ten dollars worth of articles. They too can buy large quantities at 50 percent discount and several have.

We have no present plans to expand our poetry series; we have been swamped by poetry manuscripts since our first five volumes came out in 1974. We won't do fiction or children's books either, although biographical or historical material useful in classrooms would be considered by us.

We do some of our own printing; most books are jobbed out. We pay minimum wage; our equipment is limited; our overhead is very high.

We try to do mass mailings to individuals twice a year. We have recently changed our discount policy; we do give Women in Distribution a good discount on the books they carry for us and encourage feminist bookstores to deal through them.

We have lots of dreams, but our immediate goals are to make working for *KNOW* a viable altenative to feminist who needs to earn a living. We feel there must be a way to keep us from being constantly near doom and/or losing our skilled people because they must survive and our wages are not survival-oriented. We feel that it is important for *KNOW* and crucial to the Feminist Movement to keep going. We have

146

very strong ties to NOW, and also to a couple of local feminist groups like Pittsburgh Action Against Rape.

We also strive to be a clearinghouse for local feminist news, events, etc. Our windows are usually filled with posters announcing events or meetings. Our printers are encouraged to learn to print not only for *KNOW* but also to be available to local feminist groups.

We get lots of mail and dutifully file it by topic so that is is available to local researchers. Meanwhile, we search for the definitive argument, study, essay, on a particular topic (like ERA) which can be used by feminists to sway non-feminists. Also *KNOW NEWS* serves to spread the word nationally and internationally about feminism's newest publications, causes, etc."

"We keep trying.

LES ÉDITIONS DU REMUE-MÉNAGE
Casier Postal 607
Succursale C
Montreal, Canada

Les éditions du remue-ménage is a feminist press in Montreal. Its four books are all published exclusively in French, but the content of the work crosses the language barrier, being solidly aligned with a feminist/socialist politic in any language. They see the condition women in Canadian society as housekeepers, charged with the production and maintenance of the workforce. They feel this condition is not unique to women who stay at home but also for working women who assume a double work-day, working in the world as well as at home. In either case the woman is inadequately compensated for her work, and she is channeled into extensions of her housekeeper role (nurse, teacher, saleswoman, waitress, seamstress, etc.).

By publishing and widely distributing its books les éditions hopes to contribute to the struggle to overcome this economic exploitation of women. Nicole Lacelle wrote that les éditions started two years ago with nothing: "seven feminists, a translation contract that gave us $3,500 and kitchen tables for meetings; published our first book on March 8, 1976."

147

This first book is drama, a series of scenes presented by the theater of those who work in the kitchen (le théârte des cuisines presénte) called *Môman Travaille Pas, A trop d'ouvrage!* Loosely translated this means "Mother doesn't work, she has too much work," or even looser translation, "She doesn't have a job because she works too much." Either way the meaning is clear.

The other three books from les éditions are *SORCIERES, SAGES-FEMMES ET INFIRMIERES, LA VIE D'UNE FEMME AVEC UN ALCOOLIQUE,* and *HISTOIRES VRAIES DE TOUS LES JOURS.* Les éditions has two price scales, one for groups and a higher price for libraries. "We've sold enough books by now to have a storefront office but all the women on the collective have full time jobs outside. We pay authors 10 percent on copies sold. We have the texts printed in commercial shops but we do editing, translations, sometimes typesetting, our own lay-outs."

Les editions distributes in France as well through Montreal distributor, Les Messageries Prologue, Inc. For those who read or write in French, Les Éditions du Remue-Ménage is a good press to know. The remue-ménage is les editions own dynamic version of the feminist struggle.

LES FEMMES PUBLISHING
231 Adrian Road
Millbrae, CA. 94030

Les Femmes began in November 1974 and their first book came out in the Fall of 1975. Ruth Kramer, publisher, outlines their editorial guidelines as follows: "Our purpose is to provide a literary outlet for women speaking to the concerns of contemporary women. . . We hope to encourage women to speak out, to explore new possibilities, and to apply their inborn intelligence to life's problems. We also feel many of our books will be of interest to men, believing that the emergence of the whole woman means the blossoming of all people."

Although clearly woman-oriented, Les Femmes is one of the

148

few feminist presses that in its operating policy actively encourages men to buy and read their books. In fact, of particular interest to men, is historian Jane Miller's *THE MEN BEHIND THE WOMEN*. It was her theory that the husband's of such women as Lucretia Mott, Lucy Stone and Elizabeth Cady Stanton, and others, fully supported their wives' fight for women's rights and provided a great deal of the male political clout which these women needed due to the law and social mores of the times.

Other non-fiction books from Les Femmes forcefully document partiarchal oppression of women world-wide, such as *CRIMES AGAINST WOMEN*, the shocking testimony originally heard at the first International Tribunal of Women held in Brussels in March 1976. Further books include: *IMPACT ERA, LIMITATION & POSSIBILITIES*, put together under the auspices of the California Commission on the Status of Women; *WOMEN OF THE WEST* by Dorothy Gray (history); *THE RESTLESS SPIRIT* by Barbara Kraft (autobiography). Books are perfect bound and vary in price between $3.95 and $5.95.

Historically oriented, Les Femmes publishes only non-fiction, biography and autobiography, psychology and sociology, where the works intersect personally in women's lives. They are concerned with interpersonal relationships, self-help, human sensitivity and awareness. For the future they are interested in seeing new manuscripts on psychology, philosophy, occult, women's liberation and other subjects which are of "contemporary interest. . . Our major editorial needs are for manuscripts that complement or relate to our existing booklist and for photography and art work which supplement them. We have no immediate plans to publish fiction but are willing to look at manuscripts.

The standard book format is 5½ x 8½, about 160 pages in length. Some variation is possible when warranted. They request that poetry and short works be submitted in full. All manuscripts should be typewritten and double spaced, if possible. If the writer has suggestions for art work or photography, a description or samples should be included with the manuscript. Les Femmes offers a standard royalty contract for first-time authors, with no general provisions for advances.

Distribution of Les Femmes' eight to ten books a year is through Celestial Arts of which they are a subsidiary. Celestial Arts also publishes under their own signature works by both men and women. They carry an extensive line of posters and art imprints, as well as books. Although functioning independently of each other except for distribution, the two presses can be reached through the same address. Trade sales representatives operate throughout the U.S. and many foreign countries.

MAGIC CIRCLE PRESS
10 Hyde Ridge
Weston, CT. 06880

Operating out of a workroom in her Connecticut home, writer-publisher Valerie Harms keeps Magic Circle energetically orbiting around the small press circuit. Her husband, free-lance writer Larry Sheehan, pounds his typewriter in another part of the house. Their two children inevitably get involved in the flow of press work that is a major part of their household.

> Magic Circle was started in 1972 by a friend (she was an artist and printmaker) and I who met in a rap group for artists and decided to start a business based on our talents. The two of us were the only workers for the first 3 books. Now 6 books later I have been the only worker. The Press has broken even on expenses without paying my salary. Yes, I need other jobs. Magic Circle Press is committed to publishing original work by women for people of all ages. Do not solicit manuscripts now. I pay authors according to the most recommended terms of the Authors Guild contract. I farm out manufacturing and typesetting.

Part of Valerie Harm's plan to keep Magic Circle airborne is continued publishing of well known writers. *WASTE OF TIMELESSNESS & OTHER EARLY STORIES* ($7.95) by Anais Nin is a special limited edition of stories by this now famous diarist and novelist, written when Anais Nin was in her early twenties. *A WREATH OF PALE WHITE ROSES* ($6.00) by novelist Erika Duncan is also on the Magic Circle titles list along with two works by Valerie Harms. *CELEBRATION WITH ANAIS NIN* ($6.95) documents a creative weekend spent with Nin. In *STARS IN MY SKY* ($8.00) Valerie Harms paints word portraits of three distinguished women (Maria Montessori, Anais Nin, and Frances Steloff).

Included in the publishing from Magic Circle are stories for children, such as: *LITTLE BOAT LIGHTER THAN A CORK* by Ruth Krauss, the adventures of a young child as he floats out to sea in a nutshell, illustrated by Esther Gillman ($5.50); and *DIARY OF A MONARCH BUTTERFLY* by Susan Thompson, the life history and amazing migration of this beautiful creature ($6.50).

In a special space all its own was the publication in 1975 of poetry by women housed in the Bedford Hills Correctional Facility. Collected by Anne McGovern from a poetry workshop she conducted in the prison, *VOICES FROM WITHIN*, The Poetry of Women in Prison (saddle stitched, $2.00) was a small press breakthrough, freeing the songs of long-term women prisoners, voices the public has forgotten or has never wanted to know.

Moving toward a more traditional kind of publishing, Valerie Harms recently affiliated with Walker & Company, a firm that now handles promotion and warehousing, billing and shipping of Magic Circle books nationwide, and can share production expenses for some of Magic Circle's titles. This association between Magic Circle and Walker's is similar to what Moon Books in California has done with Random House. Valerie Harms does not see this as compromising her small press. The *NEWS-TIMES* quoted her as saying. . . "I'm not doing this (Magic Circle Press) as a passionate hobby or a sideline: I want it to be a viable enterprise. I'm interested in surviving."

Surviving for Valerie Harms means more than just breaking even. She wrote that her dreams for the future might include financial success publishing more titles by well known authors, but that she has an additional idea in mind. "I have been considering, since I get requests from women, to coordinate the publishing of books other women pay for. I have the know-how and the distribution outlet but I don't have the money to understake all that I'd like. Therefore, I think I could provide a service to other women who want their work out but don't know how to do it. I think this would be a more desirable alternative than seeking sponsorship by a university or business."

MATRIA PRESS COLLECTIVE
816 Hazen S.E.
Grand Rapids, MI. 49507

Matria Press is an outgrowth from one of those miriad workshops of women writers that comes together as a press in order to meet needs of local feminists. This time the geographical location is Grand Rapids, Michigan. Given the partiarchal nature of that city, it no doubt was pure necessity for feminist writers to start their own press. Owning a Chief 15 offset press, Matria operates out of the basement of one of their members. They are turning out beautiful women's poetry anthologies in a series called *WORDWEAVINGS*. The *WORDWEAVINGS* ($1.25-$2.00) are loose-sheeted books, each page suitable for separate framing. It is difficult to know whether to call *WORDWEAVINGS* a series of books or a seasonal magazine. Printing only one or two publications a year, they are another variant in women's publishing. Rather than trying to solve the dilemma of classification, *WORDWEAVINGS* is also discussed in the magazine section of this book.

Matria's first anthology was only of Michigan women, but since then the press has been branching out nationally. *WORDWEAVINGS IV* was scheduled for Spring 1977. Payment for work is one copy. They also expect each contributor to sell at least three copies of the book in which her work appears. At the moment Matria sees this tactic as the most sensible distribution approach, a way to get their press work better known.

Sharing the financial survival of Matria with their contributors indicates a trust which a certain number of women presses have been willing to develop. We have heard of a few women's presses (not dealt with in this book) who have solicited hard cash in advance from their anthology contributors. The idea is to pre-finance publication of these anthologies (i.e. $25.00 payment from each contributor in the book for each poem of hers that is published). While sometimes these books have actually been printed, frequently contributors have lost their investment when the press folded before publication. Matria's system seems to be a low-level contributor risk and definitely furthers distribution of little-known press work. The real financial responsibility remains Matria's; as such, the contributor probably feels a real commitment to selling *WORDWEAVINGS* to friends, and maybe bookstores.

MATRIX
510 Nectar Way
Eugene, OR. 97401

Oregon is fast becoming a vital area for the exploration and development of woman spirit. Small women's communities seem to spring up daily, joining together, at least in soul, with the larger community of Oregon women. The land itself seems to beckon with its strong beauty and open spaces. The land itself is a mother, and nurturing is seen as reciprocal. Mother Earth returns the caring of her daughters.

Rising out of this spiritual climate, Northwest Matrix was organized as a women's publisher. Operating as a lesbian collective, Matrix is looking for material for a poetry anthology, feminist herstory and biography, and non-sexist fiction for young adults. They are interested in seeing more socialist-feminist writing. Already on schedule for publication is a fictional account of the SLA by Mary Beal.

At an earlier stage, the group published three limited editions of women's poetry (*MATRIX I, II, III*). In 1975, *WE ARE ALL STARS*, an individual poetry volume by Thea, ignited the women, and they expanded Matrix into an outreach press. They are es-

153

pecially desirous of printing work by Northwest women. Queries about publishing are encouraged, but financial arrangements are on an individual basis.

Matrix works closely with an all-women's print shop, Jackrabbit Press, and handles distribution through the newly formed Amazon Reality Co.

(See Print Shops: *JACKRABBIT PRESS*. See Distributors:*AMAZON REALITY CO.*)

MOON BOOKS
P O Box 9223
Berkeley, CA. 94709

Moon Books, at present almost a totally unpublicized press in the feminist grapevine, will not remain unknown for long. Interested in publishing a wide variety of feminist material with emphasis on fiction and non-fiction, their first four books are completely different except in their strong identification with women. *MOON MOON* (8½ x 11, perfect bound, $7.97) by Anne Kent Rush is the most complete exploration so far published of the moon's place in women's culture from ancient times to the present and its relationship to women's bodies, emotions, politics, and sanity. Even skeptical women admit to sensing some sort of relationship between their own female cycles and the moon's changes. To choose Moon Books as a signature for a press publishing women simply emphasized this identification.

Anica Vessel Mander in her autobiography, *BLOOD TIES* (hardcover, $10.00), explores her histroy from her earliest childhood in Yugoslavia, linking this to her grandmother, Sarika Finci Hofbauer's oral history. Together the two women present a textured view of the evolution of the new female role in society. *THE KIN OF ATA ARE WAITING FOR YOU* (perfect bound, $2.95) by Dorothy Bryant is already highly praised as a science fiction novel. A reviewer in *AMAZON QUARTERLY* wrote: "Exploring the interface between mysticism and feminism, [this] is the best yet in the newly emerging genre of women's fantasy fiction"

Moon Books' fourth book also published in 1976 is a sensitive translation of the journal and letters of Eva Forest, feminist/psychiatrist/mother, imprisoned in a Spanish prison since September 1974. Publication of *FROM A SPANISH PRISON* (hardcover, $6.95), underscores a philosophical political position of Moon Books. Co-publishers, Anica Vessel Mander, Carla Ruff and Anne Kent Rush, are planning to give 10 percent of the profits from their next book to the defense of women in jail.

"Moon Books started out of a need we felt to get feminist work into print." At this point in time that single reason lies behind the establishment of *every* feminist press. Other differences and additional reasons abound among women publishers, but there seems to be total agreement on this basic aim. One variant is on the method to accomplish this. For Moon Books that has meant teaming up with Random House. Although the imprint shows Random House as co-publishing with Moon Books, the three Moon Books women say the relationship is free of controls (i.e. what or who Moon Books prints). Random House only distributes their books; apparently quite successfully since within six months of bringing out their first four titles in 1976, Moon Books marketed over 25,000 volumes.

Marketing with Random House puts Moon Books in a special category. Although functioning with most of the same problems, they are outside of a small press classification. They are only one of two presses in this book that has this nebulous position. Magic Circle is the other.

The high volume of sales through Random House has not brought Moon Books any more financial security than the regular small press. "No, we don't survive financially, and yes, we do solicit manuscripts. Our political posture if feminist. And we are interested in publishing a wide variety of feminist material. We pay our authors the standard royalty." Moon Books works with Vera Allen for typesetting and graphics, and farms out their printing on the basis of bids.

Looking forward to publishing many more books, publisher Carla Ruff says, "Our dream for the future is to have a national feminist media network."

(See Press I: *MAGIC CIRCLE PRESS*)

NAIAD PRESS
20 Rue Jacob Acres
R.R. No. 1, Box 16522
Bates City, MO. 64011

In a society that has systematically separated its people into same-age peer groups, the women's publishing movement introduces a change, representing young, middle, old, sharing wisdom up and down the age ladder. During the years without this outlet, hundreds of women of all ages with a determined kind of stubborness kept writing, kept waiting for a day on which to be heard. Two such women, Gene Damon and Jeannette Foster, for years, quietly published *THE LADDER*, a magazine of lesbian writing. Now in a more receptive climate they are more freely moving their publishing in a couple of new directions. Much of *THE LADDER* writing is now available in book form (*THE LADDER ANTHOLOGIES*; See Press I: *DIANA PRESS*), and they have successfully launched Naiad Press, their own lesbian/feminist publishing house.

Within a relatively short period of time Naiad has publsihed seven fiction and non-fiction titles, and plans many more books. Three of these are lesbian novels by Sarah Aldridge. Two other novels are Robin Jordan's *SPEAK OUT MY HEART*, and Jeannette Foster's translation from French of Renee Vivien's 1904 novel, *A WOMAN APPEARED TO ME*. In non-fiction, *LESBIANA* by Gene Damon collates twenty-seven years of book reviews of lesbian literature. Gene Damon, Jan Watson and Robin Jordan join efforts for *THE LESBIAN IN LITERATURE*, a 96 page bibliography of lesbian literature.

Unlike the majority of women's small presses, Naiad is actively soliciting manuscripts. The editors are particularly interested in seeing more lesbian novels suitable for publication. They suggest writers query first, outlining very briefly the general plot and word-length of the manuscript, and include a SASE. At this writing Naiad was handling distribution directly. A brochure of their titles is available upon request.

OUT & OUT BOOKS
476 Second Street
Brooklyn, NY. 11215

Out & Out Books started publishing in 1975 with an explosion of four poetry titles: *HOUSEWORK* by Joan Larkin; *AFTER TOUCH* by Jan Clausen; *PERIODS OF STRESS* by Irena Klepfisz and *AMAZON POETRY*, an anthology of lesbian women's poetry, edited by Joan Larkin and Elly Bulkin. Carefully spined, but still selling for only $1.50 a copy, the books were printed at The Print Center in New York City, a nonprofit print facility funded by grants from New York State Council on the Arts and CCLM. A second printing used an all woman print shop, Tower Press.

Joan Larkin, founder, says that the reality of the press grew out of women writers sharing their work and articulating their needs: "I had been a serious poet for twenty years, but two experiences—a year in a women's writing support group (Seven Women Poets), and then Elly Bulkin's compelling proposal that she and I collect the work of lesbian poets for an anthology—finally ignited me and got the press started."

It is significant that the first four volumes published by Out & Out Books are by women poets who are both lesbians and feminists: women who have taken risk in their lives and in their writing. While Out & Out Books is not committed exclusively to lesbian writing, it will continue to reflect my primary motive in founding a press: making available to others the books we need for our survival.

For the initial four books each woman did all of the work for her own book separately, sharing information, but doing her own editing and everything else, "of course with the help of many friends," up to the point of delivering paste-ups and dummies to the printer. The four worked together on promoting

157

sales through public readings, mailing review copies, and sharing the work of filling orders.

However, Joan Larkin says that the next four books published by Out & Out Books will be done in a totally different way. "While the authors and editors of the first four will continue to help distribute their work, they are otherwise uninvolved. I am currently doing the editing alone and have a friend designing the books and another helping with a million small jobs. Both are being paid small amounts, actually out of my pocket, but in the hope that in time Out & Out will pay me back. Our first books have paid for themselves, but only that. They have not given us money to pay authors, nor to invest in new books. The recent second printing of *HOUSEWORK* was more expensive than the first, so despite a higher price, it is not bringing much in. We are going to raise prices of future books to about $3.00—variable, depending on our cost—so that we well be able to continue to survive as a press and to publish books that we don't want to see get lost. We hope to pay authors—we will pay authors a large percentage of any profit, assuming there *is* any profit. Since the authors of the next batch live outside of New York or do a kind of work that leaves them no time to help with production and distribution, the cost of those jobs will be added to the cost of producing their books."

Like many other women writers who have started presses, Joan Larkin expresses the fact that the enormity of what she's started is overwhelming. "I need one or two women of vision with unlimited time and money, to help me keep this thing alive. Since that's a dream, it's hard to predict just what our future will be. I have strong desire to keep these books, all of which I believe in passionately, in print, and to do some others, more poetry and essays, and maybe a novel. . . We do not solicit manuscripts! I hardly have time to send things back (for of course people send us tons of unsolicited stuff). I already have a backlog of things I wish I had the time and money to publish. My response to most of the excellent stuff that comes in is the same one Alta gave me when I gave her an early version of *HOUSEWORK* in 1975: publish it yourself!"

PERSEPHONE PRESS
RFD No. 1, Box 98A
Monticello, NY. 12701

Persephone Press: a branch of Pomegrante Productions Inc., is a small women's publishing house run by three women. Founded in April of 1976, their primary goal is to print quality work by women dealing with various aspects of women's spirituality.

> We see strong connections between the myth of Persephone and the Press. (Persephone was kidnapped by a male, Hades, and taken underground where she was forced to reside for six months out of the year.) We believe Peresphone, like many women, fostered by support has nurtured her Spirit, collected her Rage, built her Strength, and has now emerged from the underground to share her knowledge—in this case through the medium of print.

Marketing six books at the moment, even their titles suggest their continuing emphasis on publishing books related to women's spirituality, such as: *A FEMINIST TAROT, THE FEMINIST BOOK OF LIGHTS AND SHADOWS, THROUGH THE LOOKING GLASS, SUSAN B. ANTHONY COVEN NO. 1, THE BEGUINES, MOONDANCE* and their latest, *THE FOURTEENTH WITCH.* "Other works in planning are *AMAZONS: PAST, PRESENT, AND FUTURE* by Whitney Laughlin, a healing book, the herstory of minstrels and their relevance to today's women's music, and an exploration of the Tarot."

> Both Persephone Press and Pomegranate Production are project names for the three of us: Marianne Rubenstein, Gloria Z. Greenfield and Pat McGloin. In April of 1976, Pomegranate Productions began her activity of organizing with *THROUGH THE LOOKING GLASS: A GYNERGENETIC EXPERIENCE*, a women's spirituality gathering of 1200 women held in Boston. A fourth woman, Carol Cain, was a member at that point. Our goal was to encourage communication centering on women's spirit, or driving force, and to foster stimulating ideas. The conference was successful in establishing a network of communication and support for women exploring spirituality in its many forms.

As Pomegranate Productions, we see our role as space-makers for the sharing and presentation of revolutionary ideas. In the coming months, we well be relocating in Boston, and have an abundance of future plans, which include bringing many cultural events to the Boston women's community. Our most immediate vision is a conference on organizing—as in-depth look at the various stages and methods.

Gloria , Marianne and I have been closely working together for three years, and the organization of our businesses reflect that. We share equally in the making of all policies and decisions. Our structure is only that we utilize our varied talents in the most effective ways. All promotion, distribution, review of manuscripts for publication, editing, lay-out and fund-raising is done by us; we do not print our books ourselves, but support feminist printers by utilizing their services.

We believe strongly in the necessity of feminist communications networks; therefore we advertise in feminist media and distribute internationally in women's bookstores. In order to reach and affect as many women as possible, we also distribute to traditional, occult, and alternative bookstores. . . We are so willing to share our processes and visions. . . .

The Persephone Press women did not indicate whether they would be ⁀interested in unsolicited manuscripts. Interested writers could query with SASE.

PEOPLE'S PRESS
2680 21st Street
San Francisco, CA. 94110

A group of anti-war activists formed Peoples Press in 1969. "We began to produce literature about the struggle of the Vietnamese people against U.S. imperialism. Many of our publications, *VIET NAM: A THOUSAND YEARS OF STRUGGLE, CHILDREN OF THE DRAGON, WOMEN OF VIET NAM* and *VIET NAM: WHOSE VICTORY? WHOSE DEFEAT?*, focus on the culture, history and spirit of Viet Nam. The Vietnamese people taught the world that strength and organization of ordinary people can defeat the immense military technology of the United States in its most brutal application."

Since then the Peoples Press has broadened its base to include all peoples expoited by U.S. imperialism both in this country and abroad. "The struggles of Third World peoples, like those of Chile, Puerto Rico and Angola, and of Blacks, Latinos, Asians and Native Americans, are leading force in the fight against imperialism. The development of a militant world-wide women's movement has added great strength to our fight against imperialism and its systematic oppression of women."

As these resistance movements have grown, we have broadened the focus of our literature. Currently, we have two projects groups which are developing materials on Puerto Rico and the Middle East. We are interested in forming new groups to do the research, writing, production and distribution of other materials on peoples' struggles.

Most of the titles from Peoples Press are pamphlet size, selling for from $.50 to $1.00. Other publications are spined, but fall into a moderate price range of $3.00-$5.00. They have an impressive list of children's stories plus an excellent group of books by and about women in struggle both in this country and in other countries. They have their own printing equipment, and as far as I know, do all of their own work.

In addition to their own materials, they distribute a growing number of pamphlets and books from other groups, such as New Seed Press (non-sexist children's stories), and The Feminist Press. "We are always interested in seeing materials that we may want to distribute, or manuscripts and ideas for projects that we might help facilitate. You can contact us and send suggestions and criticism to: Peoples Press."

(See Press I: *THE FEMINIST PRESS*. See Children's Presses: *NEW SEED*)

PRESS PACIFICA
P O Box 47
Kailua, HA. 96734

It was out of a powerful desire to see Harriet Robinson's historic *LOOM & SPINDLE* once more into print that motivated Jane Wilkins Pultz to organize Press Pacifica in 1975. The book in question, long out of print, is an autobiographical account of the women who worked in the early cotton mills of Lowell, Massachusetts. As Press Pacifica's first book, *LOOM & SPINDLE* (hard bound, $7.95; perfect bound, $4.50) went into a second printing within six months. In addition to providing a press for reprinting *LOOM & SPINDLE*, Jane Wilkins Pultz energetically pursued getting this classic story into the curriculum of many high schools and colleges across the country. Often tedious and discouraging, this kind of pressure is important so that authentic books of women's herstory become a more consistent part of a student's education.

In a different vein, *I LIKE POEMS AND POEMS LIKE ME*, edited by Penny Pagliaro, was Pacifica's second title. This anthology of children's poetry tries to cover the last hundred years, a rather remarkable task to undertake (hard bound, $6.95). Two other books are already in the works. One is a novel by Rina Winslow about the trials of a juvenile delinquent boy, *BUTTER-FLIES. . . IF YOU THROW IT*. Their fourth book is *WHAT TO SAY AFTER YOU CLEAR YOUR THROAT* by Jean Gochros. This last is a parent's book on sex education. With the range of subject matter in their first four books, variety may be what can be expected from Press Pacifica.

> I make all the decisions on what to publish. I see my press as wearing two hats. My primary interest and concern are those relating primarily to women, with a special interest in women's history. So far all of my contracts have been to local women writers. The other hat is that of acting as a press where local people can go to publish. We in Hawaii feel so alienated from the mainland publishing scene. Furthermore, a number of women, in particular, have gone to vanity presses which are terribly exorbitant and cost much more than they can afford."

Press Pacifica has one part time women who contracts to do typesetting. Jane's husband, who is a publisher's representative, handles much of the administrative work for the press. "Because, like many women's businesses we are under capitalized, we cannot at this point offer big advances. We would be glad to hear from women writers who are willing to understand our problem of the moment."

RAGNAROK PRESS
3008 17th Street W
Birmingham, AL. 35208

Coming into women's publishing as early as 1970, Rochelle Holt says that the name for their press came from her friend, D.H. Stefanson's Icelandic heritage. The name Ragnarok signifies the final battle of the Norse heroes and gods against the powers of darkness. "We like the idea of working along with other private printers, poets, and artists who are engaged in that struggle to keep truth and beauty alive."

The press has largely been experimental, both in content and form. Owning their own press and concerned with color and textures as well as content, the books from Ragnarok show that a great deal of time has been devoted to creating handset small run editions. Recently, Ragnarok has been moving into various types of play publishing. The variety includes a cassette-play, a novel adapted for radio, and one adapted for the stage plus a play poem (10 new titles in all). Older titles the press is still marketing are books under series titles such as the Freya Series (3 books), Bifrost Series (2 books), and the Valkyrie Series (2 books).

Very few presses take time to handset anymore. Ragnarok is still very much committed to a slow but beautiful process. Ragnarok handles most of their own distribution and information can be obtained by writing to them directly.

SHAMELESS HUSSY PRESS
P O Box 3092
Berkeley, CA. 94703

With brilliant candor Shameless Hussy continues to print the unprintable.

Starting with Alta, who didn't fit any proper female/writer image but who has touched so many with her honesty and humor, Shameless Hussy has twenty-eight titles burning the market. Publishing first her own poems, Susan Griffin, and Lyn Lyfshin, Alta's philosophy was that the most important thing was freedom of the press for women. Early books were stapled and untrimed, inexpensive, and effectively got to women hungry for their own words. It was the kind of naked courage that helped many of us enter the fight for the right to be women writers and the right to start our own presses.

Continuing the struggle, Shameless Hussy's most recent coups are a reprint of an out-of-print English translation of that "notorious woman," George Sand, complete with the exquisite original etchings. In addition, they have a personal documentary, Calamity Jane's letters written to her daughter. Both books are perfect bound. More books about pioneer women are in future plans. Shameless Hussy was also the first press to recognize Ntozake Shange, publishing her play *FOR COLORED GIRLS* . . . when no one else seemed very interested. Alta, who calls herself the head honcho, is particularly interested in publishing creative work like Ntozake Sange's that has found no other viable outlet.

Recently, Shameless Hussy has begun to take on an interfamily look with her daughter Lorelei Bosserman as an editor; Angel dan Skarry, advisor; and John Oliver Simon, advisor. Three other women complete the group. Shameless Hussy is also broadening its media base by moving some of its initiative into video tape and film under the name Better Duck Productions. No doubt with Better Duck they will either swim or waddle into a lot more of those "shameless" places. Whatever the future brings, it will probably be as tough, warm, and humane as its past.

SUNBURY PRESS
Box 274 Jerome Station
Bronx, NY. 10468

"Sunbury Press identifies consciously with the feminist struggle exemplified in the long career of Susan B. Anthony, who was active in the abolitionist, feminist, and labor struggles combined." Publisher Virginia Scott is committed to bringing out the work of poets of intensity and excellence, who have not been given adequate voice elsewhere. With such commitment Sunbury Press has solicited work by women poets, blue-collar poets, minority poets and others whose experiences infuse their work with insight, emotion and relevance often missing in the work of establishment writers.

Unlike many feminist presses Sunbury will include work by men in the tri-quarterly magazine, *SUNBURY*, however, the poetry book series represents only women authors at the present time. For the moment Sunbury has nine poetry titles. *SOMETIMES I THINK OF MARYLAND* by Jodi Braxtion and *POEMS* by Fay Chiang are 1977 additions (perfect bound).

Sunbury sees each issue of the magazine as a separate anthology and markets these issues along with the individual books of poems. "After producing the present combination of nine books and nine issues of the magazine, we will be concentrating on sales, promotion, and distribution in order to gain a return on the investment of our energies in 18 titles in what will by four years. . . We distribute through *COSMEP/SOUTH*. We advise that self-distribution may be the most effective, or is in our experience when poets may aid the Press in selling directly to their audience."

Sunbury raises money through government grants effectively —in part because it has a "publishing consultant" who is a fundraiser and has taught the staff the skills they need. In addition, they have initiated the process of becoming a non-profit, tax exempt corporation which will enable them to solicit money from private foundations and persons. They also are at the start of a two year sales subscription and promotion effort.

With a circulation of 1500, the magazine has editors in San Francisco, Cleveland, and Buffalo, as well as its home base in New York City. The staff would like Sunbury readings, book parties in all of these cities to promote, sell, share. "We would have an amazing list of subscribers if the poets perceived their role-responsibility to the women's literary magazines in a manner similar to the sisterly support they would like to receive by our publishing them. . . imagine the magazines that could publish if 200 women poets paid $5.00 for a subscription! Becoming more truly women-supported!"

> We've learned that it ain't just editing and publishing. It's business sense, annual fiscal statements, responsible and continuing competent administration. Sunbury Press is growing as a feminist press in its 4th year.

(See Feminist Publications: *SUNBURY*)

TIMES CHANGE PRESS
Box 187
Albion, CA. 95410

Times Change Press say itself that it is somewhat ridiculous to try and incapsulate what they are because they are always changing. "Times Change Press is a not-for-profit publishing company producing only books and posters that further social change and personal growth. Our goal is to help people create a utopia: an egalitarian, loving world. If labeling is useful, I'd say we're anarcho-communist, feminist, radical ecologists. We're also into co-counselling and other growth therapies."

What is unchanging about Times Change is the publishing of books exposing the myths and struggles of men and women in a sexist culture. Coming out of the same community as *COUNTRY WOMEN* (See Feminist Publications), one of T.C.'s best sellers may be Alta's explosive *MOMMA* (perfect bound, $2.00). Other recent titles are *JANUARY THAW* (People at Blue Mt. Ranch write about living together in the mountains, perfect bound, $3.25); *THE EARLY HOMOSEXUAL RIGHTS MOVEMENT* (1864-1935) by John Lauritsen and David Thorstad (perfect bound, $2.75); and *WITH LOVE, SIRI AND EBBA* (perfect bound, $3.25) by Siri Fraser and Ebba Pederson, the story of two young women who write of their backpacking adventures in a trip across northern Africa. Among the other 20 titles, *UNBECOMING MEN* (perfect bound, $1.75) has continued to serve as a rare book on the subject of male consciousness-raising.

> Times Change Press took its name from the I Ching hexagram number forty-nine, Ko/revolution (Molting); 'Times change, and with them their demands.' This hexagram describes what we're working to bring about: 'fundamental social transformation.' As the old sage says, 'A well must be cleaned out from time to time or it will become clogged with mud.

In their brochure Times Change describes itself as a press that is trying "to expand the arena of liberation. Year after year we change what we do, yet we continue to relate to the same basic considerations: clarifying unrecognized expressions of unfreedom, examining power relationships as closely, interrelatedly and comprehensively as possible, approaching liberation from diverse perspectives, and contributing information and beauty to a growing culture that celebrates our success."

Tommy and Su Negrin, who co-founded TCP have seen changes in their own lives. Tommy, who's changed his name to Moonlight, is presently running TCP alone. "I'm living in the country as part of a ten-person commune-family, and five of us are evolving into a TCP collective. I'm excited about this development. The Press and I will greatly benefit from this new source of energy, skills, and group process." The other major change is that Su Negrin "is no longer a part of TCP. She and I have shared this publishing effort since we started it together seven years ago. Su has been the person most responsible for TCP's content and style. Her own books, the posters she designed, and the publishing company's overall output have been used and appreciated by thousands of readers. Recently, though, Su decided TCP was no longer her main interest, and that she wanted to move on to new things, one of which is her fine new book *BEGIN AT THE START* (Some thoughts on personal liberation and world change, perfect bound, $3.25)."

To those wishing to publish with TCP, Moonlight moans the standard dollar problem of most small presses. "TCP does not make much money for anybody. Authors and TCP workers get only token payment—I've been getting $40.00 a week, authors average about $150.00 per book, and all the rest goes for printing and other production and business expenses. If this dim financial prospect doesn't put you off, then by all means send us your book ideas—description first, not the manuscript—and please include a stamped, self-addressed return envelope. No poetry please."

VANILLA PRESS
2400 Colfax Avenue South
Minneapolis, MN. 55405

Vanilla Press does not fit into a neat feminist press category, but the guidelines for their press solidly support women writers. "I don't want to alienate people; but until the national average changes, we will publish two women to one man. We want to affect society. . . affect basic thinking and attitudes. . . change people's impressions of society. We're supporting things beyond traditional literature."

Jean-Marie Fisher founded Vanilla Press in 1975 by selling her house in order to raise capital. Rather than play an autocratic role, she formed the press into a collective, four women and three men. Because the press has been striving for a non-sexist position, Jean-Marie says she has felt outside of the support of feminist publishers as well as alien to much of the Small Press. "Sometimes I have felt very lonely."

Of the eleven poetry books the press has published in a year and a half all have been by midwestern writers. The most well known book at this point is *RITES OF ANCIENT RIPENING* by Meridel LeSueur. Moving into a second printing, the re-run will be 5000 books. Although most of the work from Vanilla Press represents the genre of mainstream poetry in form and style, Meridel's poetry is powerfully passionate. She rides her wise Indian soul into the roots of humanity. There is no question as to the depth of her loving.

Their anthology from *WOMEN POETS IN THE TWIN CITIES* is also selling well, plus *A COLORING BOOK OF*

POETRY FOR ADULTS. About the Coloring Book, Jean-Marie says "I want the people who haven't been exposed. It's that whole big network we're trying to get."

Designing beautiful books has a high priority at Vanilla Press. Making their press a way of living is another. In order to sell their books Jean-Marie is on the road, driving 2000 miles every other week. Personal contact with bookstores has been selling Vanilla Press books. They also supplement their income by running a typesetting service. A look at their books make clear their experience and skill. They encourage publishers anywhere in the country to write to them for a free estimate.

All of this effort is paying off. Vanilla Press pays four people full time and two part time. In addition to marketing their work through personal distribution, some of their books are carried by The Plains Distribution Service (See Distribution). Midwestern writers in particular can contact Vanilla Press about their manuscripts.

The name, 'Vanilla,' according to Webster, is a root word for vaginal sheath. Jean-Marie carries the symbolism of their press name beyond that. She hopes with Vanilla Press to be "an entry into the world, a two way street." With tongue in cheek she also admitted that "the essence of vanilla overwhelms me."

THE VANITY PRESS
P O Box 15064
Atlanta, GA. 30333

Publisher Sonya Jones is distributing a number of titles such as *THE ADVENTURE OF BOBI BEAR* and *WANDA WATER-MOCCASIN*, non-sexist stories by Jay Finley, plus two novels, *AFTER THE PROM* by Hadden Luce, and *THE LEGACY* by Sonya Jones.

> Vanity was founded as a partnership, but as women's relationships change, so do their businesses. She is currently a one-women show, in the process of setting up a 12-woman editorial board nationwide.

Vanity Press solicits manuscripts from women, preferably fiction and non-fiction. If it is exceptionally good, they will publish poetry. "No such invert as a Vanity rejection slip exists." If materal is not suitable, Sonya will return with detailed comments and suggestions. In reading manuscripts, she is most concerned with the authors' intentions. When a manuscript is accepted, the press will work closely with the author to preserve her content. "If she insists a phrase must stand after serious discussion, it will stand."

> Vanity is run out of my study. As yet, we don't need much space but would like to project into the future—warehouses, etc. . . There is the strong possibility that Vanity will publish some future works under a double Daughters/Vanity imprint. I am not saying that Daughters and Vanity are near merging, but our political perspectives are very close.

(See Press I: *DAUGHTERS*)

Vanity Press is not to be confused with the businesses called vanity presses. The choice of a particular name for a women's press is often an attempt to create positive meanings for negative concepts and/or words which have been applied to women in the past. In this case the name "Vanity Press" was chosen to give credibility and value to all those women who couldn't get published (because they were women) and so were "allowed" a "Vanity Press."

VERMONT CROSSROADS PRESS
Box 333
Waitsfield, VT. 05673

Life is hard in Vermont as it's always been, hard winters and meadows of rock to frustrate the farmer. Old stone fences built a century or two ago separate sturdy farmhouses from each other, and young calves and black and white cows still dot the hillsides in summer as they always have. Vermont has not stood still since the days of the first settlers, but it is proud of its past and is still a place of peace and scruffy do-it-yourselfism. People who were born there or move here value having the space to do their own thing. Vermont Crossroads Press is doing just that.

Their 15 titles range from personalized non-fiction: *BECOMING* (perfect bound, $2.95) by Eleanora Faison (the wonder of life from conception to birth) and *THE CENTERED SKIER* (perfect bound, $5.95) by Denise McCluggage (application of the energy of skiing as an "ideal moving meditation") to the *WOODBURNER'S ENCYCLOPEDIA* (perfect bound, $6.95, 4th printing) by Jay Shelton (extensive information about wood and stove heat as an alternate energy source). Another direction for the press is non-sexist children's stories. *SUGARCANE ISLAND* (perfect bound, $2.95; hard cover, $5.95) by Edward Packard, illustrations by Barbara Carter, can put children ages 8-12 in touch with another source of energy. The book "places the reader in the role of a character in the story. YOU make choices and decisions determining the outcome of an adventure story." *SUGARCANE ISLAND* is listed in *LITERARY MARKET PLACE* this year and foreign rights to the book have been sold.

Constance Cappel (Montgomery) and Raymond Montgomery started their press in 1973 with one non-sexist book for children, *VERMONT SCHOOL BUS RIDE*, written by Constance. "We had excellent reviews and broke even on that book. We continued the services of non-sexist, high-quality, photographic children's books and brought out *VERMONT ROADBUILDER* (Girls can drive bulldozers just as well as boys can) and *VERMONT FARM AND THE SUN* (The farm collects and stores the sun's energy)." The latter two were co-authored by Constance and Raymond. All three books are hardcover and sell for $4.95.

To supplement their children's series they also have three teaching manuals, enrichment activities books for teachers or other adults, designed to create spaces for a child's imagination. Rounding out all of ths diverse energy, Vermont Crossroads has a poetry chapbook series which has been funded by the Vermont Council on the Arts. Authors are about evenly divided between women and men both in this series and throughout the press.

Constance wrote "we are now concentrating on alternate lifestyle books, poetry, non-sexist children books, and anything else that looks good to us."

> We farm out manuscripts to a printing press. We have several women working with us on editing, billing, shipping, publicity, and whatever. We try to train people, from the printer (who had never done a book before) to our photographers and illustrators. Barbara Carter, a twenty-one year old Vermont artist, now has work from New York publishers because of her illustrations in *SUGARCANE ISLAND*. We try to give Vermonters employment with women as a top priorty."
> "Our distribution is now nationwide. We are carried by Bookpeople, Baker & Taylor, and Women in Distribution. My husband and I have had a revolving presidency, but several months ago decided to be co-presidents.

In many ways Constance and Raymond of Vermont Crossroads are very similar to Elaine and John Gill of The Crossing Press in upstate New York. Both of them have worked out a sensitive non-sexist co-partnership reflected not only in the running of their press, but in who and what they publish. The fact that both press names reflect centering and walking on in their own space brings a special kind of symbolism to this path to women's publishing.

VIOLET PRESS
P O Box 398
New York, NY. 10009

Violet Press had been printing writing by lesbian women for a long time now. Their titles are *DYKE JACKET*, and *POEMS AND SONGS* by Fran Winant; *WE ARE ALL LESBIANS*, an anthology; *TO LESBIANS EVERYWHERE* by Judy Greenspan; and their newest book *MEDUSA MVZIC* by Flash Silvermoon. All books are paperback, perfect bound and sell for $3.00 to the public, except for their anthology, *WE ARE ALL LESBIANS* (saddle stitched, $2.00). When writing for information, send a self-addressed stamped envelope.

"I am now the only person doing Violet Press," writes Fran Winant. "It is *not* surviving financially even though the books are well-distributed (Wind, Bookpeople, bookstores), all are getting sold (posibly I could go on reprinting and selling them forever) and the prices are higher than I'd like them to be. Postage, supplies, bookstores that don't pay (including Feminist one), unprofitable ads, the cost of reprinting (I don't own a press), all contribute to Violet Press being on the borderline between breakdown and losing money. There would be royalities if there were profits but there aren't."

"Violet Press is a lesbian-feminist, politically-oriented poetry press (poetry exploring the connection between the personal and the political), started in 1971, hoping to contribute to the expanding feminist culture." Fran plans to keep VP going to distribute the materials she already has, but she is not soliciting manuscripts and plans for the future suggest a different direction.

I'd like to travel and do poetry readings and sing some of my songs for feminist audiences. I don't quite know how to plan it, and I've been imaging there are probably other women in this situation. I'd like to do a book about how to get your feminist act on the road, which places will pay transportation, how to plan groups of readings in a particular area after finding the means to get yourself there. To do this book I'd need a lot of input from women in different areas who know how to plan readings for their area and women who would like to share their *on the road* experiences.

(See Distributors: *WIND, BOOKPEOPLE*).

WEST END PRESS
Box 697
Cambridge, MA. 02139

Weat End started as a magazine to print activist poetry reflecting non-classist and non-racist attitudes. Despite the fact that a number of magazines talk about being non-classist, very few actually print work written by those who have had to live with classism or racism. The joint staff for the magazine has been about equally divided between women and men. Now, John Crawford, an original staff member, has transfered his energies into starting West End Press.

With a series of chapbooks their aim is "to publish major prose writings of progressive authors both of earlier times and of the modern day. . . Two books by Meridel LeSuer have late summer 1977 publication dates. The first is *SONGS FOR MY TIME*, a collection of stories from the Forties and Fifties. "These stories deal with the period of blacklisting and political repression; most were printed in *MASSES AND MAINSTREAM*. The introduction is being done by an old movement friend and cultural worker, Adelaide Bean." The second book by Meridel is *WORKER WRITERS*, a handbook for writers published under the WPA Writers Project auspices. "We will do this book cooperatively with the Minnesota Peoples' History Project. It will be oriented for classroom use." For Fall 1977 they are also hoping to publish *INVITATION TO NIXONICIDE* by Pablo Neruda. "We have retained Stanely Faulkner (NY attorney who helped free Corvalan from Chile) to help us with the legal problems. . . We expect to work over the translations with Steve Kowit."

"We will contine to publish the best of modern poetry as well." Their current and first three chapbooks are poetry: *CHILDREN OF THE MAFIOSI* by Doña Stein from Massachusetts ($2.00); *THE STORY OF GLASS* ($2.00) by Peter Oresick, a first book by a young Pittsburgh glassworker; and *BANDAGES AND BULLETS: IN PRAISE OF THE AFRICAN REVOLUTION* ($1.25) by Antar Sudan Katara Mberi, poems by a Harlem cultural worker.

Not content to just publish, West End is reaching out through a newsletter and personal travel to set up cultural links with other like-minded presses and organizations in the U.S. Their own actions, as well as their first three books reflect a politically progressive and activist orientation. John Crawford defines West End further as "socialist-grassroots, working people and feminist-oriented. . . We pay authors in copies—so far, up to a third of the run, but will have to cut back to a few free and more on 50 percent discount/consignment. We use New England Free Press and Haymarket Press in Minneapolis—both movement shops and both feminist-oriented. Hopefully we'll grow a lot bigger. Meridel LeSuer's work is basic to our efforts right now."

Contact West End directly for information or manuscript inquiry, also to order books.

(See Feminist Publications: *WEST END*)

WOMANPRESS
Box 59330
Chicago, IL. 60645

Devoted exclusively to printing lesbian literature, Womanpress has four full length publications on the market: *WOMEN LOVING WOMEN*, an annotated bibliography of women loving women in literature, over 200 lesbian titles ($1.50); *TWO WOMEN*, poetry of Jeannette Foster and Valerie Taylor ($3.25); *WOMEN LOVING, WOMEN WRITING* ($3.95), an anthology of poetry growing out of the 2nd annual Lesbian Writers Conference 1975; and *THE ENCLOSED GARDEN* ($2.25) by Penelope Pope.

These books, as well as a brochure, can be obtained by writing Womanpress directly. They are not actively soliciting manuscripts. Lesbian, Feminist and gay organizations or bookstores and individuals ordering 10 or more copies should write to Womanpress for a special discount. Womanpress books are distributed also by *WIND*. (See Distributors).

WOMEN'S ACTION ALLIANCE
370 Lexington Avenue
New York, NY. 10017

The Women's Action Alliance is a multi-services organization that also publishes books, books particularly relevant to the women they serve. At the moment they have three full length books on the market: *A PRACTICAL GUIDE TO THE WOMEN'S MOVEMENT* by Deena Peterson (perfect bound, $5.00) an early directory of women's groups, an annotated reading list of 500 books on women's movement issues, a listing of women's periodicals current at the time of publication, and consciousness-raising guidelines; *THE FORGOTTEN FIVE MILLION: WOMEN IN PUBLIC EMPLOYMENT* (perfect bound, $5.00), an in-depth analysis of the various aspects of sex discrimination in state and local government jobs with information, tactics and resources for fighting back; *NON-SEXIST EDUCATION FOR YOUNG CHILDREN* by Barbara Sprung (perfect bound, $3.25), a practical guide designed to help teachers and parents provide non-sexist social, emotional, and cognitive experiences for children during the formative pre-school, kindergarten and primary years.

Publishing books, however, is only a small part of their on-going work. With a staff of 18 women they are "an active resource for women working for change." In their guidelines they state that they are a "national, non-profit organization. . . established in 1971 and [have], with the cooperation and support of the national women's community becomes a major and effective clearinghouse of resources and information. [Their] goal is to help women work together across organizational, cultural and economic boundaries to combat sexism and sex discrimination." They do this through the various projects in which they are engaged.

Project *SHARE* offers fundraising information and technical assistance to women and women's groups. They encourage women to write to them for help in preparing proposals for grant funding as well as to use their comprehensive information bank on funding sources. They have recently published a booklet called *"GETTING YOUR SHARE"* (36 pages, $2.00), which is an introduction to fundraising and is geared toward the novice in "grantspersonship." Two other projects are *NON-SEXIST CHILD DEVELOPMENT* and *THE NATIONAL WOMEN'S AGENDA*. The latter "coordinates the efforts of over 100 national women's organizations to achieve the goals of the U.S. National Women's Agenda."

In addition to all of the above, the Women's Action Alliance publishes a monthly resource publication, *WOMEN'S*

176

AGENDA, which reports on major issues of the women's movement—"what needs to be done and what is currently being done to achieve equality in such areas as politics, employment, education and health care."

(See Feminist Publications)

THE WOMEN'S PRESS
280 Bloor Street W
Toronto, Ontario
Canada

Unlike the United States where Feminism (and issues surrounding women's oppression) has been the overriding impetus behind the establishment of American women's publishing houses, women's presses in Canada have a different herstory. Out of ignorance the media often lumps Canadians and Americans together as if they represented a single mentality. Canadians are very sensitive to this "lumping" which is usually inaccuarte, and a simplification of a very complicated country.

In the first place Canada has French as well as British roots. The question as to whether Canada is two countries or one has not been answered. Whether books are published in French or English, or in both languages. Since these remain unresolved, Feminists in Canada have strong and useful ties with the Leftist Movement, whereas in the U.S. there has been a sizable split between Feminist and the Male Left.

Because of these differences, Feminist women publishing in Canada have not tended to focus as a *separatist* movement for women. As a result Canadian women have felt less of a need for all women publishing houses, and there are very few of them. Further, the presses that do exist favor publication of *only* Canadian women, which is another extension of their strong nationalism. In contrast, while American women seek their roots, American Feminist totally reject the U.S. form of nationalism, seeing it as another vehicle for partriarchal oppression. Since the American Feminist's experience of nationalism has been

177

so negative, it has been hard to see anything positive for women in another country's nationalism.

The Women's Press came into being with the desire to publish a book that would reflect the state of the Women's Movement in Canada. In 1970 most of the printed matter about Feminism was coming from the U.S. and there was a lot of sensitivity on that point. When the response to *WOMEN UNITE!* (a book specifically documenting women's oppression in Canada, as distinct from that in the States) was overwhelmingly favorable, the women decided they had a real, solid basis for continuing as a press.

Since 1972 The Women's Press has published fifteen adult titles, almost all of them in both hard and soft cover editions, and seven children's books (See Children's Presses). Their books are largely non-fiction with a feminist/socialist politic. Some of their titles include: *POPULATION TARGET: THE POLITICAL ECONOMY OF POPULATION CONTROL IN LATIN AMERICA* by Bonnie Mass (perfect bound, $5.50); *NEVER DONE: THREE CENTURIES OF WOMEN'S WORK IN CANADA* by The corrective Collective (perfect bound, $3.75); *WOMEN AT WORK: 1850-1930* by The Women's Labour History Collective (perfect bound, $6.00). One of their newest titles is their only piece of fiction, *THE TRUE STORY OF IDA JOHNSON* by Sharon Riis (perfect bound, $3.25). Since this novel mirrors the true story of so many women's lives in Canada, it has fit very well into their guidelines.

According to an interview in January 1977 with *THE OTHER WOMAN*, a Canadian women's newspaper (See Newspapers), The Women's Press has two target areas of concern for future titles: Canadian women's history and the economic struggle of women. "Economically, women are in a more tenuous situation than they've been for years—both in Canada and the Third World. We feel that we can publish a wide variety of materials—information about rape, birth control, novels, children's books, women in labour movements, women in the Third World —and in all of theses books confront what we see to be the primary reason for women's oppression."

As for the organizational structure of the press, Lois Pike wrote to us and spoke for the press. "We are at present a collective of 18, 4 staff (2 full time and 2 part time). The rest of the people are volunteers. In addition we have 5 people who are what we call associates: they are in various working groups but do not attend the weekly collective meeting."

> We take our books from development stage or rough draft right through to composition and lay-out. Binding and printing is done at local union shops. We have a Canadian distributor (Belford Book Distributing Co.) and sales reps who handle sales and distribution for us. We also have U.S. distribution through Bookpeople.

> Although those on the staff do have specific job area responsibilities, we operate in a non-hierarchial fashion and there are no secretaries. . . We survive financially through our trade and educational sales plus some grant and loan money from the federal and provincial governments. The government money is fairly basic to Canadian publishing and the larger as well as small publishers make use of it. Our sales are in the $100,000 to $150,000 range, but of course expenses in this business are heavy and while we've kept ourselves going for 5 years now, financially its always a fairly fine line.

WOMEN'S PRESS COLLECTIVE
5251 Broadway
Oakland, CA. 94618

Since the magical year of 1970 (when women's presses began springing up all over the country), the Women's Press Collective has printed the work of many fine feminist/lesbian poets, in addition to poet-founders, Judy Grahn, Pat Parker and Willyce Kim.

The group is an anarchist collective where every woman has had an equal voice, where decisions are made consciously, and where the politics are explicitly radical, lesbian, working-class based, revolutionary and egalitarian. It would be fair to say that everyone in the collective sees the work as political as well as cultural. Coupled with their political/personal books of poetry, the Women's Press Collective has printed such books as:*THE RAPE JOURNAL* by Dell Fitzgerold-Richards, documentation over a nine month period of one woman's long count of the days and nights that followed her being raped; *WOMEN AGAINST ELECTRIC SHOCK TREATMENT*, written by four women (two former inmates in mental hospitals and two psychiatric technicians working in hospitals) clarifying the use of electric shock to control women (women who are made to feel "crazy" when they become dissatisfied with their defined social role as women); and *SING A BATTLE SONG*, the poetic chronicle of Weather Underground Women.

Not as visible on the East Coast as Shameless Hussy Press, the collective has distributed over 60,000 copies of their books with 18 titles in print. Judy Grahn's *EDWARD THE DYKE* has sold over 6,000 copies.

Starting off with only a mimeograph machine on the kitchen table and no competence in printing techniques "y' know there was plenty of coffee and spaghetti...", they now have progressed to a Chief 22, a collator, darkroom and copy camera. A great deal of their strength continues to be the vast number of volunteers who flow through their doors giving support and energy for short periods of time.

Each book has its own financing. Often the Collective borrows money to buy the paper. Everyone keeps track of the number of days worked a month. When the money comes in from sales, the collective deducts overhead for the shop, pays what can be paid for the graphics and writing, pays off debts, and individuals take a bare subsistence wage (about $6.00 a day). Catalogues and books are available directly from the press.

Like Daughters and Diana, the Women's Press Collective maintains an independence position regarding women's cooperation with commercial (male) systems. They feel that for real change to occur, women should only publish with women's presses.

The Women's Press Collective and Diana Press have merged since this writing and can be reached at the Diana Press address.

WOMEN WRITING PRESS
RD 3
Newfield, NY. 14867

Starting with a vision of providing a press label for women poets anywhere to self-publish, Women Writing has never had enough hours to develop the dream into a venture that could support us (psychically, yes; as bread no). We have been able to make most ends meet, but we continue to need outside jobs. *NO APOLOGIES* by Polly Joan, a book of poetry and photographs coming out in 1975 was our first title. *COMING UP*, an anthology of four women's writing with Andrea Chesman, Jackie Freeman, Barbara Jasperson, and Polly Joan followed that same year. In 1976 Alison Colbert, a third member of the collective published her poetry book, *LET THE CIRCLE BE UNBROKEN*. With the help of grant money from CCLM and the New York State Council on the Arts, the *DIRECTORY OF WOMEN WRITING* was printed early in 1977.

Publishing the *DIRECTORY* was a culmination of promises made in 1973 at the First Women's Poetry Festival in Amherst, Massachusetts. At that time it was painfully evident that women writers were terribly isolated from one another. No one knew anyone else and no one knew how to get in contact with women writers she had heard about. Four of us decided to start a broadsheet newsletter to facilitate a national network of communication and support between women writers. Adding one editor and losing another, publication of the bi-monthly *WOMEN WRITING NEWSLETTER* became the first endeavor for the press. Published as a 17 x 22 broadsheet with much care taken to include drawings and photographs as well as writing, the newsletter was a very important part of our collective lives, and the lives of the women writers we now reached.

While information about women could publish, and essays geared particularly toward broadening consciousness about the specific problems of feminist writers made the *WW NEWSLETTER* valuable, we still felt (based on the innumberable letters we received) that the major need still remained for women writers to personally be in contact with each other. That was not always possible for the writer living in the country or even for writers isolated in big cities. By sharing lives and making addresses of the writers living them available, we felt we might be able to complete what we had initially set out to do.

By pulling together this information in a book we felt we could be far more useful than by continuing to print the *WW NEWSLETTER* so... The *DIRECTORY OF WOMEN WRITING* was labored and published, requiring almost eight months of work. Necessarily incomplete, the book serves as a first model for what we hope will be future directories of women writers. Since publication of the *DIRECTORY* has represented a kind of closure for us, we no longer see any need for publishing *WOMEN IN WRITING NEWSLETTER*; however WW Press will continue. *NO APOLOGIES* ($2.50) is into a second print. We expect both the *DIRECTORY* ($3.50) and *LET THE CIRCLE BE UNBROKEN* ($2.75) to have their own impact on women reading women's writing. All books are perfect bound.

Part of the reason for starting our own press in the first place had been so we could have first-hand knowledge, gain technical expertise with printing, graphics, and distribution, analyze the emotional impact of publishing on ourselves as writers, and actively exercise the politics of our beliefs as women creators of 20th century society. Another reason was to pass on whatever we learned to other women writers, to encourage them to self-publish, to risk starting their own press, to carry it on. Since we began WW Press, outlets in women's publishing have simply sky-rocketed. *WOMEN WRITING!* That's what it's all about. The fact that this *GUIDE TO WOMEN'S PUBLISHING* can now be a full length book was only a gritty hope four years ago.

(See Additional Resources: *DIRECTORY OF WOMEN WRITING*)

WYRD PRESS
131 West Street
Warwick, NY. 10990

With a publishing label like Wyrd Press one might expect literature, but that is not exactly what is intended. However, what publisher Janey Tanenbaum is trying to do is to provide a unique press label for male and female writers that she feels are creative and exciting but do not easily fit into the guidelines of existing small press publishers. As such, she is keeping a low profile as a publisher and does not solicit manuscripts.

Although Janey herself is a Feminist, she sees her press more as a creative space rather than a place with a specific political orientation. In three years of operation she has put two full length books (both by men) and four chapbooks (two by women and two by men) into print. Alta's *PAULINE AND THE MYSTERIOUS PERVERT* and Jaime Gordon's *THE CITY PLANNER AND THE MAD BOMBER* are both in the Wyrd Press chapbook series.

Using a combination of printing methods, Wyrd Press does part of each book on its own letterpress and then farms out the rest of the book to local offset printers. Since Janey also works at Gotham Book Mart, in the center of New York City, she says she is able to easily sell everything that her press publishes. Therefore distribution is not a problem for her own small press. On the other hand she is *very* concerned with the general problem of small press distribution. Her commitment to improving the market for small press books has led her to put a great deal of energy into setting up the New York State Small Press Association (See Distributors).

In the maze of women's publishing Wyrd Press is operating in a very small way to fill a gap by publishing otherwise unpublishable books, but Janey herself through the establishment of the New York Small Press Association is also trying to deal with the larger problem—more efficient marketing of any small press books being published in New York State.

YOUTH LIBERATION PRESS
2007 Washtenaw Avenue
Ann Arbor, MI. 48104

Every press listed in this book is concerned on some level with liberation, the freedom to feel one's own dignity, to grow freely into the image of self. Children's presses are trying to start at the beginning with natural images of male and female, images that won't have to be unlearned when a child grows up. Feminist and non-sexist adult presses are supporting the process as well as re-educating. Boxed in the middle are junior and senior high school students, an age group with many feelings about the meaning of respect (or lack of respect which they must face every day), with much to say, and no power of the printed word.

Very few small presses are taking an active role to pressure Boards of Education to accept non-sexist books for the classroom. Among the few making the effort are Press Pacifica (Press I) and Vertie Press (Press II). With a lot of work each of these presses has managed to get at least one of their books onto the proper lists. More publishers need to involve themselves in that unpleasant business. At the moment probably the most active and influential in this area is The Feminist Press. They have a special High School Project Committee, researching, developing and selling to educators realistic high school curriculums (See Press I).

However, as far as we know, Youth Liberation is the only press which gives youth itself a press voice. Coming out of the Midwest, Youth Liberation publishes *FPS: A MAGAZINE OF YOUNG PEOPLES LIBERATION*. In operation for over five years, the publication is a political non-sexist magazine where many of the articles are written by young people themselves. While the two editors are adult males, the staff is largely made up of youth of both sexes. *FPS* covers all aspects of youth and human liberation. Regular features include brief news items about young people, reprints from high school underground newspapers, pointed articles supplying legal information and organization tactics, comix, photographs, and book reviews. Each issue is themed for in-depth treatment of a particular subject. A look at the five year index of *FPS* indicates a wide range of topics—everything from abortion to youth employment to electorial policies, imperialism and media. Material related to women and sexism comprises the largest number of articles. The magazine is easily read by anyone who can handle newsprint, but it never talks down to its readership.

Publishing 9 issues a year, subscription to *FPS* is $10.00 for adults, but only $6.00 for youth. Youth Liberation Press also carries over eleven reprints of themed issues of *FPS*, such as "High School Women's Liberation ($1.25), "How to Research the Power Structure of Your Secondary School" ($1.00), "How to Start a High School Underground Newspaper" ($.35), "Growing Up Gay" ($.75). A brochure of the presses activities and publications is available by writing. The welcome letters and unsolicited material. Include SASE if possible.

185

FURTHER THOUGHTS

Press II is a conglomeration of publishing adventures. In this section are the single-book presses, single books that had to get out even if the woman (or women) had to create a press for that one book in order to do it. These presses may or may not continue publishing.

This section also includes the single books that have sold well through the women's network, but which carry no press name, only the vulnerability of the author herself. It takes into account presses that have plans for beginning but are only just getting through the planning stages. There are presses here that have made a great beginning, but are still too new to have more than three books in print.

I have simply listed them in alphabetical order. The section could be a bit longer, but some writers and some presses have not answered my letters. The Taurian in me has a sense of its being incomplete. I would like to include *all* of the good earth, all of the footprints.

However, of the footprints that *are* here, either in Press I or Press II, the size of it, the fact that a book comes from a large "small press," or from a self publisher, may not effect how it "sells." Regardless of where it comes from, a book can sell well in the women's market, or not at all. Women reviewers are generally not as impressed by press names as are their male counterparts. If the book is good, they will push it. If it isn't, so be it. The biggest difference in selling comes in the mass market where, if one has the money to put into advertising, it can mean big bucks for both publisher and writer. At this point, women's publishing is only beginning to scratch that broader surface, and there is a certain amount of ambivalence at this stage as to whether those big bucks should be a women's publishing goal or not.

A final thought in this *potpourri* is that neither Press I nor Press II really represents the publishing dynamic of Black women. The innovative, honest, articulate writing of Gwendolyn Brooks, Lucille Clifton, Nikki Giovanni, Toni Morrison or Sonia Sanchez, to mention a few, is painfully absent from this book. Yet women writing is not a white phenomena, or Black tokenism. However, the Black woman in her triple bind of being black, an artist, and finally, a woman, has generally published with presses sensitive to her being Black, but not particularly responsive as a press to a feminist orientation.

It is my personal hope that Black women will start some presses of their own, feminist and/or non-sexist combinations. A second hope is that Native American and Chicano women's voices will finally be adequately heard, that classism, sexism, as well as racism, will diminish because as women we all proudly brought our differences and energy to the fight—in order to end it and walk on. . . .

PRESS II

Presses Publishing One to Three Titles

AMAZON PRESS
395 60th Street
Oakland, CA. 94618

For a number of good years Amazon Press produced *AMAZON QUARTERLY*, a literary arts journal for lesbian-identified writing. When Amazon Quarterly decided to cease putting out the magazine, the editors compiled a selection of work from past AQ volumes into an anthology called *THE LESBIAN READER*. *READER* has sold over 9,000 copies to date and is the only book Amazon Press has published.

Gina Covina, one of the publishers, writes, "We have plans for others but don't now have the capital, and are *not* looking for manuscripts." *THE LESBIAN READER* (perfect bound, $4.50) can be ordered from *WIND*.

CINCINNATI WOMEN'S PRESS, INC.
3901 Ledgewood Drive
Cincinnati, OH. 45229

At the present time *SYZYGY*, a new literary arts journal (See Feminist Publications), is the only publication of the Cincinnati Women's Press, but the three women and single male who run the press have plans. . . .

> We founded the press last year (1975) as a non-profit Ohio corporation, for the express purpose of publishing *SYZYGY*. We began on a shoestring, of course, and were sanguine about our chances of

even continuing the publication. However, *SYZYGY* has had such success that we are enlarging it, and we are making plans to eventually expand the press to encompass book publication, with a paperback format not unlike that of *SYZYGY*. That is in the future. How far, it is hard to say. We hope to publish our first full-length manuscript by the end of 1977. Where we go from there is entirely dependent upon finances. Part of our logic in incorporating as non-profit was to enable us to be readily qualified for foundation or government funding. If we are fortunate in getting such funding, who knows?. . . when the time comes, quality will be the only consideration in our selection process.

Although most of our successes, individually have been in conventional publication. . . we remain committed to the idea of the small press. It is, as we know from experience, the only current outlet that is consistently sensitive to the writer, and not just to some P.R. man's idea of the audience.

FRIENDS PRESS
520 West 110th Street
New York, NY. 10025

Who ever heard of a soap opera becoming the basis for beginning a press? Well, you've heard it now. Friends Press is an outgrowth of a single book, joint-authored by two women, Esther Newton, Associate Professor of Anthropology at SUNY Purchase, New York; and Shirley Walton, journalist and moderator of a New York radio show. Like their book, *WOMEN-FRIENDS, A SOAP OPERA*, is a story , so the beginnings of their press is a story, a story best told in their own words. . . .

There has never been anything else like *WOMENFRIENDS*— the melding of two women's journals into one story, a story of friendship under pressure, friendship undergoing profound change.

Rebecca and Pauline met in college and remained close for more than a decade until Rebecca married and Pauline became a committed lesbian. Then there seemed nothing left in common for Pauline, an academic, and Rebecca, a writer, until each joined the women's movement in 1969.

A year later the two decided to re-cement the relationship through a mutual project—they would write a journal together. Almost immediately Rebecca became pregnant, just as Pauline began the painful process of becoming a public lesbian. The friendship, and the journals, were deeply threatened by the pressure of their separate lives, but the two held fast to the idea that friendship between two women could be, should be, as important as marriage, as lovers, as conventional partnerships. . . .

When the journals were through, the two began the search for a publisher. For two years *WOMENFRIENDS* made the rounds: 'Why don't you make a novel of it?'. . . 'Why don't you put more action in it?'. . . 'I love it, but I don't think I can convince the other editors to take'. . . 'I cried all night when I read it, but I don't think it's commercial.'. . . were typical comments."

So Pauline and Rebecca, who in reality are Esther and Shirley, decided to complete the cycle of their story, themselves. They formed Friends Press, Inc., reached feminist typesetters, designers, printers and a distribution firm, and published *WOMENFRIENDS* through the feminist community, entirely.

Whether Friends Press will go beyond this first book is an unknown, but the press story is an unapologetic response to the usual "no, no. . . well, we'd like to but. . . " *WOMENFRIENDS* is not your usual book. Whether the presses initially solicited are run by men or women, writers marketing a new form of literature often have problems finding a publisher. The fact that *WOMENFRIENDS* finally was unabashedly printed under a self-publishing label does not detract from its value. It is so easy (after hearing too many "no's") to give up, to shove the work into a drawer. Women in particular have heard a lot of "no's" over the years and finally assumed their writing had no intrinsic worth. Within the supportive climate of the Women's Movement, these two female writers did not feel they had to take "no" as a final solution. They simply started their own press.

Copies are available directly (perfect bound, $4.45 plus postage).

EMBERS PUBLICATIONS
c/o Maude Meehan
2150 Portola Drive
Santa Cruz, CA. 95062

One indication of the confidence that is spawned in a wo-men writer's support group is publication of a poetry anthology. *MOONJUICE* (70 pages, perfect bound, $2.00) was produced as an outgrowth of a Santa Cruz workshop. The book included poetry by all of the women in the group. Publishing under Embers Publications (an anagram of the contributor's initials), the group only printed 300 copies. Much to their amazement, they sold out in three weeks.

Maude Meehan, one of the group members, wrote that when they first started meeting as a group, all of the women were self-conscious and intimidated in the workshop. "We apologeti-cally read our efforts certain that they were inadequate and, oh dirty word, unprofessional. In an atmosphere of support and constructive criticism our confidence flourished as did our writing."

When publication of *MOONJUICE* was such a success, the group decided to continue meeting (writing and sharing their work together), and perhaps print a second anthology which would include more local women writers. *MOONJUICE II* came off the press in November 1976. More confident of the value of what they were producing, Embers printed a 1000 copy run. The new book included work by eleven women poets, grew to 120 pages, evidenced increased know-how in book publica-tion (graphics and design). The result brought another strong collaboration of women's writing into the public domain. It is only distributed locally; those out of the area can order copies directly from Embers ($3.00 plus $.25 postage).

Unabashedly a self-publishing gamble at first, some of the members of the group are now thinking of growing, expanding. "Doors seem to open as we explore, and we are seriously consi-dering starting a women's print center and press in Santa Cruz, with the profits from *MOONJUICE II* and money we raise."

A good many on-going press ventures grow out of self-publishing beginnings. It will be interesting to see what happens to Embers Publications.

THE GLASS BELL PRESS
242 Ashland
Detroit, MI. 48215

The Glass Bell Press, perhaps inspired by Sylvia Plath's bell jar, is run by Margaret Kaminski, one of the editors of *MOVING OUT*, a feminist arts journal. The Glass Bell started on its own by printing broadsides of women's poetry on its own press.

However, their first book *SISTERS AND OTHER SELVES* (perfect bound, $2.00) by Judith McCombs (a co-founder of *MOVING OUT*) was printed at Diana Press, but is published and distributed through Glass Bell. The press is not soliciting manuscripts and they handle orders directly.

(See Feminist Publications: *MOVING OUT*; and Press I: *DIANA PRESS*)

GREYFALCON HOUSE
60 Riverside Drive
New York, NY. 10024

Greyfalcon House says that they produce printed materials by women for all. As far as we know, *OREO*, a first novel by Fran Ross is the only publication (hardcover, 212 pages, $6.95). They also carry posters by Ann Grifalconi "... and ain't I a woman?" and "And God Created Woman in Her Own Image." ($2.00 and $3.00). Both the posters and the novel are carried by *WIND*.

A HARMLESS FLIRTATION WITH WEALTH
P O Box 9779
San Diego, CA. 92109

As to A Harmless Flirtation With Wealth, I (Helen McKenna) started in 1974, and am one person... I have had loans on top of loans. Also, I have received Social Security Supplemental Income, formerly Aid to Disabled, because I am homosexual and obviously disabled and mentally deranged (officially). Because I am about to show a profit and can no longer bear being spied upon, I will drop that [Social Security benefits] in June 1977... I have been working 16 hours a day for the past two years... I have had other jobs....

Under her Flirtation label Helen McKenna has published a useful, fully illustrated, (absolutely hilarious) first book called *THE TOILET BOOK*. Everything you ever wanted to know, etc., but were afraid to ask. This resource, being left visible on the dining room table at our house, motivated my adult son to proceed to the bathroom (McKenna's book in hand) and to fix (successfully, I might add) one white, leaky, whistling throne.

Helen McKenna also prints an eclectic and individualistic monthly newsletter called *BARE WIRES*. At the moment this is all the publishing she can afford under her own label beyond *THE TOILET BOOK*. A harmless Flirtation With Wealth is really "too poor to solicit mss., that is another dream." However, when a poet friend of hers died from kidney failure in 1976, Helen finished the process of publishing her book of poems: *UNHOOKED* by Connie Cox (Boondocks Press, $2.50). This book can also be ordered from Flirtation.

My political and philosophical base is so individual that I work alone. However, I do work on Stonehenge Press (former Athena Press) with one other woman, Barbara Mor. I do not own a press. I consider myself poor. But *THE TOILET BOOK* (spiral, $3.00) is distributed by Bookpeople, also by Women in Distribution. I have sold 2200 Toilet Books since July of 1975. I dream of children's books and humor books and more serious books about psychology and violence and crap. I am an animal lover and a cat just kissed my nose. He is gorgeous and his name is Felix. —Love from Helen.

(See Press II: *STONEHENGE PRESS*)

HARTMUS PRESS
23 Lomita Drive
Mill Valley, CA. 94941

Two librarians, Catherine and Ralph Moreno, have been running a very small publishing house for a number of years. Initially, the press provided an imprint for the essays, poetry and plays of Ralph Moreno. Catherine would like to see the press move into publishing poetry by women. She is advertising for submissions from women in the San Francisco Bay Area in order to do a women's anthology. The press's only other book of poetry by a woman, Judith Mosher, is now out of print.

> Doing the anthology won't be easy or fast, but once I get together about 6-8 women writers I like, I want to publish from 4 to 5 poems each plus a little biography, and ask a known woman poet to write a preface.

Catherine does all of the printing now on their Multilith 1250 which is in their house. She says that her dream for the future is complex, "but at least involves having better distribution on the small books I publish."

JAMIMA HOUSE
262 Waverly Avenue
Brooklyn, NY. 11205

Jamima House is the press label for Eloise Loftin's book of lyric poetry, *BAREFOOT NECKLACE* (saddle stitched, 40 pages, $3.00). The book can be ordered directly or from *WIND*. The author is also associated with the New York based poetry magazine, *SUNBURY*.

(See Feminist Publications: *SUNBURY*; also Distributors: *WIND)*

LYNDA KOOLISH
c/o *WIND*
P O Box 8858
Washington, D.C. 20003

Although *JOURNEYS ON THE LIVING* is a self-published book with no press imprint, it came into being with a lot of collective feminist support. Lynda put together this book of her poems, photographs and drawings in 1973 while working with the *COUNTRY WOMEN* in Albion, California. The book was printed by another women's press, the Women's Press Collective in Oakland.

The result is one of the most aesthetically beautiful books to come out of women's publishing. Perfect bound with heavy, slightly glossy pages, it is very underpriced in 1977 at $1.95. Copies can be ordered from *WIND*.

(See Feminist Publications: *COUNTRY WOMEN*. See Press I: *WOMEN'S PRESS COLLECTIVE*)

METIS PRESS
815 W. Wrightwood
Chicago, IL. 60614

Metis Press is the venture of three lesbians aspiring to be printers and publishers of women's work. Their public debut was at the Omaha Women In Print Conference where they distributed a flyer describing in story form how they progressed from being poorly paid workers in a hospital to starting a press. "Two of us, Chris Sanders and Barb Emrys, are writers, and I have a printing interest dating from age eight. . . The three of them (plus two other women) also edit *BLACK MARIA*, a feminist quarterly literary arts journal (See Feminist Publications). To expand their printing and publishing beyond the magazine seems like a logical extension.

> We are slowly acquiring equipment in our shop in the basement. We have a 320 AB Dick, a cantankerous 1250 Multi, platemaker, light table, dark room (but no camera). We farm out typesetting and camera work and cutting. We do not survive financially; the time we have to spend working to survive has been a great drawback.

When Metis is able to move into book publishing more fully, the editorial philosophy will be to support experimental self-publishing. "Each book that we put out will be an individual project, financed, created and distributed according to the desires of all involved."

Our goals for the next 6-8 months are to repair the press and improve the working conditions of our shop (in our basement). We are planning two books for Fall 1977 hopefully and two more issues of *BLACK MARIA*. One of the books planned is a 46 page fiction by Barb Emrys, collective member. . . Our priority in material is lesbian feminist, fiction rather than poetry. . . Longer range plans include merging with other women printers to expand to a job-print shop. Getting some typesetting equipment. Paying ourselves something.

MOTHEROOT PUBLICATIONS
214 Dewey Street
Pittsburgh, PA. 15218

Anne Pride, one of the founding members of the *KNOW* Collective, has recently left *KNOW* and is starting a new press. *"MOTHEROOT PUBLICATIONS, INC.* is a reality. A beginning of one, at least. I am working on the incorporation right now and have a booklet at the typesetter."

There are two of us involved, myself and Paulette J. Balogh. Paulette is an attorney, which is helpful. The first book is being done in collaboration with Pittsburgh Women Writers which is a women's workshop I have been part of for the last year or so. The booklet (it is going to be fairly brief) is tremendously significant for women writers. It is *WOMEN AND HONOR: SOME NOTES ON LYING* by Adrienne Rich. I am very excited about it and expect it to be ready in July.

The second book planned is by Donna Ippolito and is titled *THE UPRISING OF THE 20,000.*

I would like to do 4 publications per year. I want this project to stay small enough that Paulette and I can handle it personally and not have to farm too much out. I have long had the desire to be fully in control of publications from the beginning to the end. I firmly believe that publication must be considered an extension of the art and that the author should have a lot of input. The shape *MOTHEROOT* takes and the speed at which it moves will be determined a great deal by money and since I have none, we will probably move slowly to begin.

(See Press I: *KNOW*)

NEW MOON COMMUNICATIONS, INC.
Box 3488, Ridgeway Station
Stamford, CT. 06905

New Moon Communications Inc. has focused its publishing effort on women's health. Because it is a publishing effort exclusively *by* women designed exclusively *for* women, the Internal Revenue Service denied tax exempt status, charging "bias." Their major publication, *THE MONTHLY EXTRACT, AN IRREGULAR PERIODICAL* offers a communication network of global gynecological and obstetrical Self-Help. The stated purpose of this newsletter is to, "fire the Revolution by which women will rightfully reclaim our bodies." It contains: information on lawsuits, notes on new medical research or projects which positively or negatively will affect women's struggles to "rightfully reclaim our bodies" from the medical profession and male control. The *EXTRACT* includes personal letters of experiences, listings and/or short reviews or recent pamphlets, articles, or books that women need to be aware of. The publication provides a forum for information about menstruation, birth, abortion, birth control, etc., areas requiring purposeful knowledge and political pressure. The *EXTRACT* includes songs, poems and stories as well.

Contrary to large commercial trade houses or academic publishers, women publishers see no need to separate art and politics; in fact, they see the interconnectedness of the two as vital. For a female artist to speak from the truth of her own wisdom is revolutionary, and therefore her work becomes political whether she wishes it or not. Although New Moon publishing starts with political activism rather than art, for Lolly Hirsch, one of the mothers of New Moon, inclusion of women's art in *THE MONTHLY EXTRACT* has additional meaning. "Yes, art and political consciousness *must* be melded. All great artists

197

throughout time have had a political consciousness. Have you read Judy Chicago's *THROUGH THE FLOWER*? She said so many things about women and art. I was so touched by her paintings on which she wrote explanatory script knowing that so many of us had been tied home with our babies with no opportunity to visit galleries and have an art appreciation developed. Women artists must be sensitive to how so many of us have spent our lives deprived of access to the mainstream, of access to art, of access to poetry. We've been so isolated."

THE MONTHLY EXTRACT is $5.50 for six "irregular" issues (approximately bi-monthly). Two thousand copies are printed with a subscription list in the neighborhood of 1,000, the other 1,000 distributed at conferences so that eventually each issue is available only in xerox. Publishing the *EXTRACT* since 1972, New Moon Communications also carries *THE PROCEEDINGS OF THE FIRST INTERNATIONAL BIRTH CONFERENCE* ($3.00), *THE DIRECTIONS FOR A NON-TRAMATIC ABORTION* ($1.00), *THE EVOLVING LIST OF ADJUNCTS TO GLOBAL GYNECOLOGICAL SELF-HELP* ($1.00), plus plastic speculums ($2.00). In addition they help feminist artists print and publish, sharing costs and responsibilty.

New Moon operates on a very thin, almost non-existent budget. They need more space for their publishing, would like to expand. Despite all the headaches and the learning "to do it all" themselves, Mary Lee Lemke, a member of their staff, who attended the Women In Print Conference in Omaha (summer 1976), returned with a strong sense of support from more professional women publishers. "The women who had been trained professionally that there was only one way to do a lay-out or one way to print a book or one way to publish a manuscript looked as all the stuff coming out of the women's movement from those of us that didn't know how to do it properly and they said we gave them new life and awareness."

New Moon welcomes letters, information, art, ideas, donations, and support.

NEW WOMAN PRESS
Ruth and Jean Mountaingrove
Box 56
Wolf Creek, OR. 97497

Very small new publishers like Ruth and Jean Mountaingrove, continue to strengthen the back bone of a growing women's publishing network. Ruth self-published her first book of poetry around 1946. Sometime this year she will print her second one, *FOR THOSE WHO CANNOT SLEEP* (88 pages, perfect bound). "I am fifty-three. Why did I wait thirty years to publish another book of poetry?. . . The women who identify with what the poetry had to say did not exist. They do now."

> Our original money for starting New Woman Press was a gift of $900.00 given to Jean by a woman who gave eleven such gifts to individual women to love themselves with. Jean was not yet ready to love herself so she put her money into the service of publishing the *TURNED-ON WOMEN'S SONGBOOK*, a collection of feminist songs written by me over the past five years. This has since been repaid. Also the royalties from the sale of the songbook is in part paying for the publishing of the poetry book. It is a reinvestment.

Ruth and Jean Mountaingrove also are part of the collective which edits *WOMANSPIRIT* magazine. Their New Woman Press is financially separate from the magazine but spiritually very close. The press is not in a position to solicit manuscripts with writer payment, but women able to fund their own printing could certainly query New Woman Press about publishing under their imprint.

(See Feminist Publications: *WOMANSPIRIT*)

CHRISTINA V. PACOSZ
Box 354
Chimacum, WA. 98325

SHIMMY UP TO THIS FINE MUD (saddle stitched, $2.00) by Christina Pacosz is a self-published book of poems. She says at the beginning that "this book is for anyone who understands."

199

The poetry evolved out of her experience as a woman and Pat Sexton's illustrations complement the words.

Christina wrote to us for *DIRECTORY OF WOMEN WRITING* that "Putting together the book with Pat Sexton was an adventure. Everything happened and fell into place so I feel this book had some energies from the Mother. I hadn't even seen Pat's drawings when I approached her with an idea of doing a book together. She took the mss. home and when I saw the drawing ideas I knew we were meant to do a book."

SHIMMY UP TO THIS FINE MUD may be ordered directly from Christina.

PAPER TIGER PRESS
334 N. Vassar
Wichita, KS. 67208

Paper Tiger is the press name for *SQUEEZEBOX* magazine (See Feminist Publications). As part of their *SQUEEZEBOX* series certain issues of their publication are 20-30 page chapbooks of individual poets (5½ x 4¼, stapled, $1.00).

Woman-editor Mardy Murphy is open to publishing work by both sexes. Paper Tiger Press/*SQUEEZEBOX* is sponsored in part by the Kansas Arts Commission and the National Endowment for the Arts. Contributors should submit individual poems or manuscripts with SASE.

PHILMER ENTERPRISES
617 Wayfield Road
Wynnewood, PA. 19096

Philmer Enterprises is one book and one woman right now. Phyliss Shanken, a women's therapist, has written *SILHOU-ETTES OF WOMEN*, her feelings about mothering, her own mother, and other women she's known. She would not call herself a Feminist, but she relates to much that she sees in Feminism. Her book has already gone into a second printing.

She considers her book a self-publishing enterprise and relates to other work that tries "to represent human feelings," because she feels that this is the essence of her book and "even more glaringly," her second book. *"PEANUT BUTTER SAND-WICH: THE JOYS AND FRUSTRATIONS OF PARENTING*, will contain more *real* poetry as well as short stories. I feel compelled as a writer and psychologist to be understood by other human beings who want to feel *not so alone*. Consequently, my earlier work such as in *SILHOUETTES* is deliberately non-literary. My new book is a compromise. It is written in *my* language, and lo and behold, I am finding that those to whom I read it are understanding it anyway! So my sense that somehow I am too weird to be understood is gradually leaving me for a more warming feeling of acceptance."

There is one woman in my company—me! I put in at least 10 hours a week and hire a secretary for approximately 4 hours a week—just to sell one book! I do not own a press. I got into this whole business by accident. I find it absolutely exciting, challenging and engrossing... Yet I am still in conflict because I am a psychotherapist and a writer, mother, wife and neighbor and a nice person, besides publisher.

My hopes are that I would publish other people's works as long as it is emotionally oriented as well as artistic, as long as it is clean and easily understood by average everyday human beings. I would also like to continue with books that lend themselves to illustration. Ideally, what I would like to do is include work by men in my next book called *MISTER!*

Finally, at the moment, I am surviving financially because I feed my business with income from book sales as well as income from my psychotherapy practice. My reasoning is that sooner or later I will be able to show a profit! Right now, my distribution is terrible—I do not have time to run from store to store. In fact it makes me so uncomfortable, I avoid it. My time is spent promoting myself since at least this would also help my private practice and speaking engagement income as well.

PORPOISE PRESS
8501 Atlantic Way
Miami Beach, FL. 33141

Dear Polly and Andrea:

Thanks for your interest in our company. Porpoise Press is an all lesbian business conceived by Martha & Lucy Van Felix-Wilde as a means of escaping from the patriarchy. We choose the Porpoise for our logo when we found out that there are None in Captivity. Porpoises are as charming and as beautiful as dolphins, but their superior sonar enables them to remain free from man's evil ways.

We wrote and published our first work, *THE RIPENING FIG*, which is also the first book of contemporary lesbian short stories in the world, then we gave up our Long Island apartment and drove around the U.S., saying the word *lesbian* out loud, and actually getting about 500 or more individual bookstores and several distributors to accept our book. During that time we were received by countless lesbians around the country. We read to their groups, played instruments and sang for them and lived with them when we could.

We were doing great, but a calamity wiped out 4,000 of our second edition, our car, our money and any security we might have had.

Our subsequent struggle, which led to our becoming somewhat purified in the jungle refuge we were forced to live in ultimately made us happier, healthier, more capable of giving and receiving love from each other and the world. We also found out a lot of good stuff in the fields of Health, Nutrition and Spirituality, which along with our working philosophy of bliss in the here and now, will be the basis for our fantastic novel *THE AURALEANS*. We hope to have it out in June, 1977.

Our *AURALEANS* is an offering, full of deep, real characters in real world situations, recipes, remedies, methods and mantras. In it, no one has more than the lesbians, and the lesbians have everything. We see it as a movie which will terminate our financial torment and enable us to use the full powers of our love and creativity to free women.

Copies of our dear little *RIPENING FIG* can be obtained by mailing us $3.25. Martha & Lucy will have plenty of money someday, but now we don't know where our next carrot is coming from.

Hope that says it all
Love, Martha & Lucy

202

SEAGULL PUBLICATIONS INC.
1220 Ocean Avenue
Brooklyn, NY. 11230

Dear Polly and Andrea:

I'm sorry for not having answered your letter...but we (there are three of us: Peggy Bruneo, Elaine Weinreb and myself) have been very busy with two books currently in production and many more manuscripts that have yet to be read...I suppose I must tell you that we do not consider ourselves feminist press as such. For instance, we will consider and publish books by men. This is not so much out of desire as out of economic necessity, but we do carefully screen our books before seriously considering them for publication and have turned down a number of manuscripts by men that large publishers and some other presses might have jumped at the chance to contract. This is because while we find it economically impossible to function full time as an exclusively feminist press, our commitment to feminist literature is great.

This year we will be publishing 4-5 titles—three of these are by women. Women's manuscripts are always welcome at Seagull and will be given every consideration. In late 1977 we are publishing a book of poetry by Phillis Witte and we hope too, that *WONDER WOMAN BREAKFAST* will be appearing sometime late spring or early fall of 1977....

Now, to answer your questions, we have published one book to date, *SURVIVORS* by Fredrick Feirstein. A second and third book are in production—Phillis Witte's and Lousie Bell's just mentioned *WON-DERMAN BREAKFAST*. As yet we have not contracted any other books although we are hoping to contract Evelyn Schnefer's *THE COMMON BODY*, a short novel. We publish books, whenever possible, in hard cover first, usually with a smaller paperback run published simultaneously. Our hardbound books are jacketed and illustrated, and our paperbacks are smyth sewn, not just perfect bound.

We try to do quality books whenever possible and we include promotion of each book we do in the contract agreement as well. We place ads for each book whenever possible, do special mailings, and have established some distribution channels for our books with Spring Church Books, Quarto, and Serendipity. We are always trying to in-

203

crease our distribution and have plans within the year to do a cross-country trip in order to visit bookstores and talk with their owners and tell them face to face about our press.

As for future plans, we will be doing around 5 titles a year for the next year or two and hope by the third year to be doing around 8; we don't think we ever want to get larger than that. And we plan to distribute through our catalogue and special mailings, books published by women in prison and about women in prison and eventually to branch out into distributing other categories of writing as well.

We are always willing to look at good manuscripts and guarantee that every manuscript will be considered and will be answered with a personal reply no matter how busy we might be—wherever possible we will give information to women writers who ask us for it—the names of other publishers, typesetters, writers organizations, magazines, or whatever else they might want to know.

Thanks again for your letter
Sincerely, Carolyn Bennett, Vice President & Senior Editor

SHIRE PRESS
P O Box 40426
San Francisco, CA. 94140

Shire Press is really Helen Garvy, two books *HOW TO FIX YOUR BICYCLE* (48 pages, illustrations, saddle stitched, $1.00), *I BUILT MYSELF A HOUSE* (125 pages, illustrations, perfect bound, $2.50) and a whooping sales volume!

I got started by accident. I was working in a free school and not being paid so a friend and I began a bike repair shop a couple of afternoons a week to make some money. After a while of people asking the same questions about repairs (there were no books at the time) I decided to write down what I knew. Another friend worked in a print shop and one night we went there after work and printed 200 copies of my book, tied it with yarn, and began selling it ($.10 to cover costs) in the bike shop. People liked it and said I should print more and sell it to other stores, like a real book.

After procrastinating for about 6 months, I did, knowing nothing about publishing. At the time it never occurred to me to go to a real publisher, I guess I just don't work that way. I want to do something and I go do it. So I hunted around for friendly printers and found a place, The Community Press, that was excited about printing it and would teach me about printing in the process. We printed something like 2-3,000 copies and I put some in my car and began going into bookstores to see if they'd sell it. A lot did (even tho the book looked very homemade). And one place told me about Bookpeople distributors so I went to see them. And they began to distribute it, tho they gave it very little publicity. And it grew from there, with sales to bike shops accounting for a large percentage of the sales. We've sold over 100,000 so far and still going strong. I just finished doing another revision of the book (not many changes in content, tho some updating but a much nicer layout, expanded to 64 pages) which should be ready in a couple of months.

That ended it for a while. Then in 1975 (the bike book began in 1970) I bought some land in the country, an old fantasy, and began building a house. Halfway thru I decided to write a book about it, and did. Again I assumed I would publish it myself, tho by now I had learned much more about how to do that so Shire Press now has two books. (*I BUILT MYSELF A HOUSE* has sold 5,000 copies.)

And I've also decided that I like to write, and have plans for several more books, tho they have to happen when it feels right, I can't force myself to write. I've begun work on one about psychology and illness (psychological *effects* of illness not cause). I worked as a therapist for a number of years, and I think I want to write one on kids; but that's real vague now.

Now I see Shire Press as just a vehicle for publishing my own books, mainly because I'm not sure I want to get into business relationships with other people (what is a fair price to pay for a manuscript. . . ?) and because I don't have to be very businesslike if it's just me.

Right now Shire Press distributes through *WIND*, Bookpeople, and a number of others. "The money thing varies. I could survive from the two books if I hadn't bought the land that I now have to pay for, so I have to get some jobs, but I think (hope) that with this next big push around the new editions and because the bike book will be so much more appealing (I assume) I will be able to survive off book income. And perhaps each new book will

205

add a little more to make up for inflation. It has also been very important to me to keep the price of the books low. But I have few expenses other than printing costs and a little postage, so most of what I make is profit (or about half, and half goes to printing). And I live cheap, that's part of the secret."

I don't solicit manuscripts, tho I could conceivably be open to a joint venture with someone. Most likely tho, I'd want to just help them do their own. I'd be willing (very willing) to help anyone interested in publishing their own book, or just to share what I know and help people connect with other publishers.

. . . Perhaps the most important part of me is radical politics, a way of seeing this world and working for change within it. That's not real specific these days because (that's way too complicated to get into, but lots of old Movement people are stuck in similiar places) . . . I've also spent time working with people, as a teacher, therapist, and community organizer and that gets added in. And I have a strong belief in the power of people on all levels, to be able to build their own houses and fix their bikes as well as change the world.

The hardest thing for me has been learning the ropes of publishing. I only learned last month how to get a Library of Congress number, and ISBN number. I've picked up bits and pieces the long, hard way. I haven't known who to turn to to find out more. It just occurred to me that I've totally ignored Canada and I'm now trying to find out how to distribute books there.

STAROGUBSKI PRESS
P O Box 46
General Post Office
Brooklyn, NY. 11202

This is a one-woman press organized and run by Bonnie Charles Bluh. Starogubski Press has issued one book *WOMAN TO WOMAN: EUROPEAN FEMINIST* by Bonnie Charles Bluh. A review in *SIBYL-CHILD* (Vol. I, Issue 4) described the book as "the personal odyssey of one woman as she journeys across Europe in search both of feminist groups and of herself as a woman. . . Bits and pieces of conversations, fragment of women's lives, and vivid sketches of feminist consciousness-raising groups, protest marches, and abortion rallies are juxtaposed with crisp synopses of the laws and societal conditions that shape and ultimately control the vast majority of women in Ireland, England, Holland, France, Italy and Spain."

The book can be purchased from Bonnie or through *WIND* (perfect bound, 317 pages, $3.95).

WENDY STEVENS
1816 Kalorama Road NW
Washington D.C. 20009

I AM NOT A CAREFUL POET is Wendy Steven's first book of poetry (saddle stitched, $2.00). In order to produce the book she did all of the typesetting herself. "I proofed the copy three times with three different friends. . . I always kept in mind that I would kill myself if I found an error in the book after it was printed."

When Wendy's book came out in 1975, it looked and felt strange to her to see it finally done and in front of her. She wrote in *WOMEN WRITING NEWSLETTER* (Vol. II, No. 1), of her feelings. "It looked smaller than I imagined; it didn't get up and tap dance on its own. There were no eight-color illustrations. But by that time I had already lost my realistic perspective on it all. As it began to sell and I began to get feedback, it stared feeling related to me once again and I felt good that it had come from me."

"I know that the energy and emotional drain which had gone into making [this book] . . . is a part of being a woman writer that I don't want to detach myself from." Wendy's book is being handled by *WIND* as well as by herself, and is still going strong.

STONEHENGE PRESS
P O Box 9779
San Diego, CA. 92109

Stonehenge Press (which in a former life was Athena Press) has a first book out under its new label. *MOTHER TONGUE*

($3.00; 58 pages, saddle stitched) by Barbara Mor is a ritual-istic poem with sections written to be performed by a chorus of women. The initial copy run was small (200 copies) because the press has sparse access to funds. At the moment Barbara Mor and Helen McKenna (who also publishes under her own label, A Harmless Flirtation With Wealth; see Press II) handles all publi-cation and distribution for Stonehenge.

> We are now in production on our No. 1 issue of something called *REJECT*. It will include articles and poetry and things that have been rejected by the big-time establishment press. We intend to solicit mss. on this, will announce it in *REJECT NO. 1*. The first issue will have Helen McKenna's article 'My Son the Daughter: The Transsexual Hoax and How it Grew.' One of the policies of *REJECT* will be: saying all the things you probably *DON'T* want to hear.

An absence of capital seems to be the biggest problem for Stonehenge Press right now. The publishers. . . "are both individ-ualists, both have a lot of academic learning, plus a lot of outside reading, plus a lot of Welfare experience. . . . "

VERITIE PRESS, INC.
P O Box 222
Noelty, OH. 44072

The philosophical basis for Veritie Press ("Veritie" is the French word for truth) is to present true historical accounts of the extraordinary exploits of women, documented exploits which have been largely ignored by historians. In 1975 Veritie published in hardcover *MARGUERITE DE LA ROQUE, A STORY OF SURVIVAL*, the story of a French noblewoman who was marooned with her old nures on an island near Labrador in 1542.

Elizabeth Boyer, author of *MARGUERITE*, and founder of Veritie, writes that Marguerite "must have combined great charm with magnificent stamina and staunchness of soul. Her achieve-ment was incredible. And to find not one book about her among the thousands of volumes which have been written since her day, on far less worthy subjects, seems to me to be a further injustice which I have attempted to remedy."

> I started our press because when I submitted *MARGUERITE* to a couple of major publishers they seemed to want it rewritten by a co-author to 'popularize it' which I gathered to mean downplaying of facts and adding of unverifiable material, which I did not want to do. So I set up my own publishing company...We are entirely women-operated, with an all-woman board of directors, officers, etc.

In 1976 Veritie printed a second documentary historical novel, *FREYDIS AND GUDRID*, also by Elizabeth Boyer and again in hard back. This second book focuses on the turbulent lives of two women in the year 1,000 A.D., one the war-like, courageous daughter of Eirik the Red, sister of Leif Eiriksson; and the other, Gudrid, the strong, but gentleborn daughter of an Icelandic trader.

Veritie contracted with Popular Library for both *MARGUERITE* and *FREYDIS AND GUDRID* in paperback. In addition *MARGUERITE* is also being considered for a movie.

> We do not need other jobs, nor are we able to take on manuscripts at this time, due to cash-flow problems (slow pay by bookshops and wholesalers). We would pay any authors whose work we used. We use Edwards Brothers as printers, and distrubute through the usual channels. *MARGUERITE* has sold nearly 4,000 copies, and *FREYDIS* is moving toward 1,000, with many sales to libraries and schools. *MARGUERITE* was an Ohio Teachers and Pupils Reading Circle Selection, which gets it into many Ohio high schools. Both books furnish fine role models of women who learned to cope. Dreams for the future are to continue doing such books, and staying in the black while doing a bit of low-key feminist evangelizing. Women's Studies departments are starting to use the books since the paperbacks are now available.

CHOCOLATE WATERS
c/o *BIG MAMA RAG*
1724 Gaylord Street
Denver, CO. 80206

Chocolate Waters is a feminist/lesbian newspaper woman. Her single book of poetry is called *TO THE MAN REPORTER FROM THE DENVER POST* (perfect bound, $2.75). With tongue-in-cheek 14 pages at both the beginning and end of the book are newspaper squares cut out of the *DENVER POST*, pages reflecting a society that she rejects, the results of the New York Stock Exchange, ads for women's underwear, etc., etc.

TO THE MAN REPORTER FROM THE DENVER POST can be ordered from *WIND* or from Chocolate.

WOMANSHARE BOOKS
P O Box 1735
Grants Pass, OR. 97526

Womanshare Books is one book at the moment. *COUNTRY LESBIANS* is the collective adventure of five women who share their lives on the Womanshare Collective farm. A record of their collective and individual growth as women, and their experiences, the book was also an experiment in collective writing. The authors are Sue, Nelly, Dian, Carol, and Billie.

Well done graphically, including many photographs, *COUNTRY LESBIANS* is 196 pages, perfect bound and sells for $5.50. The book was printed at Jackrabbit (see Print Shops) which makes it an all-woman project. Books can be ordered directly.

ALL-WOMEN PRINT SHOPS

FEMINIST PRINTERS

Since the mid-sixties innumerable "Movement" print shops have sprung up all across the country. Almost without exception these prints shops operate from some variant of a Socialist perspective. They are usually worker-owned and have a collective organizational structure. They generally try to keep their printing costs lower than commercial printers. Some have a sliding scale based on the ability to pay. As a general rule these press shops will not print work that is classist, racist, or sexist (in so far as these are recognized).

While most of these shops grew out of the Civil Rights and Anti-war movements and represented a valuable alternative to establishment commercial presses, not all of these sixties "Movement" print shops showed equal sensitivity to what could be termed sexist. Feminist women discovered that the politics of sexism more often than not was given a lower priority in these shops, than the "big issues." As privileged members of a patriarchal society, the men of "Movement" print shops often have not wanted to consider feminism or sexism as important issues. Therefore, for most of the same reasons that women found it necessary to start women's publishing houses, women established all-women print shops. In the early 70's this feminist separatism has been absolutely fundamental in establishing a confrontation with sexism as Top Priority.

Generally, continuing to be concerned on various levels with racism, classism and corporate oppression of both women and men, all-women print shops have had overriding sensitivity to the issue of women's equality. As such, they could be categorized as the most revolutionary of the "Movement" print shops. In order for women to become politically and socially equal, revolutionary change at every level of society is required. When "Movement" print shops have recognized this fact, feminist have found it necessary to disassociate themselves from the Male Left.

With passage of time, a percentage of the men of "Movement" print shops have grown into heightened consciousness of women and the revolutionary role of Feminism. Some of these shops are now effectively run by both men and women on a healthy non-sexist basis. Feminist women looking for printers may feel very comfortable working with them.

Since both leftist "Movement" print shops and all-women print shops try to price their services lower than local commercial shops, financial survival for these shops is usually a struggle. This lower cost does not necessarily affect the quality of their printing work. In many cases the quality is superior because more care and pride are taken in the process. However, they may have a tendency to be slower than commercial printers.

It would not be feasible here to list the all-women or non-sexist "Movement" print shops. For the most part the majority function in their own local area. I would like to underscore the fact of their existence, to encourage readers to seek them out, and to become familiar with them by using their services.

However, I would like to devote space to a number of all-women print shops which are broadening their base. These print shops are advertising their printing services beyond their local area, some even internationally, such as Press Gang in Canada. Feminist publishers of both books and magazines can benefit from their printing skills and sensitivity to women's work. In fact, many already are.

At the moment one of the difficulties of present listings in Feminist sources is the fact that the distinctions between what is a Feminist press (publisher) and which are Feminist press (print) shops is usually unclear. Print shops and book publishers both go under the word "press." This if further complicated by the fact that some "print" shops also function as publishers, and some publishers do outside printing jobs. The third confusion surrounds "presses" such as The Feminist Press or Lollipop Power which (while owning and operating a press shop) limit their printing activities to their own work. The fourth bewilderment concerns publishers who print some of their work themselves and farm out other books. In this latter case the mistake is often made of assuming a joint publication rather than a publisher/print shop distinction. For instance, up until recently Women Writing Press has farmed out our printing work to Glad Day Press. Glad Day prints their logo somewhere in our books. Even locally, readers sometimes wonder if Glad Day is a co-publisher with us. In fact, we have no connection with them beyond paying them to print our material.

All of the "presses" in this section of *GUIDE* function primarily as print shops. They are all soliciting material to print and welcome contact for an estimate. As a general rule, they are not soliciting work from men, feeling that there are ample sources already for men. Their expertise goes beyond just printing to include an understanding of the particular genre of women's publishing, an important consideration when a woman wishing to self-publish, or a group of women with many books to publish, are looking for a printer.

Another variant in the Feminist print shop-publisher scene is the establishment of specific ties between print shops and women's presses and publications. Jackrabbit Print Shop in Oregon is also the exclusive printer for work from Matrix (See Press I). Tower Press in New York City is now a major printer for work from Daughters. The Whole Woman Press prints *SINISTER WISDOM* (See Feminist Publications). Megaera Press prints

213

THE SECOND WAVE, and Ms Atlas does *LESBIAN VOICES* (See Feminist Publications). There are other examples that could be mentioned. This represents a strong development in women's publishing, and I would guess that such mutually supportive Feminist collaborations will probably increase in the future.

Recently, some women's print shops with their financial base and their scheduling of press work more secure, are beginning to move toward becoming publishing houses as well. Still operating primarily as print shops, these new publishers form a distinct small group. How extensively these shops intend to go into the publishing business varies. UP Press in California only has one book on the market and rather nebulous future goals as a publisher. New Victoria Printers in New Hampshire and Press Gang in British Columbia are planning regular publishing and are soliciting manuscripts. Diana Press has operated in both arenas for quite some time (See Press I).

IOWA CITY WOMEN'S PRESS
116 E. Benton Street
Iowa City, Iowa 52240

Iowa City Women's Press is a small offset print shop. It does commercial work for women in the Iowa City area and have also done printing jobs for numerous women's groups thoughout the Midwest. Operating as a press collective since 1972, they are trying to give women access to printing tools, whether that means teaching them the skills or printing or printing materials done by women who do not have other routes to commercial printing.

They have recently begun to do publishing and are currently distributing two books that they printed, both skills manuals. The earlier book, *THE GREASY THUMB AUTOMECHANICS MANUAL FOR WOMEN* by Barb Wyatt is fully illustrated by Julie Zolot. *MANUAL* makes no assumption about the mechanical knowledge of the reader. It starts from the beginning. Iowa

City's most recent book is *AGAINST THE GRAIN*, a carpentry manual for women, written by Dale McCormick. Both books sell for $5.50. Their discount policy gives the usual 40 percent to women's bookstores and to indivdual women for ordering only five copies. All other bookstores must order 10 copies or more before the store can benefit from any discount. This policy provides a financial break for women.

Iowa City hopes in the future to expand both its commercial operation and its publishing ventures. The collective is particularly interested in publishing women's skills manuals, works of Third World and working class women, and works by lesbians. They are concerned with providing a needed access to publishing for Midwestern women, women who have material to print and are looking for a press. They do not have capital, but are willing to work on ideas, and help with distribution.

JACKRABBIT PRINT SHOP
454 Willamette
Eugene, OR. 97401

Jackrabbit is a local print shop run collectively be women. While they print all kinds of ordinary jobs, they especially love to print small runs of local women's creative material, including some of their own. Kate Jackrabbit, a member of the shop collective, has a small book of cartoons out called *GRAND JURY COMIX*.

At the moment Jackrabbit is the sole printer for lesbian-feminist publisher, Matrix, also located in Eugene. Their shop can also handle printing larger books. They have printed at least one long book, *WHAT LESBIANS DO*, a 108 page collection of drawings and writings by lesbians. Jackrabbit printers are closely associated with the Northwest feminist distribution group, Amazon Reality Co., the third link in this triple chain.

Although the Jackrabbit did not indicate whether they would solicit work to print from out of the state, we assume they would

Inquiries should be sent directly.
(See Press I: *MATRIX*; also Distributors: *AMAZON REAL-ITY CO.*)
MEGAERA PRESS
c/o W.I.T.
P O Box 745
Northampton, MA. 01060

Megaera is a women's press collective, the third member of a larger group of women called Women's Image Takeover. The other two groups are Greasy Gorgons, a non-profit car repair garage, and The Women's Film Coop, distributors of lesbian and women's films. The new Megaera Press grew out of Mother Jones Press, a Northampton feminist print collective that closed after three years. Mother Jones apparently folded because of changing politics, lack of energy and capital, and poor printing equipment. Megaera plans to focus on larger printing jobs (primarily books, magazines, pamphlets) and was planning to borrow to finance new press equipment. They will do printing jobs for women, including design and lay-out, but will publish only work by lesbians. They will continue to print *SECOND WAVE*, a feminist magazine now in its 4th year, and jobs for the Governor's Commission on the Status of Women. They encourage other women's magazines or publishers to write or call them for a printing estimate. The shop is equipped to handle regular contracts.

In addition to operating a feminist print shop, they have begun to do some publishing as well. The first book is a collection of poems and short stories, *THEY WILL KNOW ME BY MY TEETH* by Elana Dykewoman. Future plans are for children's stories, an herbal book and oral histories. One of the main goals of Megaera is to enable women to have total control over the whole publishing/printing process, from conception through design, printing, binding and distribution.

Megaera translated literally means "grudge." It is the name of one of the three Furies (or Erynnyes or Eumenides) of Greek mythology. Apparently, they are as old as creation and

216

were companions to Hecate (goddess of witches). In the Greek tragedy they represent the old order of Mother Right, which had been successfully overthrown by patriarchy. It is obvious why the press took Megaera as a name.

Old Lady Blue Jeans is working closely with Megaera to distribute their work. As a distribution company it is relatively new, and limits work to lesbian-only material.

(See Feminist Publications: *SECOND WAVE*; also Distributors: *OLD LADY BLUE JEANS*)

MS ATLAS PRESS
53 W. San Fernando
San Jose, CA. 95113

With that delicious but defiant humor that so often pervades women's publishing, the Ms Atlas logo represents a woman's hand holding up the whole world. Describing their tri-focused operation, Rosalie Nichols writes:

> Ms Atlas Press is a feminist/lesbian print shop. We have an A.B. Dick 360 press, our own camera, velox processor, and other equipment to handle everything from layout to folding. We print everything from business cards to 11 x 17 posters and can do colors, halftones, etc. We do not do full-color reproductions, however. Our only publication at present is *LESBIAN VOICES*, which is now starting its third year of publication. We do not have the financial resources yet to do any other publishing, although we have printed publications for oganizations and individuals able to finance themselves. The trouble with self-publishing, of course, is distribution—we would not pretend to be able to distribute other publications at this time, although we are happy to share information and experience we have gained.
>
> In addition to our magazine and print shop, we also operate a bookstore in front of our shop. As yet, we are carrying mostly books and greeting cards. We do not have a steady enough clientele to handle periodicals, and we have not carried many poetry books because there does not seem to be much demand. Also, when we first started the store, we decided we would not carry (or print) anything which was degrading to women (e.g. pornography), in bad taste (e.g. raunch),

217

or in sharp conflict with our value system. Unfortunately, this has meant not carrying certain women's publications and has meant recently discontinuing printing a gay male publication which was becoming increasingly trashy. We try not to hurt anyone's feelings, but there are some things we just can't bring ourselves to do.

Best wishes. . .
Rosalie Nichols

(See Feminist Publications: *LESBIAN VOICES*)

NEW VICTORIA PRINTERS
7 Bank Street
Lebanon, NH. 03766

New Victoria Printers define themselves as a feminist work collective dedicated to producing fine quality offset printing, silk-screening and graphic design. Although the printers are not specifically a resource for self-publishers, as a print shop they are very interested in printing women's manuscripts and helping women with ideas for distribution and funding. "We do not have a rate scale because specifics of jobs vary so much, but we do free estimates for anyone seriously considering having their work printed. We have a small bindery, but prefer to ship out big bindery jobs and are not really equipped to do big bindery jobs which have not been printed at the shop." New Victoria has two offset presses and facilities for silk-screening. They have a small folder, a saddle stitcher, and a manual paper cutter.

> We are also starting a publishing company which will be a separate enterprise. The publishing company is working on an anthology of local feminist writers, an excellent individual manuscript and an anthology of women's fantasy and science fiction. At the present we cannot consider other manuscripts because we need to do funding and printing on the ones we have. In the future, though, we will be interested in looking at individual manuscripts. . . We would like stories as far out as possible: Please nothing didactic, pedantic, or 'preachy.' Are there any budding Joanna Russ's, U.l e Guinn's or feminine James Tiptrees out there in Readerland?

New Victoria cannot promise to pay for material. For their

early books they are risking printing costs in the hope of starting a stable publishing fund. On the other hand "we will try to pay writers according to sales, so that they receive at least minimal monetary recognition for their efforts."

Dream:

An independent non-profit, tax-exempt publishing company to serve rural New England with fiction, non-fiction, poetry, graphic and photographic publications. A publishing company operated by women to solicit the works of non-urban writers and artists with an emphasis on works by women. A company to provide on-the-job training for women in all aspects of publishing. A company to provide nationwide distribution for authors who have less access to mainstream publishing.

A company which attracts the best in local talent and brings it to the community through benefits—readings, concerts, exhibits, and movies—as well as through low-cost publications.

OLIVE PRESS
333 S.E. Third Street
Portland, OR. 97214

Andy Wiselogle defines the work of Olive Press more as that of a women's print shop than a publisher, even though they do publish some things themselves. "We got together in fall of 1974 to do a women's printing shop in Portland. In fall of 1976 we opened up as a full time shop, after many projects and savings and some hard hard work. We do a lot of commercial printing to support ourselves, and other local women's and other political printing."

We have done a handful of books, including *NAMING* and *EYES*, at least one of which is distributed by Amazon Reality in Eugene (See Distributors). We do want to be doing more women's books. We will soon be working on a Divorce Handbook, a women's calendar, a Portland women's yellow pages, possibly a poetry/essay book and a history for children. We are more printers than publishers, in that we don't have the financial capability to back large projects like books, aside from the ones we're working on currently. But we are interested in printing (maybe publishing) good stuff that needs to get out.

Please note that many women's print shops have agreed to refer authors to the women's print shop nearest them geographically—so with that in mind we would be printing material from the Northwest.

PRESS GANG PUBLISHERS
821 E. Hastings Street
Vancouver, B.C.
Canada

With a leftist/feminist perspective Press Gang, as a print center, does the usual variety of print jobs: posters for events, flyers and handouts. They also print small books for other people and do an assortment of newspapers and periodicals. Examples of their work indicate maximum competence. They are highly skilled in their craft, and capable of doing color separation well. *MAKARA*, one of the periodicals they print, evidences this in a number of beautiful multi-color reproductions.

Like many feminist printers, Press Gang is gradually moving toward becoming a publishing collective as well. Their first paperback *WOMEN LOOK AT PSYCHIATRY*, edited by Dorothy E. Smith and Sara J. David, critically examines the role psychiatry plays in the oppression of women in Canada. "It gathers together the experiences of 9 women victims, patients, therapists, theorists, and formulates a challenge to psychiatry's basic assumptions about women." The book demands that society reassess its concepts of mental health and illness. Two books of individual women's poetry are also in the works for Press Gang.

Since establishment as a feminist collective in Spring of 1974 Press Gang "has been committed to the development of printed media as a way of presenting for discussion the concerns and aims of the Women's Movement in Canada. As publishers we want to make available a wide variety of literature that critically examines the role of women in Canada, that counters the confining sexual stereotypes that oppress us and our children, that explores creatively our perceptions of ourselves as women."

Acting as distributors, Press Gang handles the work of a

number of individual women, plus they are an access in Western Canada for The Women's Press (Canadian Women's Educational Press). They also distribute some five non-sexist children's titles from the Before We Are Six Collective. Both Press Gang and Before We Are Six distribute through The Women's Press as well, a good example of cooperative distribution.

Press Gang Publishers is growing and moving in a number of directions consistent with their politics and their past history of high level energy. They are open to printing work from American publishers and encourage women to write them for an estimate. Brochures about their *own* publishing are available upon request. "We accept women's manuscripts for [publishing] consideration. Please send a copy only, as we cannot insure return, and a SASE." Under their own label they are looking for work by Canadian women only.

(See Press I and Children's Presses: *THE WOMEN'S PRESS*; also, Children's Presses: *BEFORE WE ARE SIX*; Feminist Publications: *MAKARA*)

SNAILS ANKLES' PRESS
248 Seaside Street
Santa Cruz, CA. 95060

Snails Ankles' represents three women and a "just getting off the ground" print shop. "Our press has been in our plans and work and dreams for about two years." Charlotte, a member of the collective, bought a house with a big shed and Laurie, another member, bought a press. "We've been working on both ever since. We're finally putting more energy altogether into the shop and the collective, which includes Catherine as well. We plan to be operating within a month, e.g., press and our equipment working."

> We would like eventually (6 months? a year?) to be working enough to provide salaries as well as maintenance and overhead (which is low with no rent). We feel three is as many 'to pe paid' women we can deal with but we're open to working with/learning from/and teaching others when we know more ourselves.

221

"We want our equipment to be available to women in the community. We want only to work with women though where vital skills are needed we're willing to work with men. We will be setting up a list of priorities for jobs." Though the group sees themselves largely as a job shop, they all have individual plans that include doing some of their own publishing. In the immediate future this would be calendars, posters, and prints. "We have a Davidson 220 now with a 10 x 16 plate. We do all our own pre press and press work and really want to move into publishing someday." Charlotte's long range goal is "to work for international exchange of lesbian literature, publishing translations, etc."

Like many women's print shops, Snails Ankles' is a collective business, this time in the very beginning stages. They are receptive to ideas and ready to grow. It is too soon to know whether and when they will be soliciting manuscripts to print under their own label, but maybe by the time the next *GUIDE TO WOMEN'S PUBLISHING* is written. . . .

UP PRESS
1944 University Avenue
East Palo Alto, CA. 94303

For four years UP Press has been offering its community quality printing and, within a certain range, printing at lower than commercial rates. As an all-women's business "We would like to see more feminist work coming into our shop." They are equipped to print cards, leaflets, small books, and posters up to 17 x 22. At the moment UP Press is the exclusive printer for New Seed Press, non-sexist publisher of children's stories, and feminist cartooner Bulbul of Arachne Publishing. During the summer of the great Bicentennial year, UP Press found themselves drawn to publishing, too.

The story is that as early as 1974 another group of women in the area (of different races, backgrounds, and political beliefs) were gathering together to express concern over the commercialization of the Bicentennial and what they could do about it.

222

They were tired of being told through television commercials what the "great moments" in their history were. "All of our lives we've been fed history in which minority people's struggles have been either omitted or negated, in which women have been degraded, and in which imperialist conquest, monopoly and militarism have been viewed as heroic. We wanted to portray the *people* as making history: the nameless, countless members of movements and struggles that have affected the soul and character of America." So wrote Connie Young Yu in *THE PEOPLE'S BICENTENNIAL QUILT: A PATCHWORK HISTORY.*

This group of women made their response to these feelings by designing and sewing a large bicentennial quilt. In order to share the meaning and beauty of their work with others who could not see their handiwork, they turned the process and the history behind each of the 45 pictorial squares in the quilt into a 60 page book (saddle stitched, $3.00). UP Press completed the story by becoming their publisher.

Whether UP Press, having gotten into the publishing business, will support more books with their own imprint is a question. In any case UP Press continues to print, and their finished work shows that highly trained technicians guide their press.

(See Press I: *ARACHNE PUBLISHING*; also Children's Presses: *NEW SEED PRESS*)

NON-SEXIST CHILDREN'S PRESSES

CONCERN FOR SONS AS WELL AS DAUGHTERS

The growing need for non-sexist literature for young children has emerged side by side with feminism in the Women's Movement: Along with the realization that feminist presses were essential in order to put into print a realistic view of women, many feminist mothers felt the need for and started children's presses in order to counteract rigid sex-role stereotyping in children's literature. Realizing that sons along with daughters have been channeled from earliest childhood through the stories they are read at bedtime, these presses print stories that present a wide variety of choices upon which children can build images of themselves and the world. Boys can be helpful and expressive of their feelings, show fear and love; girls can be creative, aggressive, and adore adventure.

Broader in their scope than the attempt to deal with sexism, children's presses emphasize stories free from racist and class stereotyping as well. All of Us states in their editorial policy that their "purpose is to put forth some of the realities of society not shown in Dick & Jane. The plurality of life styles, family structures, occupations and values existing in this culture are under-represented... This leaves many children without any books with which they can readily identify." Furthermore, omission of these lifestyles leaves the impression that they are unnatural or wrong. Wishing to cope with this devaluation by omission children's presses tend to look for stories that deal with varied types of family structures: one parent families (the parent being either male or female); families where both parents are the same sex; extended families, interracial families; families with adopted, foster, physically or mentally handicapped children;

224

communal families. Contrary to the impression left by most children's stories on the commercial market, the typical family unit is *not* made up of a father, a mother and a white picket fence.

Another children's publisher, Lollipop Power, says in its guidelines that they look for stories that represent the fact that "many mothers work; many fathers are nurturant; many families have only one parent; some children spend their days in child care centers; not all families are white or middle class. . . People of a variety of races, cultures, and family types need to be depicted with dignity and respect. . . Children's presses also tend to support publication of stories that present cooperation rather than competition as a value.

It is interesting to realize that the promotion of non-sexist children's presses has been almost totally by women. Although many men are extremely supportive of the effort, it has been women who have taken the lead role in establishing publishing houses for non-sexist, non-stereotypical children's literature.

Because of their own herstory, perhaps, women are more conscious than men of oppression, its many tragic and subtle forms. Because women can be mothers, and traditionally have been the most responsible for the early education of children, they have seen non-sexist children's presses not only as a necessity for a changing world but also as a natural arena for female involvement. Interestingly enough, by identifying the value and potential of women, children, and men to grow and be themselves, these children's presses support a radical transformation of our present society toward more humane and realistic environments for all beings. While it seems to many of us as simply a most logical direction for the movement (and about time, too), promotion of these changes in society through children's stories is obviously rather threatening to mainstream society. Who would thought, even five years ago, that writing and publishing stories for children could possibly be considered revolutionary? The fact that it is, would seem to merit a whole belly-full of female (particularly motherly) chuckles.

ALL OF US
P O Box 4552
Boulder, CO. 80306

All of Us began in the spring of 1973 in Mommouth, Oregon. "It was born out of a desire to provide our children with non-sexist literature to read. . . Five women started it as a collective and it has always remained that way. Our beginning monies was $1700 that came from a women's fund in Portland. We have revolved on that money ever since. We are non-profit and only occasionally pay ourselves for the work we do. We were in Oregon for three years and in that time published, printed (All of Us originally owned their own press), and distributed 3 books, and a research paper (Sex Role Stereotyping in Children's Literature). We have always solicited manuscripts from everywhere but to date we're only satisfied with our own and have only printed from our group (or from very close to it). We read many many manuscripts and always give a personal reply, educating as we go."

Early in 1977 the collective moved to Colorado. Two of the five founders are continuing plus a new third member. "Time has scattered the original five women all over the nation and there were two of us who wanted to carry it on."

> We survive financially only through outside jobs. The books survived all right on their own, but not us! We are looking for quality children's literature that is free from sex, race and class stereotyping. We pay $50.00 a book to be split between author and illustrator. We do distribute out of our homes and also through Women in Distribution.

All Of Us has not published any new books since 1974, but they are hoping to begin publishing again soon. They have three priorities integral to their future plans. They want their writers to be feminists. Secondly, the collective has a commitment to become bilingual. One of their first books, *ZENAIDA* was written with a combination text using both English and Spanish. "It has to do with our own love of culture and a basic belief that the women's movement underlies all movements for change and harmony."

A third priority is to involve children in the writing and binding of their books. The women of this collective live in a multi-cultured, multi-lingual housing project. They are beginning to work with the children there, teaching skills, and beginning to encourage the children to write their own stories. "We have a dream of expanding this beginning into production of books that would have the wonderful quality of hand-crafting and the unique perspective of children. The three new ideas really come together in the children, in our unusual community and will hopefully manifest themselves in our new books."

BEFORE WE ARE SIX
P O Box 33
Hawkesville, Ontario
Canada

Before We Are Six, as a children's press, is trying to supplement existing gaps in available non-sexist, non-racist literature for children. Three of their five books specialize in one parent family situations. *IRENE'S IDEA* deals with the emotional impact on a child of drawing Father's Day cards at school when there is no father at home. *PLEASE MICHAEL, THAT'S MY DADDY'S CHAIR* is the poignant story of the mixed feelings a child has when there is a new parent image in a household. *MINOO'S FAMILY* represents a divorced family situation. The book treats the attempt of both mother and child to get beyond sadness and loneliness.

The other two books are also specialized topics. *THE LAST VISIT* handles a child's feelings when a grandmother dies, and *FAMILIES GROW IN DIFFERENT WAYS* is about adoption. New titiles from Before We Are Six will be *MY FEET ROLL*, a story of two sisters, one confined to a wheelchair. This book has no text, but has rather large detailed illustrations. *MADELINE & ERMADELLO* is the other new title. Young Madeline lives with her father (another single parent model), and has a

227

terrific imaginary friend, Ermadello. Before We Are Six books are saddle stitched with plastic-coated covers, and sell retail from between $2.50 to $2.75.

The press is in a process of transition right now. Having moved through various stages from a non-sexist collective to a women's co-operative, and then to a women's partnership, the press at the moment is run by Susan Shaw Weatherup alone. She is in the process of setting up a 12 women board and is incorporating as a non-profit press. (The saga of Before We Are Six is re-told in Susan's own words at the beginning of the press section of *GUIDE* as "One Story.")

The press has sold approximately 10,000 copies of its books. Susan says, "Yes, we solicit manuscripts... Authors and illustrators are paid as much as we can get together plus royalities (We are just starting that procedure)... We farm out our work to a press shop (helping in any way to cut costs)." The Women's Press in Toronto (See Childrens's Presses and Press I), is their exclusive Canadian agent. With that agent-connection BWA6 books are distributed through Press Gang (See Print Shops) and through Belford Distributors. Belford has a separate catalogue of six Canadian children's presses. Kids Can Press and The Women's Press (often called The Canadian Women's Educational Press), also distribute with Belford. In the U.S. BWA6 works with Bookpeople. (See Distributors).

THE FEMINIST PRESS
Box 334
Old Westbury, NY. 11568

The Feminist Press involvement, as a strong arm for re-education on the role of women and as innovative researcher in non-racist, non-sexist, non-classist curriculum for wider public use, has been influential and exciting. Not ever content to sit still, the collective is always on the brink of some vibrant change. They have always taken their non-profit educational status extremely seriously. Recently, they turned a studied eye and

228

heart toward their role as a children's book publisher.

"Six years ago, when *THE DRAGON AND DOCTOR* was published, books with active, adventurous, female protagonists were considered radical children's literature." So recorded Sharon Wigutoff, Feminist Press children's book editor, in the Spring 1977 Feminist Press *NEWSNOTES*. However, since that first revolutionary non-sexist children's book with a female doctor in 1971, the social climate has undergone changes. Most of these were positive she felt. "New books from major publishing houses suggested an increased awareness of sexism and a sensitivity toward issues previously considered controversial." On the negative side Sharon said she began approaching each day thinking, "Please don't let there be another manuscript about a girl trying to be accepted in the little league."

These realities suggested re-evaluation of the children's books section at The Feminist Press. "We wanted to determine whether the major publishers were, in fact, interested in producing non-sexist books; if they were willing to handle only 'safe' themes while still avoiding others; and whether or not the complex society with which children today are struggling is being reflected adequately in the literature available to them. The last point was crucial—as a small, non-profit press we cannot compete economically with major publishing companies. If we publish books on themes that are appearing elsewhere, we defeat ourselves in the marketplace, and we fail to answer the continued needs of people who turn to us when no one else hears them."

After an extensive study, Sharon continues in *NEWSNOTES,* "we learned. . . while commercial publishing is receptive to non-sexist ideas, the job of raising levels of awareness has only begun. The role of the small press as an innovator, a creator of new markets, and a publisher of the 'sticky-issues' book remains."

In a further explanation to me, Brett Harvy, another staff member at the Press, wrote that book production expenses and other small press competition were additional factors recommending policy and strategy changes. "Our children's book program has undergone a big re-examination recently because, although The Feminist Press began publishing with children's books, as time went on they became increasing expensive to produce, and the competition became fiercer—from both directions: establishment houses got on the bandwagon and were able to do more non-sexist books, and do them cheaper—and more small feminist presses began to do inexpensive books for children. Our kids books are, as you probably know, extremely expensive, because we want them to be good-looking and solid enough to get into libraries, and we have no capital to do large print runs. At any rate, all these things needed to be re-evaluated, which we have done. The result is that will will be trying in the future to do cloth-bound children's books which will—we hope—pay for, or carry, less expensive paper versions of the same book. We are still accepting and reading children's book manuscripts and, in fact, are specifically looking for manuscripts which are not quite so heavy-handedly propagandistic as our earlier children's books —which *had* to be that way!"

Their newest children's book, *MI MAMA LA CARTERA* ($3.50), is a good example of the direction the Feminist Press would like to go in. Translated, the title means *MY MOTHER THE MAIL CARRIER*. The story has a completely bilingual text and deals with the shared love and admiration of a five year old girl and her mother. According to the press description "Lupita is aglow with involvement in her mother's world. Daughter and mother live together in their bright city apartment in complete parity as persons. Whether they are preparing tamales, painting Lupita's room, or just cheering each other up, their exuberance transforms everyday life into adventure."

In addition to *MIA MAMA LA CARTERA*, there are eight, previously published, children's titles from Feminist Press, ranging in price from $2.00 to $3.50 such as: *FIREGIRL* (a little girl who wants to be a "fireman," $3.25). *A TRAIN FOR JANE* (she wants a train for Christmas, not a doll, $3.50), plus the inimitable *DRAGON AND THE DOCTOR* (she's the doctor and her brother's the nurse, and together they fix the dragon's tail, $2.00).

"We are also publishing some time next summer, a lovely book for 9-11 year olds—a much neglected age group—called *THE LILLITH SUMMER*. It's about the relationship between a 10 year old girl and a 70 year old woman." By the time *GUIDE* is out, this book should be on the market.

To receive the Feminist Press book list, order books, or submit children's book manuscripts write to the Press at their Long Island address. (For more information about The Feminist Press, see Press I).

JOYFUL WORLD PRESS
468 Belvedere Street
San Francisco, CA. 94117

Shirley Boccaccio is the founder and only writer for Joyful World Press. Attempting to fill what she felt was the gaping hole in children's literature, Shirley Boccaccio, through her press, is integrating her personal life with art and her feminist convictions. In her three stories (*THE PENELOPE BOOKS*) she has centered on her own two children, Penelope and Peter. "The scope of each succeeding book increases as the children mature—a reflection in microcosm of a growing social consciousness and awareness." These books are uniquely illustrated using a combination of actual photographs of the children and pen and ink drawings.

> I create and manage the press. It is essentially a one person operation but my children are involved too in many ways. Friends help in special situations such as typesetting and promotion parties. . . also we are very much tied into the Bay Area Women's Movement activities. Mainly, we try to make the press pay for itself which doesn't always happen. We do not publish outside work, mainly because of financial limitations. We contract the printing out and distribution is rather a constant problem. For a future, we hope to continue the "Penelope" series and continue to educate boys and girls in the joy and freedom from constricting sex roles.

Joyful World books all sell for $2.95 each plus a "Penelope" poster which is $2.00. Bookstores and interested individuals can contact Joyful World directly.

KIDS CAN PRESS
830 Bathurst Street
Toronto, Ontario
Canada

Kids Can Press produces delightful children's books, creatively illustrated and non-sexist. The press was founded by a group of Canadian women who were concerned about sexism. The group felt a real need for an alternate literature for children in which the concepts of positive sex role indentification, multi-cultural-ism, and Canadian content would be given priority.

They published their first five books in the summer of 1973. In 1975 they added five more books to their list of titles. One of these was the popular seller *THE YAK/LE YAK*, a bilingual dialogue on freedom between a yak and a character called Idea. With more books in the works, three recent titles for 1977 are *THE GREEN HARPY AT THE CORNER STORE* by Rose-mary Allison, a story about an irascible, sentimental, indomit-able Harpy; *KIDS CAN COUNT* by Angela Wood, a multilingual counting book; and *THE CHRISTMAS TREE HOUSE*, written and illustrated by Ian Wallace. These three books are priced at $2.95. Other titles range from $2.75 to $3.50. All of the Kids Can Press books are perfect bound paperbacks, and like most children's stories, fully illustrated. These books are distributed in Canada by Belford Book Distributing Company and by Book-people in the U.S. They also handle orders directly.

Guidelines for the press reiterate the fact that the members, "coming from a variety of backgrounds, are united in the effort to produce books of high quality and relevance for Canadian urban children. Working as a collective, we write, illustrate, typeset, edit, design, layout, print, and distribute our books. We are committed to the process of continued response to com-munity needs, and strive to provide books which reflect the diversity of city life and which explore new possibilities in human relationships."

Priscilla Carrier from the collective writes that they do solicit mss, but that they "must be authored by Canadians and reflect the Canadian experience. We think, however, that our stories have universal appeal since they deal with questions of sexual stereotyping, prejudice, alternate lifestyles, etc."

"We do not print stories *by* children." Because of their publishing label, Kid Can Press, they are often asked whether their stories are written by children. They farm out all of their printing to Canadian companies. "We follow the Writer's Union of Canada contract for authors who are not members of the Press and that includes a progressive royalty. Our sales are still small, but growing."

> . . . and, I guess our goal is to become an important voice in independent Canadian children's publishing.

LOLLIPOP POWER
P O Box 1171
Chapel Hill, NC. 27514

Along with women's liberation, men's liberation, Black, gay, Third World and power to the people symbols, it seems quite in keeping with the times to have a lollipop in hand as a liberation symbol for young children. Since 1970 Lollipop Power has published thirteen illustrated paperbacks for pre-school and elementary-age children.

"Lollipop Power is incorporated as a non-profit, tax-exempt, literary and educational organization. We work as a collective and average about 10 members. We avoid a hierarchy, share decisions, and rotate responsibilities as much as possible. Lollipop Power started as an all-volunteer organization; neither collective members nor authors nor illustrators were paid for their work. Now we pay a small wage for specific jobs, such as printing, distribution, and brochure mailing, but all editorial work and collective meetings are still done on a volunteer basis. We also now pay $100 per book, split between author and illustrator, and hope to begin royalty payments in the future." The publishers do their own printing and distribution. At the moment they say they place about 16,000 books per year.

Since large publishers are now beginning to incorporate some of their goals, Lollipop Power is searching for manuscripts to meet specific needs: strong female protagonists, especially Black, Spanish-American, and Native American girls and women; non-traditional family situations; non-heterosexist values; girls or women who are struggling to change values and behavior. "The books we have published have all been fiction, but we would also like to receive non-fiction, especially biographies for children."

Lollipop has a careful process for each manuscript sent to them which might serve as a model. "When a manuscript is received, it is reviewed and discussed by the group and is either rejected or accepted for workshops. In the workshops, suggestions for editing may be made, which could include anything from punctuation changes to major rewriting of passages. We then work with the author (by mail, phone, or in person) to reach agreement on a final version of the story. A board meeting is called to review the manuscript when it is in final or almost-final form. A decision is made by the board either to reject the manuscript or accept it officially and sign a contract with the author. The acceptance for publication pends illustrations, if they are not included with the manuscript."

Copies of the manuscript are then sent to people who have indicated an interest in illustrating for us. Several passages are selected for sample drawings, only one of which must be completey finished. In conjunction with the author, the group then selects an illustrator based on the sample drawings. At this time, a contract between Lolli-pop Power and the illustrator is signed. The illustrator makes preliminary sketches and layouts, which the group reviews in workshops. Again, some changes may be required before the final drawings are accepted.

When both the manuscript and illustrations are in final form, a board meeting is called. The book can be rejected or approved for publication. If accepted, the book goes to press as soon as possible. Although the step of the final board meeting is usually only a formality, it is necessary to insure that both the text and illustrations are acceptable to the entire collective in their final form.

We maintain an active file of prospective illustrators. If you would like your name included, write us at the above address. Everyone in the file is given an opportunity to submit drawings for an accepted manuscript for which we must solicit illustrations.

No one has ever said that operating a collective is the fastest way to get things done. Everyone also knows that small press publishing is not the way to get rich. However, presses like Lollipop Power with their slow and careful step by step processing try to print gentle words on the foreheads of everyone involved. An invisible pen may stamp similar words on every book of theirs that reaches the public.

NEW SEED PRESS
P O Box 3016
Stanford, CA. 94305

New Seed is a very small publishing house supportive of positive images for young children. For future books, "We want to respond to the specific need for stories reflecting the lives of lesbians. While we think such stories are important for all children, we. . . want to publish books with which children of lesbians can readily identify."

We seek manuscripts by lesbians and children of lesbians which portray children in supportive living situations with lesbian adults; stories which deal positively with conflicts children experience arising from lesbian oppression in a heterosexist society; feminist herstories of lesbian women for children. These manuscripts might or might not deal with sexuality.

New Seed has three titles for distribution: *PETER LEARNS TO CROCHET* by Irene Levison (saddle stitched, $1.25), the illustrated trials and troubles of a grade schooler who is fascinated by the art of crocheting, finally learns, and proudly makes himself a carry-all for his books; *FANSHEN THE MAGIC BEAR* by Judy, Becky, Ric and Bob ($1.25). The latter story has group authorship which itself models the possibilities when people work together rather than competing with one another.

New Seed Press started in Madison, Wisconsin in 1971 in a parent-controlled pre-school—as a fund raising project for the school and as a way to get cheap, non-sexist books into the school. Two of the New Seed people moved to California and brought the idea with them. One apprenticed in a women's print shop here and New Seed was reborn.

New Seed is a collective of five women (over 28 people have been a part at one time or another since the beginning). "We are anti-profit—not a business—are not yet self-supporting— People get paid off and on but all $$ go into putting out new books or reprinting old ones. We all work at other part time jobs. We pay artists and writers a nominal amount—either small fixed fee or tiny royalty."

The press edits, designs, does all the pre-press and binding work on their books, and most of the distribution. Distribution is also handled by Women in Distribution (See Distributors) and People's Press (See Press I). The group shares worker space with UP Press, a worker-owned-controlled feminist print shop in East Palo Alto, California. UP Press does all the printing for New Seed (See Print Shops).

OVER THE RAINBOW PRESS
Box 7072
Berkeley, CA. 94707

Most of us probably retain at least one rainbow myth, fondly carried over from our childhood. Over the Rainbow Press has a small but growing list of non-sexist children's fairytales, complete with very human princesses and princes. The most well-know, and the first book from the press, is THE FOREST PRINCESS by Harriet Herman, now accompanied by a color filmstrip and 20 minute cassette recording. The price for this package is $25.00 (quite prohibitive for most of us). The book is also still sold as a separate item (saddle stitched, $2.95). A sequel to this fairytale, RETURN OF THE FOREST PRINCESS, has been added by Harriet Herman.

Books by Over the Rainbow can be ordered through WIND (See Distributors) or direct from the press. Essentially a one-woman operation, Over the Rainbow is not actively seeking manuscripts.

WOMEN'S PRESS
(Canadian Women's Educational Press)
280 Bloor Street W.
Toronto, Ontario
Canada

Six non-sexist children's presses in English-speaking Canada have joined together under Belford Distributors in order to market their children's stories more effectively. Three of these are women's presses. Along with The Women's Press are two others, Before We Are Six and Kids Can Press. This joint marketing in a special children's catalogue has been a very efficient method of getting their books into local libraries.

In the seven books specifically published by the Women's Press (CWEP) the non-sexist message is very low key. One of their best known titles, *MANDY AND THE FLYING MAP* by Beverly Allinson and illustrated by Ann Powell (saddle stitched, $2.50) is very simply the story of a little girl who flies all over her town on a map of the area. While CWEP stories are honest and acceptable to non-sexist parents, they have little imaginative content to hold a child's attention.

CWEP had little to say about their children's books in correspondence. This may be because they are more psychically envolved with their socialist/feminist adult titles. However, they make no organizational distinctions within their collective between the adult and children's books produced.

In the past the press has only solicited material from Canadian women, but recently they contracted to publish a Canadian version of an American children's book, *WHAT IS A GIRL? WHAT IS A BOY?* Increased sharing of children's book materials might favorably expand the market for both Canadian and American non-sexist children's books. Presses interested in such exchanges might write directly.

(For more information about other work being done by The Women's Press, see Press I.)

237

distribution

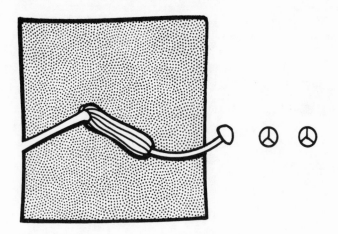

GETTING THE WORD OUT

In dealing with distribution I have not made any attempt to be complete in terms of providing listings or analysis of all possible options. Distribution is a knotty problem and could be a whole book in itself. What I have tried to do is to explore the all-women distribution models that have been organized specifically to deal with the growing number of Feminist presses; and, secondly, to provide some examples of companies operating within the general area of small press distribution who are open to carrying Feminist press books. Unfortunately, there are very few in either category.

Each press needs to be very aware of its own potential readership and to find ways of making its books accessible to those buyers. For Feminist publishers this has usually meant making contact with Feminist readers, wherever they could be found. In the past regular bookstores did not like dealing with small presses in general, and Feminism in particular. As a result there has been almost as big an explosion in the formation of women's bookstores as there has been in women's presses. At the present time there are over a hundred women's bookstores with new ones beginning every day. Establishing women's distribution companies to efficiently link these presses and bookstores is the logical third step in women's publishing. Women in Distribution is the largest women's distributor, but others are beginning.

Effective distribution of a book is extremely important, but "selling" is a joint endeavor shared by both publisher and distributor. The publisher cannot simply dump an unpromoted, unadvertised, unreviewed book on the distributor's doorstep and grumble if the book does not sell. The publisher still holds a great deal of the responsibility for "selling" a book to the public. Publishers would sometimes like to forget this fact and blame distributors when books sales are not high. On the other hand small press distributors have an equal responsibility to initiate contact with presses who have books they would like to carry and to advertise extensively those books that they do.

The whole genre of small press publishing is in a better position now than it was ten years ago, and this has had a positive effect on women's presses. One very important step was the development of *COSMEP*. Joining small presses together has given them a greater single voice to compete with the over-ridingly loud voices of big commercial houses. Membership in *COSMEP* is open to both book and magazine publishers. Many women publishers have become a part of this network. Along with coordinating information and sharing support, the formation of *COSMEP* has helped to facilitate the highly successful small press *BOOKFAIRS* held on the East and West coasts. Through these bookfairs, not only has the public had an opportunity to get a better idea of the value of small presses, but it has opened up better access for small presses to the large market and readership represented by sales to libraries.

This growing public awareness of small press books has also helped to support small press distributors. There are varying opinions as to whether a press felt satisfied with the number of books these small press distributors have sold for them. There are still a number of distributors that, while maintaining their close association to the small press in general, have carried none, or else very few works from women's presses. In correspondence one of these distributors maintained that in their case this was because women's presses did not contact them, rather than a reluctance on their part to carry Feminist books. For the most part though, my queries to distribution companies were not answered, even repeated after requests for information. This lack of interest could mean a number of things. Either they don't take women's presses seriously enough to warrant a reply or, more negatively, they do not want to be associated with a book about women's publishing. Perusal of their catalogues showed few or no books by women listed. Even though viewpoints are changing about women writers and publishers, women can still assume that their books are not as acceptable as work done by men. In this transition period it seems to be that it is up to distributors who have non-sexist policies to make them better know to Feminist publishers.

A great number of fine books are coming out of women's presses. Unlike early books in the late sixties, most of these are well packaged and are being well reviewed in Feminist literary and culture journals. They have a ready market that could be easily expanded by a distributor if these reviews were given the credibility they deserve. However, continuing disinterest or refusals from distributors would suggest that all-women distribution companies are extremely important. At the present time they make up the smallest part of this book.

Women traditionally have not had capital to begin businesses, yet we now have over eighty women's publishing houses. What would happen if we plowed back a small amount from sale of our books to the women distributors who carry them? With more capital perhaps women's distribution companies could fly. Our books would develop broader wings. It would be seed money well spent.

We have come too far to allow ourselves to be stymied now by disinterested or negative distribution. Even as this book could not have been written ten years ago, I hope that within not too many years, some one will be able to write the exciting story of how our books are getting out, a book about *WOMEN'S DISTRIBUTION.*

WOMEN INVOLVED IN DISTRIBUTION

WOMEN IN DISTRIBUTION
P O Box 8858
Washington D.C. 20003

After the glow of publishing and out of the pain of discovering that "a writer can't eat on the Feminist Spirit" some hardnosed thinking is developing to conquer the distribution problem, focusing on bread for sustaining writers and publsihers.

Straight bookstores have always voiced an aversion to dealing with small presses; but, even women's bookstores, imbued with Feminist consciousness, have found it a lot of paperwork to deal with 80 women's small presses. In addition, some presses would like to get out of the distribution business as much as possible and concentrate on their publishing.

To provide a partial answer for the growing number of Feminist presses, Women in Distribution began in July 1975. Set up to handle women's writing exclusively and willing to handle single-book presses, they have been the first women's distribution company on a major scale to get off the ground.

WIND, as they have grown to be affectionately called, consists of three women, Cynthia and Helaine (full time) and Chris (part time). After two years in operation they are distributing over 300 women's titles and are working with 100 publishers, 80 percent of which are women's presses. Only 40 percent of their accounts are with women's bookstores, but in terms of quanity of books ordered, women's bookstores still take up over 60 percent of the sales volume.

The *WIND* women are gradually building to the point where

244

they have on-going accounts outside of women's bookstores with local, counter-culture, and chain bookstores, as well as increasing support from libraries. Getting women's press work into the mainstream culture is where the bread money exists. *WIND*, presses and writers will all benefit from this breakthrough.

The *WIND* contract with presses and individuals is generous. They consign work at 50 percent of the retail price, re-selling at 40 percent. This low consignment rate, however, has made it hard for *WIND* to show any survival profit. By only taking 10 percent of the retail amount of a book, they only make $500 distributing $5,000 worth of books. Most distributors take 20 percent.

> It's very difficult to cover expenses on this. In order to grow, to better sell the books we carry, we have to put as much money as we can into advertising and promotion. Since we barely cover expenses, you can see the bind we're in. As far as paying ourselves. . . at the moment, we are paying 3 of us small amounts of money, intermittently. The first two years, we all had to work full time jobs in addition to running *WIND*. We have been able to work more or less full time on *WIND* in the last eight months.

One of *WIND*'s problems has been not enough initial capital. "If we had started the way we wanted to, we would have had several hundred titles at the outset. We would have been carrying some popular trade titles, to help sell the small press/women's press unknowns (often a store will place an order for something they have heard of, and then add on a few *experimental* copies of books they haven't seen). As it was, we started with 30 titles, all of them women's/small press and fairly unknown to local or chain bookstores."

WIND gives an account to presses on what has been sold every 60 days, accompanied by a check. Each press and independent publisher receives a catalogue advertisment and this catalogue is updated and re-produced every six months. All merchandise is insured for the wholesale cost while stored in their warehouse.

Hoping to further increase their book sales, they are developing areas of promotion such as installing a *WIND* booth at the American Booksellers Association (ABA) Conference and the American Library Association's Annual Conference. At the "ABA" all the chain/large bookstores in the country shop for the books they will offer the next year. At the latter, over 10,000 librarians attend, also "shopping" for new books to put on their shelves.

Another promotional idea that *WIND* wants to continue is the cooperative advertising they did in 1976. They are very open to contributing whatever they can to cooperative advertising with both bookstores and publishers. "In our opinion, advertising/reviews/promotion are as crucial to getting a book out, as distribution... Reviews in the women's press and in trade magazines mean greatly increased interest in the book(s) reviewed. We have been trying to get books we carry reviewed in various publications, with some luck. We have concentrated these efforts on those books we distribute under an exclusive contract."

This additional willingness of *WIND* to help presses get books reviewed in women's publications and trade journals is superlative distributor support. While women's presses are becoming more conscious of getting their books reviewed in Feminist publications, getting through the protocol of having these same books reviewed in trade magazines has been quite minimal. However, most local and chain bookstores and libraries limit their perusal of new books to these trade magazines. If women's press books aren't there, they lose a big hunk of their "access." Women's presses interested in pursuing the process of getting reviewed in trade magazines, especially *PUBLISHER'S WEEKLY* and *LIBRARY JOURNAL*, are encouraged to write *WIND*.

Such overt willingness to help presses work to get "known" differentiates *WIND* from most other small press distributors. Some small press distributors even take a much higher press cut for books they feel are under-reviewed, because the distributor feels these books will be harder "to sell." It is understandable but underscores how the support systems operating in

Feminist publishing reciprocally continue to reinforce each other.

On the other hand, some of the inexperience in women's publishing creates hassels all around. For *WIND* "the main hassels with small presses have centered around business practices. . . sometimes different values (we greatly value efficiency, planning, organization—some small presses don't); sometimes lack of skills (packing, bookkeeping). Particular examples. . . i.e. a press raises the price of 3 books. They don't tell us. The old price remains imprinted on the books. We continue to sell at the old price, finding out 3 months later that the price has changed. Major and constant hassel: We order books from a press and don't hear from them for 6 months. We don't know whether the book has gone out of print or what. We continue to tell our customers *it should be coming*, and our customers get frustrated. I'd say the root of a lot of these problems is that presses don't seem to realize that what they do with their books greatly affects us (or whoever else is distributing them) and that we need to be kept informed. Also, I think this whole problem has improved a lot in the last 6 months. . . We seem to be getting more feedback and information from most of the presses we carry."

The other major hassel seems to be payment. "I think often these troubles come from similar value differences, mentioned above, i.e. when a store buys from us on 30 day terms, we expect that they expect to pay within 30-40 days. We have found out that some stores purchase books from us with no intention of paying within a time period, a 'well we are all bucking the system, so they aren't going to mind if we ignore these rules' type of attitude. We have learned that some bookstores always pay the large publishers (e.g. Random House) before they pay *WIND*, or independent producers. There are also stores which sometimes have trouble paying us, but are responsible in how they deal with us. I think these stores need to be more widely supported by women (financially)."

On the other hand Cynthia of *WIND* wrote "I'd say the main joy working with small presses has been the sharing of a sense of adventure, and the willingness to take risks (you might say an I'll try *anything* attitude). That, and seeing many women (ourselves included) stand back in amazement at what we *can* do."

> . . . It's an exciting, frustrating, fascinating bizness. We are totally wrapped up in it (probably too much at times. . . occasionally have to take drastic measures to get physically and psychologically away from *WIND*). I think for a lot of people the paperwork, constant little problems would make the work unbearable, but for some reason we seem to get thru these and still like what we're doing.

AMAZON REALITY
P O Box 95
Eugene, OR. 97401

Amazon Reality is one of two new women's distribution companies developing distribution specifically for lesbian work. At the moment the number of titles Amazon Reality is marketing is small, but they feel that outlets for Northwest women need to be increased and they are hoping to do this.

The association with the women's work they carry is apparently so close that their promotion folder does not even mention the press names of the books and materials they are distributing. However, from other contacts it is known that they market at least two titles for Matrix Press (see Press I) and perhaps four books, printed and published by Jackrabbit (see Print Shops). They also distribute some five posters. Contact directly.

OLD LADY BLUE JEANS
c/o W.I.T.
200 Main Street
Northhampton, MA. 01060

A second new women's company for exclusive distribution of lesbian work is Old Lady Blue Jeans. Closely associated with Megaera Press (see Print Shops), their first book for distribution is a collection of poems and short stories by Elana Dykewoman, *THEY WILL KNOW ME BY MY TEETH.*

Still in the formation stage Old Lady Blue Jeans is handling an *ALMANAC AND LUNATION CALENDAR* printed by the Iowa City Women's Press (see Print Shops) and a musical tape of Linda Shear.

The work they distribute is "to be shared by and sold to women only." They expect to be handling more graphics, music, photography, magic, fiction, fact, wit, etc., with the belief that whatever lesbians create reflects "herstory, our present and our future and must be shared." Interested lesbians should write Old Lady Blue Jeans directly.

FIRST THINGS FIRST
2427 18th Street NW
Washington, D.C. 20003

First Things First is chartered as a not-for-profit educational corporation "to educate people about feminism, the sexist nature of society, the discrimination and oppression that exists—to get as much of this information into the hands of as many women (men & children) as possible and to encourage the increased work of women writers, publishers and researchers."

First Things First is a mail order house for women's literature. Started in 1973 they were the first real attempt to form a distribution link between women's presses and the public. During the early years their catalogue advertised over 2500 books by and about women, women's liberation, sexism and non-sexist children's materials. It was the only source for "hard-to-get" Feminist books and the only place where independent publishers could market their work nationally.

With time, Feminist books have become more acceptable through the open market. They no longer need to come in through the back door. Reviews of books in Feminist magazines have increased, and addresses of Feminist presses have become more readily available. Large numbers of women's bookstores are sprinkled around the country. Establishment of women's distribution companies and ties with small press distributors have facilitated ties with bookstores and libraries. With these changes First Things First has gradually done some phasing out of their mail order business, concentrating their efforts on the bookstore part of their operation. Such alterations are to be expected, but many of us remember, and will always carry a soft spot in our hearts for First Things First, as one of the first, to reach out their women's hands to Feminist presses.

RESPONSIVE DISTRIBUTION MODELS WITHIN THE
SMALL PRESS CIRCUIT

BOOKPEOPLE
2940 Seventh Street
Berkeley, CA. 94710

Bookpeople in California provides distribution for over 500 small, independent publishers with over 2000 titles in the category. In their Distribution Agreement (contract) they state that in order to effectively market they "must order on a consignment basis. These consignment titles are offered to retail bookstores at a 40 percent discount off the retail price. The publisher receives 80 percent of the net (after our discount to our accounts) sale proceeds and we receive 20 percent. This is equilvalent to our taking 52 percent discount off the retail price." What this means for a publisher is that from a book that sell retail for $4.00, the take home pay on each book sold is $1.60. For the distributor to take 20 percent is usual in the business, but it points up exactly how much of a break Women in Distribution gives to publishers by only taking 10 percent of the retail. With Women in Distribution on the same $4.00 book, the publisher receives back $2.00.

With Bookpeople the publisher receives a Monthly Sales Report which includes all sales, returns from bookstores, and the publishers inventory. Payment for these sales is within 90 days of the Monthly Sales Report. This allows Bookpeople a reasonable period for collection from their customers.

Like all distributors, Bookpeople will periodically review the sale of a publisher's books. If they feel that it is no longer mutu-

251

ally beneficial to continue to carry a book(s), they will return all unsold copies to the publisher and complete their payments due to the publisher up to that date. This points up the continuing need for publishers to keep promoting their books on their own so that sales volume can continue to be good from the distributor's point of view.

Bookpeople's organizational structure is worker-owned and controlled. In their own words they state: "The Association was formed as a labor organization to protest the indiscriminate firing of the entire staff by the corporation's outside owners in the summer of 1971. In a rapid series of developments, the Association incorporated itself and bought all the outstanding shares of Book People, a California corporation. Later, we merged the two companies."

> Having experienced enough of the oppressive effects of private ownership, we divised a system of capital stock control that, in effect makes the very idea of ownership extinct. Each employee, after a brief apprenticeship in the business, acquires 50 shares of stock. No one may purchase any additional shares; everyone must sell his shares upon leaving the company. Control of the company is thus always equally in the hands of the people doing the work. This scheme is not an instant panacea for routine conflict and problems that arise in the course of operating a successful business. But the fact of totally shared control and responsibility is the essential basis of our working together with respect toward the goals of maximizing our freedom, happiness and dignity, both individually and collectively.

Bookpeople continue in their business to try to be humanistic. They encourage publishers to write to them, sending copies of books they would like Bookpeople to handle. They do not require exclusive distribution rights.

NEW YORK STATE SMALL PRESS ASSOCIATION
P O Box 151 Village Station
New York, NY. 10014

Establishment of the New York Small Press Association is a brand new idea for New York State as well as for the genre of the small press. Effective distribution is considered the major problem for the small press. This particular group will specifically serve New York State small presses, but their contact will be nationwide. Their uniqueness is that they "will advertise in mainstream and small press review publications such as the *NEW YORK TIMES BOOK REVIEW, SAN FRANCISCO REVIEW OF BOOKS, PUBLISHER'S WEEKLY, MARGINS, LIBRARY JOURNAL, NORTHEAST RISING SUN, CHOICE, THE SMALL PRESS REVIEW* and others. That is, for perhaps the first time small press book and magazine publishers will have access to the same trade publications and trade services as major publishers. Since most small presses and magazines cannot afford to advertise, we'll be opening up wider and new markets for your publications."

This type of distribution services could be a real breakthrough and model for small press distribution. In order to get it off the ground, Janey Tannenbaum, publisher of Wyrd Press (see Press I), is serving as director of the project. The day to day operation of the distribution is being handled by Ted Greenwald. The first catalogue (including 62 NYS small presses) went out to over 3000 libraries, wholesalers, bookstores and individuals.

The Association has received a grant of $24,793 from the New York State Council on the Arts to set up this service. Although the Arts Council is at present willing to pick up a substantial portion of the cost of this pilot project, obviously the service will eventually need to be self-supporting. In order to begin this process a $25.00 membership fee is required of each small press publisher using the service, a fee that the organizers feel will be fully returned to the small press by the increase of their book sales.

Payment will be based on the 50 percent discount rate with sale to retail outlets at the standard forty percent trade discount. Interested Feminist and small presses in New York State can contact the address given and receive information.

THE PLAINS DISTRIBUTION SERVICE
P O Box 3112
Block 6, 620 Main Street
Fargo, ND. 58102

The Plains Distribution Service is an example of regional, mail order, small press distributors that operate in various parts of the country. Plains selects about 60 books a year to distribute, largely to individuals. They feature fifteen of these in each of four seasonal catalogues. In order for a book to be considered for inclusion "it must be published by a small, university or non-commercial press located in, an author living in or from, or about some part of the following states: Wisconsin, Minnesota, North Dakota, South Dakota, Iowa, Montana, Wyoming, Nebraska, Kansas, Missouri, Illinois, Indiana, Ohio or Michigan."

> In the past we have been accused, correctly, of not carrying enough titles by women. The problem is that we depend on submissions from presses and writers for the selection of what we promote and distribute—we receive very few books written by women. Possibly if more people knew that we are willing and looking for books, need books, send 'em.

Books (poetry, fiction, history), must meet their standard of quality, however. Joseph Anderson, the director of Plains, and one of two full time employees, says that their main purpose is "to provide an exposure for Midwestern writers and publishers that would otherwise be too difficult to obtain individually. With distant market centers and a scattered readership it makes good sense to have a mail order service that can bring books to folks in rural areas that haven't any book stores. We also mail to the coasts where people looking for Midwestern writing and publishing have a difficut time finding them since publishers are unable to service the bookstores."

They also try to bring back to the small publishers they deal with as much profit as possible. Their policy is sensitive to the financial needs of small presses. Since Plains is set up as a non-profit enterprise, they are in a better position to do this. "We

254

purchase from independent small presses at a 30 percent trade discount in an effort to return as much to the producers as possible. We purchase from university presses at a 40 percent discount in order to provide the better discount for the independents."

The present actual sales volume of Plains is very small. For the 60 titles they carry they sell about 4,000 volumes a year. This calculates out to around 66 volumes sold per title per year. They are hoping to double this volume by getting a book bus and taking to the road.

In addition to carrying books, Plains distributes ten Midwestern literary magazines. Magazine distribution is always a problem and Plains offers an alternative to independent magazine publishers. They have a separate catalogue with information on each magazine they service.

As for distributing women, in recent catalogues Plains has carried books by Meridel LeSueur (*RITES OF ANCIENT RIPENING*), Gwendolyn Brooks (*REPORT FROM PART ONE*, a summary of her life), Kathleen Wiegner (*COUNTRY WESTERN BREAKDOWN*), *WOMEN POETS OF THE TWIN CITIES: AN ANTHOLOGY*, and a couple of others.

> Although we are in need of books by women, we will not compromise simply because a book is authored by a woman. Hell, you know what I mean—we don't plan on setting up a patronizing quota system for anyone, however we, sure could use some strong books by women. I wish that more were being published or that more of those that have been published would be sent here for possible distribution.

This latter comment is a rather lame duck response to the question of why small distributors are not carrying a larger number of women's titles. It seems to me that if distributors want to swell the number of women authors they distribute, then they could easily learn about new books by women by reading Feminist publications, and/or contacting women's presses, encouraging direct contact with their distribution services.

COSMEP VAN PROJECT AND
COSMEP/SOUTH DISTRIBUTION
c/o Judy Hogan
Box 209
Carrboro, NC. 27510

Although the COSMEP Van Project (national) and COSMEP/ SOUTH (regional) are distinctly separate distribution services, they are both being handled by Judy Hogan (see Press I: *CARO-LINA WREN*) and information can be received by writing the same address.

The COSMEP Van Project is getting underway as of August, 1977. Under a $30,000 grant COSMEP (Committee of Small Magazine Editors and Publishers) has purchased a tractor-trailer bookmobile from a library in Minnesota. Any member of *COS-MEP* National (see Additional Resources) can carry one title with the Van for distribution. Later it may be possible for the Van to carry more than only one title from each press or magazine, but at this initial stage there is a necessary limitation.

Obviously, the hope is that a mobile distribution service such as the Van can move into geographic areas not previously reached by independent publishers. The Van can set up house in shopping areas, go to local fairs, become a traveling bookstore in isolated country areas, starting with the deep South.

The COSMEP Van Project, while intending to reflect the wide diversity in self-reliant publishing in this country, has a democratic base. The intention is that no materials that are blatantly intolerant (i.e. racist, classist, or sexist) will be sold from the Van. COSMEP members will have continuing input as to criteria. Indications from past COSMEP history would suggest that the Van Project will no doubt have many scrappy and vocal watchdogs.

The Van will carry five copies of a single title on 50 percent consignment and will request further copies as required. Any unsold copies after a year will be given to the COSMEP Prison Project.

COSMEP/SOUTH DISTRIBUTION is also handled by Judy Hogan, but her position is regional coordinator rather than director. Largely a small mail order service, business has about a $100 a month turnover. Set up specifically to work as a Co-op with Southern presses and magazines, the group has a catalogue that is freely distributed, serving as good promotional exposure. Buyers are urged either to order directly from the publisher or to funnel orders through Judy's Carrboro, North Carolina office.

The Co-op deals with 37 presses and carries 200 titles. Over the course of a year Judy says she sells approximately 600-800 books. She has no way of knowing how many orders go directly to the publishers rather than to her, but she says the positive spin-off from wide distribution of their *COSMEP/SOUTH* catalogue probably does increase direct sales to the publishers.

Few of the presses and magazines in the catalogue are feminist-oriented, but that is due to the fact that there are few in the South. If the present service broadens to include presses in other parts of the country, Judy would be very supportive of increasing the number of feminist presses. Since COSMEP/SOUTH is a Co-op, this cannot simply be a personal decision.

THE SMALL PRESS BOOK CLUB
P O Box 100
Paradise, CA. 95969

Book clubs are another viable, but limited, option for small press distribution. The Small Press Book Club, recently added to the extended activities of Dustbooks, has Ellen Ferber acting as editor-in-chief of the operation. Book clubs carry a limited number of books and do their selling through membership. The member is required to purchase a certain number of books or magazines a year in return for certain advantages. In the case of the Small Press Book Club, according to Ellen, "You become a member when you buy· a book. Any inquiry about the club is answered by sending a packet with a description of the club, a note on small presses and a copy of the most recent selections list. If you buy a book from the list, you become a member for six months." In order to remain a member the participant must buy at least one book every six months.

For the select number of books the Book Club will choose each time, they are mainly interested in literature (poetry, fiction) but "we do also carry at least one title that is how-to, some kind of feature (psychology, criticism, travel), and we are on the lookout for children's books."

The book club will look at *any* book or magazine, as long as it is published by a small press. "We will not use books by large presses, or those who have access to the distribution facilities of large presses... We do try for a balance of all kinds: poetry/fiction, parts of the country, methods of production (we're even thinking of trying a mimeo corner), prices, presses."

Ellen is aware of keeping a non-sexist balance, too. "I like to think that there will be a natural balance of male/female, in both presses and authors, because of the natural equality of the distribution of talent and hard, careful work. Example: we picked four poety books for our first list: two by women, two by men. Our fiction anthology was edited by a woman, and contained stories about equally divided by sex of author. The novel we picked was by a man. I think I would become conscious of a disparity if it appeared, and I would make a conscientious and deliberate attempt to rectify it, but I don't think it will happen. Given the phenomenal growth of women's presses in the last say, five years, and the emergence of incredible numbers of talented women writers, artists, thinkers, photographers, editors and publishers, the problem is one of narrowing the choice down to a number we can handle on any given list, not worrying about whether we can find any, or enough."

The Small Press Book Club Agreement with publishers is generous, and the arrangement is similar to the excellent terms offered by *WIND* and the NYS Small Press Association. They will take copies of titles selected at 50 percent discount, only a 10 percent take, over and above the usual bookstore discount. They report to publishers on sale of any title they carry each month, and send payment with each report. They reserve the right to return unsold copies after a certain number of months (this is stated in the contract), but they make it a policy to hold and keep active on their back list any titles that continues to draw subscriber interest. This is a particularly important fact for publishers to be aware of.

For titles on their list they want as much information as possible. They encourage the publishers of titles chosen to send them complete promotional material, including reviews, pictures, excerpts the publisher has chosen as especially effective, and biographical information on the author(s). They try to include this information when they make up the listing.

In addition to dealing with books that are sent to them, "we might solicit a review copy of a book we see a notice of or hear about. . . The only books we won't offer through the club, besides those done by big presses, are those we (Dustbooks) publish. Somehow it seems to us unfair to choose our own books."

(See Press I: *DUSTBOOKS*; also Additional Resources: *INTER-NATIONAL DIRECTORY OF LITTLE MAGAZINE AND SMALL PRESSES, SMALL PRESS RECORD OF BOOKS, SMALL PRESS REVIEW*.)

OTHER NATIONAL DISTRIBUTORS*

SMALL PRESS

The Benjamin & Matthew Book Co.
Box 191, RFD 1
Freeport, ME. 04032

Book House Northwest
P O Box 296
Portland, OR. 97205

The Distributors
702 S. Michigan
South Bend, IN. 46618

---

*The policies and practices of these distributors is not known.
The addresses are listed as information.

Pacific Pipeline
Box 3711
Seattle, WA. 98124

Serendipity Book Distribution
170 Shattuck Avenue
Berkeley, CA. 94707

WIN
Box 547
Rifton, NY. 12471

CANADA

Belford Book Distributing Co.
11 Boulton Avenue
Toronto, Ontario
Canada

METAPHYSICAL-RELIGIOUS

Devorss & Co.
P O Box 550
Marina Del Rey, CA. 90291

SAN FRANCISCO AREA

L-S Distributors
1161 Post Street
San Francisco, CA. 94109

PHOTOGRAPHIC BOOKS

Light Impressions
P O Box 3012
Rochester, NY. 14614

RELIGIOUS

Samuel Weiser
625 Broadway
New York, NY. 10012

TEXBOOKS

Western Paperback Co.
444 Bryant Street
San Francisco, CA. 94107

MAIL ORDER DISTRIBUTORS

These distributors specialize in selling directly to individuals

Before Columbus Foundation
c/o Shawn Wong
The Combined Asian-American Resources Project
P O Box 18621
Seattle, WA. 98118

The Book Bus
Joe Flaherty
c/o Visual Studies Workshop
4 Elton St.
Rochester, NY. 14607

Casa Editorial
3128 24th Street
San Francisco, CA. 94110

Cold Mountain Press
4705 Sinclair Avenue
Austin, TX. 78756

COSMEP West
c/o A.D. Winans
P O Box 31249
San Francisco, CA. 94131

De Colores
c/o Jose Armas
2633 Granite NW
Albuquerque, NM. 87104

Gotham Book Mart
Small Press Department
41 West 47th Street
New York, NY. 10036

LPSC (Literary Publishers of Southern California)
1639 W. Washington Boulevard
Venice, CA. 90291

NESPD (New England Small Press Distribution)
45 Hillcrest Place
Amerst, MA. 01002

Quarto Book Service
P O Box 4727
Columbus, OH. 43202

Sand Dollar Booksellers & Publishers
1205 Solano Avenue
Albany, CA. 94709

Small Press Center
c/o Intersection
756 Union Street
San Francisco, CA. 94133

Spring Church Book Co.
P O Box 127
Spring Church, PA. 15686

University Place Book Shop
821 Broadway
New York, NY. 10003

Washington D.C. Area Distribution Project
c/o Candyce Stepen
The Writer's Center
Glen Echo Park
Glen Echo, MD.

Women's Distribution Group
Barbara Baracks
c/o Maureen Owen
Box 672
Old Chelsea Station
New York, NY 10011

additional
resources

NETWORK OF SUPPORT

By now it should be perfectly clear that women's publishing encompasses many arenas. Our vision of feminist publishing her-story begins with women writing poems and gathering these poems into magazines and books which they printed and published themselves. With these books and magazines, women began to learn the techniques of distribution. We are now at a point where our diversity is great, and women all over the country are aware of the existence of a "feminist press." And still the picture is incomplete.

There are networks of support which run in and out of women's publishing. Most of these networks are ad hoc, informal; it is a co-operative field. Publications exchange advertising mailing lists, copies. Presses share expertise. But there are also some organized support systems. To a certain extent these support networks are also a part of small press publishing in general. These are the public funding institutions, the organizations of publishers, the directories which spread the work and facilitate growth. However, with the advent of the Feminist Writer's Guild, we may be entering a new era of formalized feminist support structures which will further implement an autonomous feminist press.

This chapter talks about a few such networks. To tell the whole story would entail another book. This chapter samples the directories and review publications which spread the word, the libraries and archives which preserve our words, and the organizations that help to make all of the publishing possible.

DIRECTORIES, WRITER'S RESOURCES
AND REVIEW PUBLICATIONS

SPREADING THE WORD

As an established literary institution, the current small press movement is close to 15 years old. The feminist press is somewhat younger. In a society attuned to mass marketing techniques and the idea that "bigger is better," neither the small press nor the feminist press has received a fair share of grants, publicity, or access to libraries. In turn, this has diminished their impact on the literary public. Distribution is a problem shared by both the small press and the feminist press.

One aspect of distribution is book reviewing, which brings a book to the attention of a buying public. Many feminist literary publications carry book reviews and reach a feminist audience. There are other publications, outside of the feminist publishing community, specifically designed to promote small press publishing; this chapter will focus on a few of them.

Libraries are slowly becoming aware of small press books. Traditionally, librarians have relied on such trade journals as *PUBLISHER'S WEEKLY* and the *LIBRARY JOURNAL* for buying directions. These publications notoriously ignore small press and feminist press books. However, there are other journals, some read specifically by librarians, others read by a more general public, which are willing to provide the necessary service of promoting small/feminist presses. It is important to get one's book reviewed. In my opinion, no book or magazine is adequately distributed until everyone has free access to it in a public library.

Of course having a review in a review publication does not insure distribution. As long as many presses distribute directly through the mail, and as long as most reviewers neglect to include addresses, prices, etc., in reviews, it is necessary to be listed in a record of books in print. There are two such books dedicated to the small press: *ALTERNATIVES IN PRINT* and *SMALL PRESS RECORD OF BOOKS IN PRINT*.

But spreading the word about small and feminist press publishing involves more than book reviewing and selling to libraries. Writers need to know where to send their work to be published. Subscribers, the financial base of most publications, need to know what magazines are available. Thus, directories of publications and writers' resource magazines are another aspect of spreading the word.

Finally, there is another way of spreading the word—through directories where writers are offered the ideas and address of other writers and encouraged to share expertise directly, instead of through the more formal support structures set up in the section on "Organizations."

Again, this section is incomplete. But hopefully, it is the start of a documentation of small press distribution.

****

ALTERNATIVES IN PRINT

New Glide Publications   6 x 9½, 346 pages, perfect bound
330 Ellis St. $8.95 plus $.50 handling
San Francisco, CA. 94102

Compiled by the American Library Association's Social Responsibilities Round Table (SRRT), this directory is specifically addressed to librarians. *ALTERNATIVES IN PRINT* is an "annual catalog of social change publications" from "nonprofit, anti-profit, counter-culture, Third World, and movement groups." Books are listed under the press name and an indexing system enables librarians to locate specific books under subject headings from "abortion" to "vegetarianism."

To be listed in *ALTERNATIVES IN PRINT*, write to the ALA/SRRT, 50 E. Huron Street, Chicago, IL. 60611, for guidelines.

BOOKLEGGER
555 29th Street
San Francisco, CA. 94131
> For publication information, send inquiry with SASE

In the cyclic way that feminist magazines come and go, *BOOKLEGGER* stopped publication in 1977 until they can establish a more secure financial base. As Celeste West wrote me, "Re *BOOKLEGGER:* flower bent but not broken!" At this writing, *BOOKLEGGER* is about to resume publication.

Made "by/for workers," *BOOKLEGGER* provides information, discussion, and reviews, interesting to anyone who works with books. From a radical feminist perspective, *BOOKLEGGER* promotes small press books. Each issue contains short essays with bibliographies organized around specific topics. The topics vary extensively and include: "Do-it-yourself Law," "Hotels," "Homosexuals," "Films—Women," "Houses—Homemade," "Native Americans," "Radical Magazines," "Senior Power," etc. In addition to the bibliographies, there is always a large section of small press book reviews, as well as an occasional article on a political topic such as "Class and Professionalism."

A complete index to *BOOKLEGGER* is available from Booklegger Press at the above address for $1. Back issues are available for $1.50 (Nos. 1-12) and $2.00 (Nos. 12-16) pre-paid. Each issue is a valuable reference. Also from Booklegger Press is *POSITIVE IMAGES:* An evaluative Guide to 400 Non-Sexist Films for Young People ($5.00), *REVOLTING LIBRARIANS* ($2.00) and *WOMEN'S FILMS IN PRINT*: An Annotated Guide to 800 Films Made By Women ($4.00).

THE BOOKLIST
50 E. Huron Street
Chicago, IL. 60611

Write for publishing information

Reflecting an increasing awareness of small press books on the part of libraries, *THE BOOKLIST*, a bi-monthly review journal of the American Library Association, now features a column of reviews of small press books: "The Alternative Press Scene" by Val Morehouse. Books, journals, tabloids, poem cards, assemblings, audio magazines, posterpaks and other mixed media are all reviewed in this column. Materials for review whould be sent to Ms. Morehouse at 117 Worcestor Park, Falmouth, Ma., 02540.

Single books of poetry should be sent directly to *BOOKLIST* for a review in a recently established poetry column.

THE DIRECTORY OF WOMEN WRITING
Andrea Chesman and Polly Joan
Women Writing Press   8½ x 11, 96 pages, perfect bound
RD 3 $3.50 plus $.35 handling
Newfield, NY. 14867

A meeting place for women writers, three hundred women share their lives, their dreams, their poetry in the *DIRECTORY OF WOMEN WRITING*. Recognizing the need for more contact between writers, this *DIRECTORY* was conceived to be a place where isolation can end and communication begin. This *DIRECTORY* is not a who's who; the women listed are all interested in contacting other women, some are published writers, some are not. In addition to the annotated listing of three hundred women, there is a mailing list of seven hundred women who were all subscribers to the *WOMEN WRITING NEWSLETTER*.

(See Press I: *WOMEN WRITING PRESS*)

271

The Dustbooks Information Series
Dustbooks
P O Box 1056
Paradise, CA. 95969

As a small press, Dustbooks is best known for its Information Series. In addition to *THE GUIDE TO WOMEN'S PUBLISHING*, Dustbooks has three directories and one periodical devoted to promoting small presses. *THE INTERNATIONAL DIRECTORY OF LITTLE MAGAZINES AND SMALL PRESSES* (12th Edition, $6.96/paper, $9.95/cloth) was used in researching this book. The 13th edition is now available, $8.95/paper. Librarians, students, writers all frequently use this book as a guide to the ever expanding collection of small and independent book and magazine publishers. Each listing, which is free, contains: name, address, editor(s), price, circulation, frequency, type of material used, payment rates, rights purchased, discount schedules, size, personal statement by editors, number of issues, titles published in the previous year and projected into the coming year. The entries are indexed by region and subject, as well as alphabetically. It is a very complete guide to small presses. *THE SMALL PRESS RECORD OF BOOKS IN PRINT* (6th Edition, $8.95) lists books, magazines, pamplets, broadsides, poemcards by small presses. A listing in this directory, also free, enables book buyers and librarians to locate small press books; it is under-utilized by feminist publishers. Updating the *INTERNATIONAL DIRECTORY*, the *SMALL PRESS REVIEW* is a monthly magazine featuring listings of new presses and magazines, reviews of small press books (100-250 words) and news from the small press world. *THE SMALL PRESS REVIEW* costs $8.00 per year. Dustbooks also publishes the *DIRECTORY OF SMALL MAGAZINE PRESS EDITORS AND PUBLISHERS* (8th Edition, $6.95). To be listed in any of these Directories, write for their form.

(See Press I: *DUSTBOOKS*)

EMERGENCY LIBRARIAN
c/o Sherrill Cheda
46 Gormley Avenue
Toronto, Ontario M4V 1Z1

Published bi-monthly
$7 per year, Canadian
$9 per year, U.S.
8½ x 11, 24 pages, saddle stitched

Addressed specifically to Canadian librarians, the *EMERGENCY LIBRARIAN* is sympathetic to small press and feminist press needs. A recent issue on Feminist (including lesbian) publishing establishes the feminist orientation of this all-women publication. A review in *EMERGENCY LIBRARIAN* might be helpful in reaching Canadian audiences. Each issue contains articles, book reviews and bibliographies.

MARGINS
P O Box A
Fair Water, WI. 53931

Published monthly
$6 per year
8½ x 10½, 72 pages, saddle stitched

"A Review of Little Mags and Small Press Books," *MARGINS* publishes commentary, reviews, interviews, criticism and letters, all focusing on small press books and little magazines. Some issues of *MARGINS* have focused on one particular aspect of small press publishing. A very special issue was edited by Beth Hodges on lesbian-feminist writing and publishing, and there are plans to do a second one.

THE MEDIA REPORT TO WOMEN INDEX/DIRECTORY
The Women's Institute for Freedom of the Press
3306 Ross Place NW
Washington, D.C. 20008

$8/$4 for persons listed in it
8½ x 11, 60 pages, spiral binding

Best known for its *MEDIA REPORT TO WOMEN* and its *INDEX/DIRECTORY*, the Women's Institute for Freedom of the Press is an organization "devoted to research and to publishing practical and theoretical works on the communication of information. Its purpose is to engage in research on all aspects of communication; to study ways in which freedom of the press may be extended to more people, worldwide; and to inform women who have a special interest in media or who work in it of new developments in the field.

Communication between women in media is greatly facilitated by the annual *INDEX/DIRECTORY* of the *MEDIA REPORT TO WOMEN*, this book updates a list of some 500 women's periodicals, presses and publishers, news services, radio-tv groups, video, cable, art, graphics, music and theater groups, bookstores and other women's media groups and individuals. A vital support network, each listing is a brief 25 word description by the women themselves, with addresses, phone numbers, and contact persons. This Directory was used extensively in preparing this book. To be listed in the *INDEX/DIRECTORY* write to the Women's Institute for Freedom of the Press.

(See Feminist Journals: *THE MEDIA REPORT TO WOMEN*)

WRITE ON WOMAN!
A Writer's Guide to U.S. Women's/Feminist/Lesbian
Alternative Press Periodicals
Lynne Shapiro
92 Horatio Street 4S $3.50
New York, NY. 10014   5½ x 8½, 32 pages, saddle stitched

Designed to inform writers of their feminist markets, *WRITE ON WOMAN!* lists 45 publications. The basis for each listing is a questionnaire sent by Ms. Shapiro and includes names, addresses, types of work solicited, publication schedule, circulation and readership. *WRITE ON WOMAN!* was also used in researching this book.

Ms. Shapiro plans an update of *WRITE ON WOMAN!* and publications who wish a listing should contact her.

WRITERS' RESOURCES   Published bi-monthly
c/o Ann Morganson/Bruce Shatswell
48 Kinnaird Street, Apt. 3 $5 per year
Cambridge, MA. 02139   5½ x 8½, 24 pages, saddle stitched
          Free to mental hospital and prison programs on request

274

WRITERS' RESOURCES is just that—a bi-monthly publication of information and ideas for writers (and publishers) involved in the small press. Each issue contains articles of opinion or analysis concerning the small press, book reviews, a calendar of east coast/Canadian literary events, listings of publications received, special announcements and writers' classifieds.

All listings, announcements are free (*WRITERS' RESOURCES* also accepts paid ads). They are an excellecnt form of publicity and *WRITERS' RESOURCES* is happy to exchange publications, receive regular mailings, etc. They are also soliciting small press reviews, essays/articles on topics of interest to writers, and graphics that do not require screening.

LIBRARIES AND ARCHIVES

PRESERVING OUR WORDS

Few of us who studied history in high school are likely to forget the image of women suffragettes that was so glibly taught and dismissed in those classes. Suffragettes were grim-faced women who hated men and wore outlandish bloomers. Relentless, they pursured temperance with the same uncompromising determination with which they pursued the vote. They were not courageous; they were laughable. This image, preserved in text books, was the product of male press of the time. In fifty years, when young women are studying the feminist movement of the sixties and seventies, what image of us will be preserved? Will they also inherit a view, courtesy of the male press, that feminists are "strident, men-hating bra-burners?" History is nothing more than a series of political choices determining what truth is preserved, what buried.

Fortunately, today there are a few libraries and archives determined to preserve an accurate history of women. Some of these collections reach into our past, uncovering original documents, making the truth available to writers and researchers. Other libraries are specializing in preserving our current works. Whatever the focus, these collections are vital links with our future.

This section focuses on a few libraries and archives, not a complete listing. However, these libraries are unique. They have been listed in women's publications and directories. Hopefully this means that they are willing to preserve our words in all our cultural fullness. Researchers should explore them. And publishers should consider ensuring their works a position in these collections. It is one of the very few gifts we can give to future generations of women.

THE LESBIAN HERSTORY ARCHIVES
P O Box 1258
New York, NY. 10001

Recognizing that lesbian culture is still a hidden voice in many feminist archives and resource centers, The Lesbian Herstory Archive is defined as the one place where lesbians are seen and heard in all their complexity. Records of lesbian lives and activities are gathered and preserved in the Archive to insure future generations of lesbians ready access to materials relevant to their lives.

Operating out of a back room in an apartment owned by a LHA collective member, the archive is an informal room open to all women. It is a room filled with over 200 books, including a collection of 1950's and 1960's paperbacks, lesbian feminist newsletters from across the country, feminist publications with lesbian content, photographs, tapes, records, bibliographies, an over-flowing file cabinet with clippings, organizational announcements and flyers, etc. There is a desk and a quiet space for women to read and do research.

The collection is a unique one. Special emphasis is given to preserving the lesbian voice—not just in published works but also in the form of letters, doodles, "rejected" writings that grow out of a struggle to survive. They strive to represent women of all cultures and class so that "old myths about who lesbians were can not be used to separate us." Although the collection is primarily in English, some international resources are available.

A key goal of the Archives is to facilitate research on lesbians. They are working to develop bibliographies in special interest areas and to maintain files organized by specific subjects. News of these activities is filtered through a newsletter published three times a year. In the newsletter they also list new archive acquisitions, research queries, lesbian culture bibliographies, and announce new publications. Write to them to be included on their mailing list.

Survival of the archives depends solely on donations. The

Archives welcome donations of materials as well as money to meet basic on-going expenses such as mailings, printings, the post office box and buying new materials.

Access to the archives can be made by writing for an appointment.

WOMEN'S COLLECTION
Special Collections Department
Northwestern University Library
Evanston, IL. 60201

A familiar statement to be found on many feminist periodicals is: "This publication is on file with the International Women's History Archive, Special Collections Library, Northwestern University. . ." The permanent home of the original *HERSTORY* collection (compiled by The Women's History Research Center) of women's publications published between 1956 and 1974, the Women's Collection is an up-dated extension of the original collection. Considered one of the largest arrays of contemporary women's periodicals, this collection also contains position papers, posters, buttons, brochures, etc.

The Special Collections Department subscribes to all the newsletters, journals and newspapers formerly donated to The Women's History Research Center. Contact Sarah Sherman, librarian, at Northwestern University for more information.

WOMEN'S HISTORY LIBRARY
Archive of Contemporary History
The University of Wyoming
Laramie, WY. 82071

Almost 4,000 files on contemporary women are available at the Women's History Library with topics ranging from "Affirmative Action" to "Women's Studies." A large part of the collection is the original source documents compiled by The Women's History Research Center. Their files on Women and Law and Women and Health/Mental Health have joined with other women's collections of material on the nation's feminist politicians and public figures, photographs of activists from the 1870's to the present, and material on 20th century suffrage leaders, critics, activists, and writers.

The entire collection is available to researchers by phone, mail or visit. A query to the Research Historian of the Library will result in a list of all subject headings of the Library so that specific requests for information can be made. The major areas covered are: women in countries, in ethnic groups, in history, groups, projects, protests, events, services, roles, religion, sports, business, fashion, etc. The staff of the archive will photocopy or microfilm, at cost, any material in their collection.

The Women's History Library is actively seeking donations of women's writing, graphics, clippings, pamphlets, booklets, theses, term papers, tapes, photographs, journals, leaflets, songs, brochures, bibliographies, newspapers, etc. Send all material to the Research Historian.

THE WOMEN'S HISTORY RESEARCH CENTER
2325 Oak Street
Berkeley, CA. 94708

"So much has been written about women. But so little has shown up in the libraries." From 1968 to 1974, The Women's History Research Center collected over a million documents relating to women in our society. Although the collection has since been dispersed (See Northwestern University and The Women's History Library, Laramie, Wyoming), the Research Center has much of their collection on microfilm.

With these collections on microfilm, more women have access to them, but only through libraries; the cost of microfilms is prohibitive. The collection is divided into three series. *HER-STORY*, "the only comprehensive record is ideas of the current women's movement," consists of 821 newsletters, journals and newspapers published by and about women's liberation, civic, professional, religious, and peace groups. *WOMEN AND LAW*

279

provides information on legislation, employment, education, education, housing, rape, prison, prostitution, Black and Third World Women, gathered from mass, alternative and professional publications. *WOMEN AND HEALTH/MENTAL HEALTH* deals with physical and mental health and illness, sex roles, biology, life cycles, birth, population control, sex and sexuality, Black and Third World Women, etc.

Other publications of the Research Center includes an annotated *DIRECTORY OF FILMS, BY AND/OR ABOUT WOMEN, INTERNATIONALLY PAST AND PRESENT*. Women who want to see their local library collections up-dated with reference to women should encourage the library to consult The Women's History Research Center. Microfilms can be ordered directly from Barbara Baisley, Northeast Micrographics, 27 Palmerwoods Circle, Branford, CT. 06405.

OTHER WOMEN'S COLLECTIONS

The Arthur and Elizabeth Schlesinger
Library on the History of Women in America
Radcliffe College
3 James Street
Cambridge, MA. 02138

Business and Professional Women's
Foundation Library
2012 Massachusettes Avenue NW
Washington D.C. 20036

Catalyst Library and Information Center
14 E. 60th Street
New York, NY. 10022

Center for the American Woman and Politics
Eagleton Institute
Rutgers University
New Brunswick, NJ. 08901

Feminist History Research Project
P O Box 1156
Topanga, CA. 90290

Midwest Women's Historical Collection
University of Illinois
Box 8198
Chicago, IL. 60680

The New Alexandria Library for Lesbian Women
3512 N. Halsted
Chicago, IL. 60657

Overbury Collection
Barnard College Library
Broadway at 117th Street
New York, NY. 10027

The Sophia Smith Collection
Women's History Archive
Smith College
Northampton, MA. 02138

White Mare Archive
Preston Hollow, NY. 12469

Women's Action Alliance Library
370 Lexington Avenue
New York, NY. 10017

ORGANIZATIONS

Just as the women's movement has been a loose confederation of local political/support groups, women's publishing has been more characterized by their informal organizations. Small press publishing, on the other hand, has quite a few formal structures which nurture their group interests. This section focuses on a few writer's/publisher's support structures.

There is one Feminist organization, just forming, which may revolutionize feminist publishing—The Feminist Writer's Guild. The first national feminist writers organization, and one of the few national feminist organizations of any type, the Feminist Writer's Guild may symbolize the start of a new era in publishing.

CENTER FOR ARTS INFORMATION
80 Center Street
New York, NY. 10013

The Center for Arts Information acts as a clearinghouse for information on the arts in New York State. Their many services include a free newsletter which contains much information of special value to art organizations on funding, legislation, etc. Recently, the Center for Arts Information published a nine page list describing fifty-six service organizations which provide assistance to New York State poets, playwrights and fiction writers. The Center has a similar list for visual artists and has plans to compile one for photographers. These lists are available to New York State residents free of charge; send a self-addressed, stamped envelope to the Center.

Other services of the Center for Arts Information include answering questions and maintaining an arts administration research library. The services of the Center are available to all members of the arts community as well as the general public.

CODA: POETS AND WRITERS NEWSLETTER

201 West 54th Street
New York, NY. 10019

Published 5 times per year
$5 per year
8½ x 11, 36 pages, saddle stitched

An indispensible resource tool for writers, *CODA* provides news of and for the writing community. Up-to-date information is supplied on prizes and grants awarded or available, anthologies looking for submissions, soliciting magazines and publishers, low-cost print centers, jobs available or sought, etc. In addition to the news items, each issue features a carefully researched article pertinent to writing: copyright laws, self-publishing, vanity presses, distribution, the economics of writing, taxes. They will print any news they have the space for, and that includes travel plans, job openings, changes of address, research queries; writers should contact them directly.

Poets and Writers is a publically supported information center for poets, writers, playwrights, publishers, and editors. In addition to publishing *CODA*, they print biennial directories of American poets and fiction writers; and under a grant from the NYS Council for the Arts, they help arrange readings and workshops in NY State.

CONCILIO MUJERES

725 Rhode Island Street
San Francisco, CA. 94107

Because not much information about Spanish-speaking women's groups is collected in most feminist publications, Concilio Mujeres is an important resource. "Our priority is defined to promote the image of La Raza women in education, communication, publishing and in the arts."

Concilio Mujeres is an information, education, publication distribution and communication network for La Raza women which is committed to the development of the Latino individual and the community. The organization was formed in 1970 by a group of Spanish speaking women attending San Francisco State College as a task force to encourage Raza women to enter non-traditional professions and to offer psychological and sociological support to one another.

By collecting and distributing information regarding Raza women, Concilio Mujeres hopes to educate individuals and groups such as educators and community culture workers. Their resources include a newspaper of news and poetry, *LA RAZON METIZA*, poetry anthologies, bibliographies, television series scripts, and a monthly bulletin *ESCUCHAR MUJER* ($3 per year). They will also share or trade their mailing list of 6000 educators, organizations, movement people and social change advocates.

COSMEP
Box 703
San Francisco, CA. 94101   Membership: $20 per year

COSMEP stand for Committee of Small Magazine Editors and Publishers. It is an international association for small magazines and presses (including self-publishers) and has close to 1000 members. Operating on the principle of strength in numbers, COSMEP seeks to "promote in any practical way possible the furtherance of our 'cause.'" To the outside world, COSMEP represents the small press as a lobbying group in Congress and among the large press review media. Internally, COSMEP works to increase communication among members; they organize book fairs and conferences. They have published a series of technical pamphlets designed to initiate newcomers to the fields of distribution, promotion, finances and the technicalities of printing.

A monthly newsletter keeps COSMEP members informed of their activities. It includes information for all publishers: lists of libraries and bookstores, new publications and presses, information about distributors, etc.

One of COSMEP's special projects is the COSMEP Prison Project run by Carol and Joe Bruchac. They supply free literary magazines, books and newspapers on a monthly basis to inmates wishing to receive reading material. They also supply an ever-growing list of editors and publishers interested in inmate writing, inform people of writing contests, etc. Anyone wishing to contribute to the project (especially poetry publications which are likely to be approved by prison officials) or learn more about the project's activities should contact Carol and Joe Bruchac directly: COSMEP PRISON PROJECT, Greenfield Center, NY. 12833.

THE FEMINIST WRITER'S GUILD
c/o Carol Murray
Redland and Murray
1182 Market Street, Suite 408
San Francisco, CA. 94102

Perhaps nothing attests to the vitality of women's publishing as well as an indigenous, independent support structure such as The Feminist Writer's Guild. Newly organized, the Guild is an organization with a two-fold purpose: as a political body it will represent the interests of writers in trade magazines and funding institutions, and as a service organization it will provide information on support structures for professional and non-professional writers.

As a political organization the Guild will protest the review bias against feminism in major review publications such as the New York Times. They will pressure publications with national distribution to review books by the feminist presses and will work against the suppression of writing by lesbians. Essentially the Guild will work to open more doors of acceptance to the feminist presses, always aware of the special requirements of a feminist/women's press. Thus, when lobbying for more grants for women writers, the Guild will encourage the creation of grants which take into consideration the special needs of women, such as money for child care.

285

As a service organization the Guild will assemble a list of minimal rights and percentages, draw up standard contracts, and put together a handbook on how to read contracts. A file on feminist writers and agents will be compiled and a newsletter will be sent four times a year to provide information on publishing, grants, and Guild activities. Eventually we hope to provide medical insurance and even a retirement plan for members.

The growth of community among writers is a key goal of the Guild. They hope to see local chapters formed. One of the Guild's first activities will be to organize local writing workshops throughout the country.

It is hard not to get very excited about the prospect of the Feminist Writer's Guild, although at this time it is still in the planning stages. Just as women's publishing begins to enter a more professional phase, the Guild has formed to help women *be* professional. And not only does the Guild aim to work with professional writers, it recognizes the need for feminist community, for local support structures, and especially for support of the non-professional writers.

Membership in the Guild is $10 per year ($5 for unemployed women). Contact the Guild directly.

THE WOMAN'S SALON
c/o Erika Duncan
463 West Street
New York, NY. 10014

Harking back to the old European tradition of literary salons, The Women's Salon is a meeting place where feminist literary art is forged and refined. About once a month women gather at the Salon, which operates out of private homes, to hear women read their own works, published and in progress. They discuss criticism and theory, and read fiction, poetry and drama. One of the Salon's priorities is to support young and emerging writers, and to honor older women whose writing lives have been spent defining a feminist esthetic.

At each Salon, women share announcements of future events

that would be of interest to writers. There is usually a book table where women can display their recent publications. The Salon is more than a meeting place, it is a support network also. Therefore, the Salon would like to serve as a contact for out-of-town writers.

Operating on a membership basis, the Salon is open to all women. The $10 membership fee entitles the member to free access to all Salons, plus a monthly newsletter which contains announcements about writing events and blurbs about future Salons. In addition, members receive all Salon publications,such as a booklet of essays by Salon members. Non-members are always welcome; a $1 donation or gift of food or wine is expected.

BOOKSTORES AND MAIL ORDER

ARIZONA

Antigone Books
415 N. 4th Avenue
Tucson, AZ. 85705

Womansplace
2401 N. 32nd Street
Phoenix, AZ. 85008

Womansplace
9 E. 5th Street
Tempe, AZ. 85281

CALIFORNIA

Awakening Bookstore*
469 Bascom
San Jose, CA. 95128

Califia Inc.*
3415 Highland
Manhattan Beach, CA.
90266

The Full Moon
4862 18th Street
San Francisco, CA. 94114

Ici-A Woman's Place
5251 Broadway
Oakland, CA. 94618

Modern Times Store
3800 17th Street
San Francisco, CA. 94112

Mother Right
538 Seabright
Santa Cruz, CA. 95060

Ms Atlas Bookstore
53 W. San Fernando
San Jose, CA. 95113

Old Wives Tales
532 Valencia
San Francisco, CA. 94130

The Oracle
22640 Main Street
Hayward, CA. 94541

Page One
26 N. Lake Avenue
Pasadena, CA. 91101

Rising Woman Books
600 Wilson Street
Santa Rosa, CA. 95401

Riverqueen Women's Books*
17140 River Road
Monte Rio, CA. 95462

---

* Bookstores whose existence hasn't been verified recently.

Sacramento Women's Books*
1221 20th Street
Sacramento, CA. 95814

Sisterhood Bookstore*
13716 Ventura Blvd.
Sherman Oaks, CA. 91403

Sisterhood Bookstore*
The Women's Building
743 S. Grandview
Los Angeles, CA. 90057

Sojourner
538 Redondo Avenue
Long Beach, CA. 90814

A Women's Bookshop*
404 Town & Country Village
Palo Alto, CA. 94301

The Women's Store
2965 Beech Street
San Diego, CA. 92102

COLORADO

Lilith Feminist Bookstore
1743 Walnut Street
Boulder, CO. 80302

Militant Bookstore
916 Broadway
Denver, CO. 80203

Radical Information Project
737 E. 17th Street
Denver, CO. 80203

Satisfy
1431 Ogden
Denver, CO. 80206

Together Books
636 E. 17th Street
Denver, CO. 80203

Woman To Woman
2023 E. Colfax
Denver, CO. 80206

CONNECTICUT

Feminist Bookmobile
76 Cross Highway
Westport, CT. 06880

DISTRICT OF COLUMBIA

Lammas
321 Seventh Street SE
Washington, D.C. 20009

FLORIDA

Feminist Connection
1208 W. Platt Street
Tampa, FL. 33606

Her Store Inc.*
434 W. College Avenue, No. 4
Tallahassee, FL. 32301

Womanstore
12 NW 8th Street
Gainesville, FL. 32601

IDAHO

Observer Books*
1406 Eastman Street
Boise, ID. 83702

ILLINOIS

Lesbian Feminist
Center Bookstore
3523 N. Halsted
Chicago, IL. 60657

INDIANA

A Room of One's Own
309 E. Third Street
Bloomington, IN. 47401

Women's Literature Alliance*
3232 Valley View Drive
Bloomington, IN. 47401

MARYLAND

31st Street Bookstore
425 E. 31st Street
Baltimore, MD. 21218

A Women's Bookstore*
12 West 25th Street
Baltimore, MD. 21218

MASSACHUSETTS

New Words Inc.
186 Hampshire Street
Cambridge, MA. 02139

100 Flowers Bookstore
15 Pearl Street
Cambridge, MA. 02139

Sweetcoming Books
P O Box 745
Northampton, MA. 01060

Women's Educational Center*
46 Pleasant Street
Cambridge, MA. 02139

MICHIGAN

Her Shelf
2 Highland
Highland Park, MI. 48031

HerStory*
3660 Kenbrooke
Kalamazoo, MI. 49007

Verbal Spears*
21 Sheldon NE
Grand Rapids, MI. 49502

A Woman's Bookstore
211½ N. Fourth Avenue
Ann Arbor, MI. 48108

MINNESOTA

Amazon Bookstore
2607 Hennepin Avenue S
Minneapolis, MN. 55408

MISSOURI

New Earth Bookstore
24 E. 39th Street
Kansas City, MO. 64111

Woman's Place
225 N 9th Street
Columbia, MO. 65201

NEW MEXICO

A Woman's Gallery
3007 Central NE
Albuquerque, NM. 87106

NEW YORK

Djuna Books
154 West 10th Street
New York, NY. 10014

Emma
2223 Fillmore Avenue
Buffalo, NY. 14214

Feminist Book Mart, Inc.
P O Box 149
Whitestone, NY. 11357

Gotham Book Mart
41 West 47th Street
New York, NY. 10036

Kay's Book Studio
86 Front Street
Binghampton, NY. 13905

Smedley's Bookshop
119 E. Buffalo Street
Ithaca, NY. 14850

Sister Bear
401 1st Street
Liverpool, NY. 13088

Womanbooks
201 West 92nd Street
New York, NY. 10025

OHIO

Coventry Books
1824 Coventry Road
Cleveland Heights, OH.
44118

Fan The Flames
127 E. Woodruff
Columbus, OH. 43201

Labyris*
2545 Seegar Avenue
Cincinnati, OH. 45225

OREGON

Book & Tea Shop*
746 24th Avenue
Eugene, OR. 97405

Mother Kali's
541 Lair
Eugene, OR. 97401

A Women's Place Bookstore
1300 SW Washington
Portland, OR. 97215

PENNYSLVANIA

Alexandria Books
2041 Walnut Street
Philadelphia, PA. 19103

Giovanni's Room
1426 Spruce Street
Philadelphia, PA. 19102

Know, Inc.
P O Box 86031
Pittsburgh, PA. 15221

Penelope & Sisters* .
603 South 4th Street
Philadelphia, PA. 19147

Women's Cultural Trust
3601 Locust Walk
Philadelphia, PA. 19104

UTAH

The Open Book
1025 Second Avenue
Salt Lake City, UT. 84103

VERMONT

Tigris-Euphrates*
Box 6
Plainfield, VT. 05667

VIRGINIA

Higher Ground*
7 Elliewood
Charlottesville, VA. 22903

WASHINGTON

It's About Time
5502 University Way NE.
Seattle, WA. 98105

Madwoman Feminist Bookcenter*
317 Pine Street
Seattle, WA. 98101

Past-Time Feminist Bookcenter*
151 South Lincoln
Spokane, WA. 99202

Women's Resource Center
243 Simons
Richland, WA. 99352

WISCONSIN

People's Book & Crafts
1625 E. Irving Place
Milwaukee, WI. 53202

A Room of One's Own
317 W. Johnson Street
Madison, WI. 53703

CANADA

Everywomans Books
2033 Oak Bay Avenue
Victoria, BC
Canada

Toronto Women's Bookstore
85 Harbord Street
Toronto, Ontario
Canada

Vancouver Women's Bookstore
804 Richards Street
Vancouver 2 BC
Canada

Women's Bookmobile*
195 Seaton Street
Toronto, Ontario
Canada

Women's Place*
25 Dupont Street E
Waterloo, Ontario
Canada

INDEX